Vast, Intricate Machines Click

faultlessly through their electronic paces, echoing the tempo of a highly technical age.

These manufactured "brains" maintain inventories, calculate payrolls, keep track of plane reservations, guide missiles, play games, compose music, translate. Thousands of people are influenced by their work, but only a handful of people understand *how* they work. The technical literature is almost unintelligible to the layman.

In this fascinating book, Irving Adler explains the theory of computers in terms that can be easily understood by anyone who has had elementary algebra. He begins with the simplest mathematical concepts—everyday arithmetic, the binary scale of numerals, the brief essentials of logic, showing how these concepts are used in the building of mechanical calculators. From this, he takes the reader into the algebra of classes, propositions, and switching circuits. Finally he illustrates how Boolean algebra is used to design circuits that can calculate and perform deductive reasoning.

Here is a book that unveils a modern mystery, that explains how the art of mathematics engendered great mathematical brains which can think faster than man, calculate more accurately, and follow a process of logic without any of the fallibility of human thought.

Other SIGNET SCIENCE LIBRARY BOOKS

Irving Adler

THINKING
MACHINES

*A Layman's Introduction to
Logic, Boolean Algebra and
Computers*

With diagrams by Ruth Adler

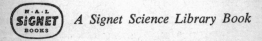 A Signet Science Library Book

Published by THE NEW AMERICAN LIBRARY

Published as a SIGNET SCIENCE LIBRARY BOOK
By Arrangement with The John Day Company, Inc.

FIRST PRINTING, FEBRUARY, 1962

SIGNET TRADEMARK REG. U.S. PAT. OFF. AND FOREIGN COUNTRIES
REGISTERED TRADEMARK——MARCA REGISTRADA
HECHO EN CHICAGO, U.S.A.

SIGNET SCIENCE LIBRARY BOOKS are published by
The New American Library of World Literature, Inc.
501 Madison Avenue, New York 22, New York

PRINTED IN THE UNITED STATES OF AMERICA

THINKING MACHINES

CHAPTER 1

Hardware Brains

WE HAVE entered the age of "thinking" machines and automation. Organized collections of hardware, made mostly of metal and glass, carry out activities that used to be the monopoly of the living human brain. They make long and involved calculations, weigh possible courses of action in complex situations, and exercise functions of guidance and control. What is more, they do these things faster and more accurately than the unaided brain can do them.

Electronic Clerks

In the simplest jobs that they do, electronic "brains" serve as clerks and bookkeepers. In many offices, factories and stores, they maintain inventories of supplies. In railroad and airline offices they keep track of ticket sales and reservations. In these activities, the computers operate at their lowest levels of skill. They add and subtract numbers, and store the results in their "memory" devices. They get more of a chance to show their powers when they are put to work calculating payrolls. Using stored information about rates of pay, number of hours worked, social security tax rates, and rules for withholding-tax deductions, they cal-

culate the paychecks of individual workers. In these calculations they use all the basic operations of arithmetic:
addition, subtraction, multiplication and division.

Guides for Missiles

Firing a missile at a moving target is no simple matter.
The path of the missile depends on more than the speed
and direction with which it is launched. From the moment
the missile leaves the ground it is pulled by gravity, blown
by the wind, held back by air resistance, and turned by the
rotation of the earth. All these factors must be taken into
account when the path of the missile is calculated. Of the
many possible paths that the missile may be given, one must
be selected that allows it to intercept the moving target.
The calculations needed to make this selection are carried
out before the missile is fired. In the case of a guided
missile, there are more calculations made after the missile
is fired. The path that the missile follows is compared with
the path that it should follow. As fast as errors in the path
are detected, the course of the missile is altered to make up
for them. Only electronic computers work fast enough to
make these corrections while the missile is in flight. The
computers that plot and correct the path of a missile do
more advanced mathematics than those that merely keep
inventory or calculate payrolls. They solve what are known
as *differential equations*.

The Robot That Beats Its Master

In order to show what a computer can do, and to help
explore new areas of activity for computers, the companies
that make them have designed some that play games. One
of these was wired to play a good game of checkers against

a human opponent. The machine looks ahead several moves. It examines all the moves that it may make, and all the possible countermoves of its opponent. After weighing all the possibilities, it chooses the move that seems to be best. The machine remembers every move of every game, so that in future games it may avoid the moves that didn't work out so well. In other words, this machine "learns" from its own mistakes. Because of this built-in ability to learn, the machine has improved its game so much that it now plays checkers better than the engineer who designed its circuit.

Factories without People

In an ordinary factory, there are machines that do much of the work, but there are men and women who control the operation of the machines. In an automated factory these men and women are displaced, because even the job of control is taken over by machines. So far, automation has proceeded the furthest in the oil and chemical industries. There is a continuous flow of materials moving and being changed according to a definite plan. Measuring instruments at key stages of the process report the temperature, pressure, rate of flow, and other relevant measurements. If any of these measurements is not what it should be, the machine that is in control of the process immediately takes the steps needed to make a correction. For example, if one of the materials is flowing in too slowly, a valve is opened to permit it to flow faster. If it is flowing in too fast, a valve is partly closed to slow it down.

Composers and Translators

The variety of jobs that computers can do increases from day to day. When a giant radio telescope tunes in on the messages sent from a rocket in interplanetary space a computer guides the turning of the telescope to make it face in the right direction. There are computers that can play chess, and computers that compose simple songs. Some computers are pilots that guide ships. Others are language specialists that translate books and magazine articles from one language into another.

The Thinking of a Computer

We refer to automatic computers as "thinking machines" or "electronic brains." These terms are dramatic, but not very accurate. They make it seem as though the computers can do the same kind of thinking that the human brain can do. Actually, this is not so. Roughly speaking, there are two kinds of human thinking. There is *creative* thinking, based on imagination and insight. This is the thinking displayed in its highest form by a Beethoven when he composes a symphony, a Shakespeare when he writes a play, or an Einstein when he formulates a new scientific theory. This kind of thinking follows unpredictable channels, and follows no fixed rules. There is also routine thinking, that requires no special talent to carry it out. It proceeds according to fixed rules along a course that is easily foreseen. Any school boy who knows the rules can think out a sum in arithmetic, can solve a quadratic equation, or can translate a paragraph of simple French. It is only this kind of routine thinking that a so-called "thinking machine" can do. The fact that it is routine thinking, however, does not make it unimportant. A large part of the thinking we do in our daily lives is of this routine type. And often, while it is routine, it is also complex and time-consuming. We save a lot of time and energy, and avoid many errors, by letting the machine take this thinking off our hands, or rather, off our minds. Moreover, it is no routine matter to design a machine that can do routine thinking. Behind the routine thinking of the machine is the creative thinking of the men who invented it.

The thinking machine is one of the great marvels of the twentieth century. How do we succeed in making it think? To answer this question we must first answer two other questions. What is a machine? And, what is the nature of the routine thinking that we are turning over to the machines? These questions are explored in the chapters that follow.

CHAPTER 2

Tools with Self-Control

Extensions of the Body

THINKING machines are tools of a special kind. Like other tools, they serve as inanimate extensions of the human body. Hammers are extensions of the hand; they increase the force with which the hand can strike a blow. Tweezers are also extensions of the hand; they reduce the force with which we grasp things, so that we can handle small and delicate objects without crushing them. Telescopes and microscopes are extensions of the eye. Telephones are extensions of the ear. Automobiles and railroad trains are extensions of our legs. Similarly, thinking machines are inanimate extensions of the human brain.

The Evolution of Tools

The tools we use have gone through three stages of evolution. The first stage is that of the hand tool. The hand tool is specially designed to do one or more specific jobs. A hammer, for example, can drive a nail in. It may also have a claw for pulling nails out. But a hand tool does not do its work alone. A human muscle must wield the tool, and a human brain controls the muscle.

The second stage is that of the power tool. This is the stage that is usually meant when we use the word "ma-

14

chine." In this stage the human muscle has been replaced by an engine, an inanimate source of power. But the tool and the engine that moves it are still guided by the human brain. Often the power tool is capable of performing several distinct operations. It may be set to carry out all these operations in a fixed sequence. Or it may perform different operations chosen for different occasions. But the choice is always made in the brain of the person who operates the tool.

The third stage is that of the automatic machine. The main feature of the automatic machine is that it is a machine *with self-control*. If it performs only one operation, it decides for itself when to start or stop. If it can perform many different operations, it decides for itself which ones to do, and in what order to do them. These decisions are not free decisions. They are made according to fixed rules that are built into the working of the machine. In this stage, the built-in control mechanism has taken over the guidance function formerly exercised by the human brain. It operates as an inanimate extension of the brain. All machines that are referred to as "thinking machines" are tools in this third stage of development.

Here is a simple example of the evolution of a tool passing through all three stages of development: Assume that the heat for a room is supplied by an oil burner. Suppose we form a closed circuit of the oil burner and a voltage supply, and then break the circuit by cutting one of the connecting wires. We can close the circuit again and turn on the oil burner by grasping the cut ends of wire, one in each hand, and pressing them together. This is not a wise way of doing it, even if the wires are insulated, because there is the danger of getting an electric shock. A better way of doing it is to connect the two ends of wire to the terminals of a toggle switch. Then we can close the circuit by throwing the switch. The switch is a tool that takes over from our hands the job of closing the circuit. It is a hand tool because we use the muscles of our hand to make it work. We can convert it into a power tool by attaching a clock to it, so that the clock closes the switch in the morning to turn the oil burner on, and opens it at night to turn the oil burner off. Finally, we can convert the switch into an automatic tool by introducing a thermostat. Then the thermostat has control of the switch that turns the oil burner on or off. The thermostat "decides" to turn the oil burner on when the room is too cool. It "decides" to turn the oil burner off again when the room is warm. It makes these decisions because of the way in which it is constructed. One of the contact points of the switch is mounted on a thin bar made of two sheets of metal that are joined back to back. Each sheet of metal expands when it warms up, and contracts when it cools. But they expand and contract at different rates. As a result, when the bar grows warmer it curls and pulls the contact points of the switch apart. Then the switch is opened and the oil burner is turned off. Later, if the bar has cooled sufficiently, it straightens out again. The contact points are brought together until they touch. Then the switch is closed, and the oil burner is turned on. A thermostat switch is an automatic tool because it has this built-in self-control.

Controlling a Car

To understand what is required to give a machine self-control, let us examine another familiar situation, that of driving an automobile. Consider first the actions of a person who is learning how to drive. His instructor sits at his side and tells him what to do. After he starts up in first, the instructor says, "Take your foot off the gas. Step on the clutch and shift into second. Let out the clutch slowly, and step on the gas." Later, as they cruise in traffic, the instructor may say, "You are getting too close to the car ahead of you. Step on your brake gently." Under these conditions, who is in control of the car? Obviously, it is the instructor, and not the driver. The instructor is making all the decisions. His instructions are signals that activate the movements of the driver. The driver does not control the car until, after having acquired experience, he begins to make his own decisions and give himself the signals that activate his movements. The experienced driver hears the sound of his engine as he starts up in first, and sees his car picking up speed. He recognizes when to shift into second

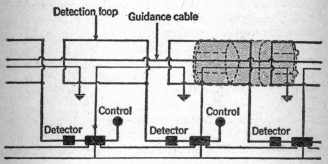

Automatic control of auto traffic

from what he hears and sees and feels. *The basis of his control of the car is the fact that he observes the results of his own actions, and these observations become signals that initiate his next actions.* When a mechanism can detect the results of its action, and is guided by these results, engineers say that it has *feedback*. Now, if we can build a feedback system into the car itself, we can dispense with the driver, and have a car that controls itself. A step in this direction has already been taken by General Motors and the Radio Corporation of America. They have developed a system for automatic control of a car that is riding on a highway. The car detects the results of its own movements through an electronic feedback system built into the roadway and the car. A guidance cable in the roadway warns the car when it is straying from its lane. Detection loops in the roadway sense the presence of other cars ahead. If the car gets too close to a preceding car, the feedback system puts on the car's brake to slow it down.

The Key to Self-Control

Feedback is the key to self-control. To make a machine automatic, we have to provide it with a feedback mechanism. This means we must provide it with a means of observing the results of its own actions. Each type of result has to generate a distinct signal. The action of the machine has to be guided by these signals according to a predetermined plan.

Automatic Calculators

The term "thinking machine" is used most often to refer to automatic calculators. These machines "think" in a double sense. First, as tools that carry out computations, they serve as extensions of the brain. Secondly, as automatic tools, they carry out the guidance function formerly supplied by the brain. These two types of thinking are distinct, and are carried out by separate parts of an electronic brain. One part is a calculator, that can do arithmetic when it is told what to do. The other part is the control unit, that tells the calculator what to do.

CHAPTER 3

Getting an Idiot to Think

Making the Complicated Simple

A TYPICAL tool can carry out only a few easy operations. A calculating machine is like other tools in this respect. It moves in certain predetermined ways. These are simple in nature and few in number. The machine is like an idiot that moves only on command, and can understand and follow only a few commands. Nevertheless, we are using such machines for carrying out very complex calculations. We have transformed the idiot into a competent mathematician. How is this transformation accomplished? How do we get a simple machine to carry out a complicated job? We do it by first making the complicated job simple. We break the job down into a sequence of small steps, each of which is simple and is in the range of what the machine is capable of doing. Then we see to it that the machine carries out these steps in the proper sequence.

A familiar example of this procedure is seen in the operation of a knitting machine. Sweaters may be knit in a great variety of complicated patterns. But all of these patterns, no matter how complex, are built up out of sequences of a few simple knitting operations, such as *knit, purl, increase, decrease, slip,* and *yarn over*. The knitting machine is designed to carry out these simple steps. To have the machine knit a complex pattern, we first identify the sequence of steps in the pattern, and then instruct the machine to follow this sequence.

If a machine is electrically operated, its action may be controlled by opening and closing switches. A particular set of switches will control a particular step that the machine can perform. The switches themselves can be opened or closed by electrical signals. By supplying these signals to the machine in a definite sequence, we can get the machine to perform a particular sequence of steps.

When a machine knits a sweater, every step it performs can be charted in advance. Such a machine can be given a single complete set of instructions before it starts working. The situation is somewhat different for a machine that makes calculations. It is not possible to list in advance all the steps it must perform, because some of the later steps depend on the outcome of the earlier steps. For example, if the machine is adding some two-digit numbers, we do not know whether it will have to carry a number to the second column from the sum of the first column until we know what that sum is. To deal with this situation, we give the machine several sets of instructions. Then, we give the machine the general instruction that, after each step it performs, it should observe the outcome of that step and then choose the appropriate instructions for the next step. This is where the feedback mechanism of the machine comes into play.

The Turing Machine

To show concretely how a simple machine can be given the ability to perform complex calculations, we shall describe one designed by the late British mathematician A. M. Turing. Turing's machine is a purely imaginary one. He invented it for theoretical purposes. A working model can easily be made, because hardware is available that can carry out the acts that the machine is required to perform. However, we do not propose that you make a model to see how it works. We suggest, instead, that you cast yourself in the role of the machine. Make believe that you are the machine. Follow blindly the instructions that the machine is given, just as an inanimate mechanical device would. In this way you will get a full appreciation of the nature of the mindless thinking that the machine performs.

The Turing machine has these parts: a tape, divided into squares; a motor, for moving the tape; a scanning device for reading what is written on the tape; a writing device that can write X's or 1's or can erase them; a numbered dial with a pointer; and a control unit that tells the machine what to do. The machine can perform only these simple acts: It can write an X or a 1 in a blank square. It can erase an X or a 1 that is already there. It can move the tape one square to the left or to the right. It can flash an appropriate signal and then stop when its work is done. In a mechanical model, the control unit would be an electronic device that receives signals from the scanner and the dial after each step. These signals would activate switches that initiate the next step the machine should take. For our purposes, the control unit will simply be a table which you can read to obtain the machine's instructions.

In order to play at being the machine, first prepare these pieces of equipment: a pencil, an eraser, a narrow strip of paper divided into squares, a blank sheet of paper, and a card. The blank sheet of paper will be your dial. Write the number 1 on it. When you are instructed to change the dial setting, cross out or erase the number that is there, and write the new dial setting in its place. The card will serve to fix the position of the scanner. Place the tape under the card so that part of the tape is exposed to the right of the card. The first square next to the right edge of the card will be the square that is being scanned.

Numbers are written on the tape in the most primitive possible way, as a sequence of 1's. The X's are used to indicate where a number begins and ends. Let us begin by entering on the tape the numbers 2 and 3, as shown in the drawing below. Place the tape under the card so that the last 1 on the extreme right is in the position of being scanned. This is the starting position for the machine. Now we show how the machine is launched on the job of performing some operation in arithmetic with the numbers that are on the tape. A program for this operation is worked out, and it is embodied in a control table. The table is independent of the numbers that are entered on the tape.

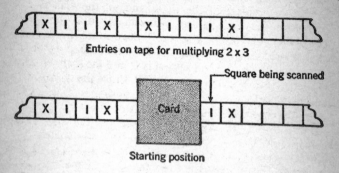

Entries on tape for multiplying 2 x 3

Square being scanned

Card

Starting position

The Turing "machine"

No matter what the numbers may be, the machine need only follow the instructions given by the table, and it will automatically carry out the operation and stop when the job is done. The answer will appear as a single string of 1's on the tape.

The program for doing addition is given in the first control table on page 24. The numbers 1 to 6 in the first column represent dial settings of the machine. The symbols at the top of the table, a blank square, a square with an X, and a square with a 1, represent what the scanner may see. By entering the table in the row indicated by the dial setting, and in the column indicated by what the scanner sees, the machine obtains the instructions it should follow for each step. The instructions are made up of two parts, a letter and a number. The letter may be D, X, E, R, or L. D means write the digit 1 in the square being scanned. X means write an X. E means erase what appears in the square. R means move the tape one square to the right. L means move the tape one square to the left. The number in the instructions means change the dial setting to that number. A question mark in the instruction box means, "What happened? You made a mistake somewhere." An exclamation mark means, "Stop. The job is done." For example, in the starting position, the dial setting is 1, and the scanner sees a 1. So you look for instructions in the row labeled 1, and the column headed 1. The instructions are, "$R1$: Move the tape one square to the right, and set the dial at 1." After these instructions are followed, the dial setting is again 1, and the scanner sees a 1 once more. So the instructions for the second step are the same. After the third step is carried out, the dial setting is 1, and the scanner sees an X. Now the instructions are, "$E2$: Erase the X, and set the dial at 2." As a result, the dial setting is 2, and the scanner sees a blank square, so the instructions for the fifth step are, "$R2$: Move the tape one square to the right, and set the dial at 2." The reader is advised to continue, following the instructions step by step until the computation is completed. If you have the time and the patience, do another addition example with larger numbers. Remember to begin with the dial set at 1 and the tape in the starting position described above.

The other tables on page 24 give programs for carrying out multiplication and exponentiation (raising to a power). When the exponentiation table is used, the right hand number on the tape is the base, and the left hand number is the exponent. For example, if the numbers 2 and 3 are written as shown on page 22, with the 2 to the left of the 3, then 3 is raised to the second power. To raise 2 to the third power, write the 3 to the left of the 2.

When you work out a complete addition example, you will observe that the machine adds the two numbers written on the tape by combining the two strings of 1's into a single long string. If you use the control table for multiplication, you will see that the machine multiplies by doing repeated addition. Similarly, the machine does exponentiation by doing repeated multiplication. The more complex operations are accomplished through repetition of the simpler ones.

The Turing machine is not a practical calculator. It writes numbers by the laborious method of putting down long strings of 1's. It makes calculations by moving these 1's, one at a time, across lengthy stretches of tape. The

CONTROL TABLES FOR THE TURING MACHINE

Program for Addition

		X	1
1	D6	E2	R1
2	R2	E3	?
3	R3	E4	E5
4	L4	?	R6
5	L5	?	R1
6	X6	1	R3

Program for Multiplication

		X	1
1	?	R2	R1
2	R2	E3	?
3	R3	E12	E4
4	L4	L5	?
5	?	?	E6
6	L6	L7	L6
7	D8	?	L7
8	L9	R8	R8
9	L9	R10	E6
10	D10	R11	R10
11	R11	E12	E4
12	L12	E13	?
13	L13	L14	E13
14	X15	L14	L14
15		1	

Program for Exponentiation

		X	1
1	R2	R1	R1
2	R2	E3	?
3	L3	L4	L4
4	D5	L4	L4
5	X5	R6	L5
6	R7	R6	R6
7	R7	R8	E8
8	L8	L8	E9
9	L9	L10	L9
10	L10	L10	E11
11	L11	L12	L11
12	D13	?	L12
13	L14	R13	R13
14	D15	R15	E11
15	D15	R16	R15
16	L17	R16	R16
17	?	L18	E9
18	?	L18	E19
19	X19	L20	?
20	?	L21	E19
21	X21	R22	L21
22	D23	R22	R22
23	D23	R24	R23
24	R24	E25	E8
25	L25	E26	?
26	L26	E27	E26
27	L27	E27	R28
28	X28	1	

action of a working model would depend on mechanical motion, shifting the tape back and forth one square at a time. For all these reasons, a Turing machine would be too slow to do the calculating jobs described in the first chapter. A really practical calculator would have to meet two major requirements: 1) It would have to have an efficient system for recording numbers. 2) It would have to be able to make computations very quickly. The first requirement is met by using a place-value system of writing numbers. The Arabic numerals that we use every day constitute a place-value system. It is not the only one, however. Of the many possible place-value systems, there is one that is best suited for use by calculating machines. We shall get acquainted with this system in the next chapter. The second requirement is met by building a calculator out of parts that can act without mechanical motion. Machine components that have this property are those made of electronic circuits. The action in them consists of pulses of electric current. Electronic devices can easily generate and manipulate as many as one million pulses per second. Since each pulse corresponds roughly to one step in a simple computation, an electronic calculator can carry out about a million steps in a second. At this rate, even complex calculations that require many steps are carried out at high speed.

The Components of an Automatic Calculator

Although the Turing machine is not a practical calculator, we can learn from it. We find in it all the major components that an automatic calculator should have. When we observe them in action, they suggest questions that should be answered before analogous components can be designed for an electronic calculator.

Every automatic calculator has a *calculating unit* that performs the actual computations. In the Turing machine the calculating unit consisted of the tape that moved back and forth, and the pencil and eraser that entered and removed 1's and X's. The calculating unit took this peculiar form because of the method that was used for writing numbers. So we see that the system employed for writing numbers determines, in part, the design of the calculating unit. Since we shall be using a place-value system for writing numbers, we shall have to look into the question, "How can electronic circuits be designed to represent numbers written in a place-value system, and to carry out computations with them?" To answer this question, we first get acquainted with different ways of writing numbers (Chapter IV) and various devices, both mechanical and electrical, for making calculations (Chapter VI).

Every automatic calculator has a *control unit* that guides the calculating unit through the sequence of steps it performs. In the Turing machine, the control unit gave the instructions that were recorded in the control tables. In an electronic computer, the control unit is itself an electronic device. So we have to look into the question, "How can an electronic device give such instructions to a calculator?" We find additional questions that we should explore when we notice the form that the Turing machine's control system took. The instructions for each step depended on what the dial setting was, and what the scanner saw just before the step was taken. When the machine was doing addition, the dial might be set at 1 *or* 2 *or* 3 *or* 4 *or* 5 *or* 6. The scanner might see a square that was blank, *or* contained a 1, *or* contained an *X*. The table that gave the instructions is essentially a condensed way of writing statements of this form: *If* the dial is set at 2, *and* the square being scanned contains an *X, then* erase the *X and* set the dial at 3. In the sentences above that describe what the dial does, what the scanner sees, and what the control table says, the key words are *or, and, if,* and *then*. These words represent certain logical ideas. We shall have to investigate the part that these ideas play in logical thinking, and then look into the question, "How can we get an electronic circuit to do this kind of thinking?" That is why we take up Logic and Boolean Algebra, and their relationship to circuit design, in Chapters VII, VIII, IX and X.

Every automatic calculator has a *memory unit*. In the Turing machine, the dial was a primitive memory unit. It stored information derived from its earlier steps, when this information was needed to guide its later steps. In an electronic computer, the memory units are electrical or magnetic devices. We shall have to look into the question, "How can these devices store and deliver on demand such things as numbers and instructions for the calculating unit?" This question is taken up in Chapter XI.

Every automatic calculator has an *input unit* and an *out-

put unit. The input unit supplies to the machine the data it works with, and special instructions for the job to be done. The output unit delivers the results of the machine's calculations. The input and output of the Turing machine were the written symbols on the tape. The form that they take in electronic calculators will be described in Chapter XI.

CHAPTER 4

Numbers and Numerals

ALL THE numbers we use are derived from the natural numbers, the numbers we use for counting. These are the numbers we call *zero, one, two, three,* and so on. To represent these numbers, we use two different kinds of symbols. One kind is the *number name,* which we can say out loud, or which we spell out when we use written words to stand for spoken words. *One, eleven, one hundred,* and *one million* are examples of number names. The other kind of symbol is a *numeral.* It is a written symbol only. When we read it out loud, we really say the *number name* that corresponds to it. 1, 11, 100, and 1,000,000 are examples of numerals. Notice that as you read them you say "One, eleven, one hundred, and one million," which are the corresponding number names.

There are many ways of assigning number names to the natural numbers. In fact, every language has its own set of number names. The number that is called *two* in English is called *deux* in French, *zwei* in German, and so on. Similarly, there are many ways of writing numerals for these numbers. Where we use the numeral 2, the Romans used the letters II, and the ancient Hebrews used the symbol ב, a letter of the Hebrew alphabet. In this chapter we shall be discussing different systems of numerals. Consequently we may use several different written symbols to stand for the same number. To avoid confusion, let us agree at the same time to use only one number name for each number, the one that it has in the English language. Thus, although we may use different symbols for the number we ordinarily write as 2, we shall always refer to the number by the name *two,* so that there will be no doubt about what number we mean.

An Alphabet for Numbers

The list of natural numbers *zero, one, two, three,* and so on, is endless. Since we want to be able to write a numeral for each of these numbers, we need an infinite collection of numerals. One way of getting such a collection is to assign a different symbol to each number. This way of writing numbers would be analogous to the Chinese way of writing words. In the Chinese language, there is a separate written symbol for each word. In order to learn how to read Chinese, it is necessary to memorize thousands of symbols. We avoid this difficulty in the English language by using a mere twenty-six symbols as an alphabet. Then we build all written words out of these symbols. In the same way, a more efficient system for writing numbers is obtained by using just a few symbols as a kind of alphabet for numbers, which can be put together to form all the numerals.

We may, for example, use as an alphabet for numbers the symbols 0, 1, and +, with their ordinary meanings. Then we can write all numbers above 1 by adding enough 1's. In this system, $1 + 1$ would be the numeral for two, $1 + 1 + 1$ would be the numeral for three, and so on. This is the system that we used in the Turing machine, except that we omitted the plus signs. Primitive man used the same system when he cut notches on a tree or made scratches on the ground. The system is useful as long as we use only small numbers. It becomes very cumbersome as soon as large numbers are needed. For this reason, the method of repeating 1's was discarded in all parts of the world in favor of better alphabets for numbers.

New alphabets for numbers arose out of the habit of counting things out in groups. Because we have five fingers on each hand, the groups used most often were groups of five or ten. However, groups of twelve, twenty, and sixty have been used by some peoples in various parts of the world. The use of groups for counting suggested that special notations be used for designating the number of things in a group. In most cases, the notation took the form of new symbols. In the Roman system of numerals, for example, five is designated by V, ten is designated by X, and so on. However, in a few systems of numerals, the group number was designated not by a new symbol, but by an old symbol put in a special place. Systems that use this method are called place-value systems. The Arabic system, which we use today, is a place-value system.

Arabic Numerals

In the Arabic system for writing numbers, as we count up from 0, we introduce a new symbol called a *digit* for each number up to 9. Then we start using the fact that we group things by tens. To write the number ten, we write 10, which is an abbreviation for "one group of ten plus no units." Eleven, which is one group of ten plus one unit, is written as 11, and so on. The meaning of a digit in a numeral depends on its position in that numeral. If it is in the first column from the right, it designates a number of ones. In the second column it designates a number of tens. In the third column it designates a number of hundreds. Thus, 325 means 3 hundreds plus 2 tens plus 5 ones. The basic group of the system is the group of ten. The larger groups are all compounded from groups of ten. One hundred is ten times ten. One thousand is ten times ten times ten, and so on. The number *ten* is called the base of the system.

If We Had Eight Fingers

The choice of *ten* as the base of our system of numerals is the result of a biological accident. We happen to have just ten fingers on our hands. If we had eight fingers on our hands it would have been natural for us to use the number eight as the base of a place-value system for writing numbers. In such a system, we would need separate symbols 0, 1, 2, 3, 4, 5, 6, 7 only for the numbers up to 7. To designate the number eight we would write 10, to mean "one group of eight plus no units." Then 11 would mean one group of eight plus one, or nine. 12 would mean ten, etc. In this system, where eight is the base, 10 means *eight,* 100 means *eight times eight,* or sixty-four, 1000 means *eight times eight times eight,* or five hundred twelve, etc.

Once we recognize that a number other than ten may be used as the base for a place-value system, then the way is left open for devising many more place-value systems. Any natural number larger than one may serve as the base for a place-value system of numerals. The number of digits required in the system is equal to the base. In the Arabic system, where the base is ten, we use ten digits, 0, 1, 2, 3, 4, 5, 6, 7, 8, and 9, to stand for the numbers less than ten. In a system with base eight, we need eight digits, 0, 1, 2, 3, 4, 5, 6, and 7, to stand for the numbers less than eight. In a system with base five, we need only five digits, 0, 1, 2, 3, and 4, to stand for the numbers less than five. Then five itself is represented by 10. This should be read as "one-oh." It should not be read as *ten.* The symbol 10 always means the base of the system of numerals. Hence it means *ten* only when the base is ten. It means *eight* when the base is eight. It means *five* when the base is five. It could also mean *two,* if we choose two as the base.

The Binary Scale

We shall now pay particular attention to the place-value system with base two. It is known as the *binary scale* for writing numerals. It is the simplest of all place-value systems because it uses as base the smallest number above one. It requires only two digits, 0 and 1. They are often referred to as *bits,* a contraction of *binary digits.* We have a special interest in the binary scale because binary numerals can be represented easily by means of electrical devices. A lamp, for example, can be used to represent a bit, by letting it stand for 1 when the lamp is on and for 0 when the lamp is off. For this reason, binary numerals are the natural ones to use for work with electronic computers.

In the binary scale, a 1 in the second place from the right stands for *two.* In the third place it stands for *two times two* or four. In the fourth place it stands for *two times two times two,* or eight, and so on. The numbers, one, two, four, eight, sixteen, etc., are called *powers of two.* So a binary numeral really represents a number as a sum of powers of two. For example, 111 means one four plus one two plus one one. 1010 means one eight plus no fours plus one two plus no ones. Therefore it means eight plus two, or ten.

Lazy Man's Arithmetic

Doing computations with binary numerals is a lazy man's dream. There are only a few binary number facts to memorize. For addition: $0 + 0 = 0$; $1 + 0 = 0 + 1 = 1$; $1 + 1 = 10$. For multiplication: $0 \times 0 = 0$; $0 \times 1 = 1 \times 0 = 0$; $1 \times 1 = 1$. These facts are summarized in the following tables:

Addition				*Multiplication*		
+	0	1		×	0	1
0	0	1		0	0	0
1	1	10		1	0	1

To do binary arithmetic, follow the ordinary rules of arithmetic, except that you use these tables instead of the base ten tables that you learned in school.

Binary Numerals

To get better acquainted with the binary scale, suppose we write the binary numerals for the numbers from zero to eight. We can use the addition table to help us figure out what these numerals are. Begin by writing 0 for zero. Then proceed by adding 1's, one at a time. Adding 1 to 0, we get $0 + 1 = 1$. Adding 1 to this result, we get $1 + 1 = 10$. To add 1 to 10, first write the addends one over the other. Then add, column by column. The next few additions are written out in the same way. Keep in mind that when you add 1 and 1, since the sum is 10, you put down the 0 and carry the 1 to the next column to the left:

10	11	100	101	110	111
1	1	1	1	1	1
11	100	101	110	111	1000

Then the binary numerals for the numbers from zero to eight are written as follows:

zero	0	three	11	six	110
one	1	four	100	seven	111
two	10	five	101	eight	1000

To acquire facility with binary numerals, the reader is advised to continue adding 1's until he reaches 32.

There are short-cuts that can be used to write any given number in the binary scale. We give two methods, and demonstrate each by using it to write the number *fifty-nine* in the binary scale.*

* For practice exercises, see *Magic House of Numbers,* by the same author, The John Day Company, New York, 1957.

Method I. Decompose the number into powers of two by first subtracting the highest power of two that is not larger than the number. Repeat the process with the remainder, and continue until the remainder is 0 or 1. The highest power of two that is not more than fifty-nine is thirty-two. When we subtract, the remainder is twenty-seven. The highest power of two that is not more than twenty-seven is sixteen. When we subtract, the remainder is eleven. The highest power of two that is not more than eleven is eight. When we subtract, the remainder is three. The highest power of two that is not more than three is two. When we subtract, the remainder is one. Writing the numbers in Arabic numerals (base ten), we can now write 59 as a sum of powers of two as follows: $59 = 32 + 16 + 8 + 2 + 1$. To take into account the powers of two that are missing, we rewrite it in this way: For every power that is present, write 1 times that power. For every power that is missing, write 0 times that power. Then we have $59 = 1 \times 32 + 1 \times 16 + 1 \times 8 + 0 \times 4 + 1 \times 2 + 1 \times 1$. The numbers that multiply the powers of two are the bits we should use to write 50 in the binary scale. So we have 59 (base ten) = 111011 (base two).

Method II. Write the number in Arabic numerals and divide by 2. Write the quotient underneath, and write the remainder, which is 0 or 1, at the side. Then divide the quotient by 2, and record the quotient and remainder. Continue dividing successive quotients by 2 until you get a quotient that is 0 or 1. The successive remainders and the last quotient give you the bits of the binary numeral in reverse order.

Moving a Bit

In a binary numeral, the meaning of each bit depends on its place in the numeral. What happens to the meaning of

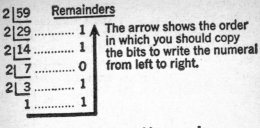

Converting to binary scale

the bit if it is moved one place to the left? To answer this question, let us start with the bit 1 in the first place on the right. Here it stands for the number *one*. Now move it one place to the left, and fill the place it has vacated with the digit 0. The new number we get is 10, or *two*. If we move the 1 again, we get 100, or *four*. After the next move, we get 1000, or *eight*, and so on. It is clear that when a bit is moved one place to the left, the number it stands for is multiplied by *two*. (Similarly, in the decimal system, when a digit is moved one place to the left, it is multiplied by ten.)

Now take any binary numeral, shift every one of its bits one place to the left. Since the place on the extreme right is left empty when this is done, fill it with a 0. The shifting doubles the meaning of every bit. As a result, it doubles the meaning of the entire numeral. For example, consider the binary numeral 101. The number it stands for is four plus one, or *five*. When we shift the bits one place to the left, it becomes 1010, which stands for eight plus two, or *ten*. We shall see later (page 142), how electronic calculators use the shifting of bits as a simple way of multiplying a number by two.

If shifting a bit one place to the left doubles the number that it stands for, then shifting a bit one place to the right divides the number by two. To be able to shift all bits to the right, without losing sight of which bit is in the units place, we put a dot immediately to the right of the units place, just as we do when we write Arabic (decimal or base ten) numerals. Then bits which stand to the right of the dot stand for binary fractions, just as in Arabic numerals they stand for decimal fractions. Thus, in the binary scale, 1. stands for one, 0.1 stands for one half, 0.01 stands for one fourth, and so on. With this notation, we can use binary fractions to represent common fractions, at least approximately, just as we usually employ decimal fractions for the same purpose.

CHAPTER 5

Algebra of Numbers

Basic Operations

IN EVERYDAY arithmetic, we often have occasion to do four different things with natural numbers: we add them, subtract them, multiply them, and divide them. Each of these operations "combines" two given numbers in a special way to obtain a third number called *sum, difference, product* or *quotient,* respectively. When we add two natural numbers, the sum we get is also a natural number. When we multiply two natural numbers, the product is a natural number. To express the fact that we do not have to go outside the natural number system to find the sum or product of any two natural numbers, we say that the natural number system is *closed* under the operations addition and multiplication. We cannot make the same assertion concerning subtraction or division. While we can subtract 2 from 5 in the natural number system, we cannot subtract 5 from 2 in that system. The latter subtraction becomes possible only in an expanded number system that contains the negative integer -3, a number that is outside the natural number system. Similarly, while we can divide 6 by 2 in the natural number system, we cannot divide 2 by 6 in that system. The latter division becomes possible only in an expanded number system that contains the fraction $\frac{1}{3}$, a number that is outside the natural number system. We see, then, that the natural number system is *not closed* under the operations subtraction and division.

Because of this distinction with regard to closure, the operations addition and multiplication are considered the basic operations in the natural number system. They are considered basic for another reason, too: The other operations can be defined in terms of them. The statement "Subtract 2 from 5" really means "Find the natural number which, when *added* to 2 gives 5 as the sum." The statement "Divide 6 by 2" really means "Find the natural number which, when *multiplied* by 2 gives 6 as the product." So all questions involving subtraction and division can be expressed in terms of the basic operations, addition and multiplication. We designate these basic operations by means of the familiar symbols $+$ and $\times$.

General Statements

We know from the addition table of ordinary arithmetic that $2 + 3 = 3 + 2$. There are many true statements of the same form: $3 + 5 = 5 + 3$, $4 + 9 = 9 + 4$, and so on. In fact, the relationship expressed in these statements is perfectly general, and may be expressed as a rule in these words: Write the sum of two natural numbers. Then write another sum by interchanging the two numbers. The two sums are equal. This rule can be stated in another form: If x stands for any natural number, and y stands for any natural number, then $x + y = y + x$. In this formulation of the rule, the letters x and y serve merely as place holders. They indicate places that may be filled by natural numbers. Letters used as place holders in this way are called *variables*. The use of variables makes it possible for us to state in very brief form general rules like the one we just observed. In the abbreviated statement of the rules it is customary to leave out the prefatory phrase, "If x stands for any natural number, and y stands for any natural number." Although the phrase is omitted, it must be understood as part of the statement of the rule.

The Rules of Arithmetic

The rule we have just observed is important enough to have acquired a name. We call it the *commutative law of addition.* There is an analogous *commutative law of multiplication,* which may be written in this form: $xy = yx$. Here xy is to be read as "x times y." We are using the usual convention of omitting the multiplication sign between variables, to avoid confusing the multiplication sign with the letter x.

Here are some more general rules about natural numbers, expressed by means of variables:

$x + (y + z) = (x + y) + z$. (Associative Law of Addition)

$x (yz) = (xy) z$. (Associative Law of Multiplication)

$x (y + z) = xy + xz$. (Distributive Law)

The associative law of addition merely expresses the familiar fact that when we add three numbers, it doesn't make any difference whether we first add the first and second number and then add in the third number, or first add the second and third number and then add in the first number. It is because of this law that we are sure that adding a column of figures from the bottom up gives the same result as adding it from the top down.

The distributive law merely expresses the fact that the number of objects in a rectangular array is unaltered if the rectangle is decomposed into two rectangles, as in the diagram below:

$$3 \cdot 7 \text{ or } 3(5 + 2) \quad = \quad 3 \cdot 5 \quad + \quad 3 \cdot 2$$

The distributive law

Distinguished Numbers

The number 0 has a peculiar property in relation to addition. When you add 0 to any natural number, that number is unchanged. Using a variable, the rule about 0 takes this brief form: $0 + x = x$. Let us call this rule the Law of Zero.

The number 1 has an analogous property in relation to multiplication. When you multiply any natural number by 1, the number is unchanged: $1x = x$. Let us call this rule the Law of One.

The Algebra of Natural Numbers

We have just observed that the natural number system has these characteristics: 1) It is a collection of elements that is closed under two operations, each of which "combines" any two elements to form a third element in the system. 2) These operations obey the seven laws displayed above: the Commutative Laws, the Associative Laws, the Distributive Law, the Law of Zero, and the Law of One. Any system which is closed under one or more operations that obey laws somewhat like these is said to have an algebraic structure, or, more briefly, an *algebra*. The seven laws we have examined, together with some others we have not mentioned (since we shall have no need for them in this book), are the foundation of the *algebra of natural numbers*.

The Algebra of Integers

The *negative* of a number is defined as the number you must add to it to get 0 as the sum. In the natural number system, a number that has a negative is a rare thing indeed. In fact, the number 0 is the only natural number that has a negative. However, there are other number systems in which numbers that have negatives are the rule rather than the exception. One of these systems is the system of integers, consisting of 0, the positive integers $+1, +2, +3,$ $\ldots$, etc., and the negative integers $-1, -2, -3, \ldots$, etc. Here every number has a negative. For example, since the sum of $+3$ and -3 is 0, -3 is the negative of $+3$, and $+3$ is the negative of -3. A minus sign is used as the symbol for the words "the negative of," so that if the variable x stands for some integer, then $-x$ stands for the negative of that integer.

The reader will recall from his high school mathematics days that integers can be added and multiplied, and the result in each case is an integer. In other words, the system of integers is closed under the operations addition and multiplication. Moreover, in this system, the same seven laws that we observed in the natural number system are also obeyed. Consequently there is an *algebra of integers,* and these seven laws are among the properties of that algebra. However, because every integer has a negative, the algebra of integers obeys some additional laws that do not apply to the system of natural numbers. Among these are the four laws listed below, which you will recognize as rules that you learned when you studied high school algebra:

$$-(-x) = x. \qquad -(x+y) = (-x) + (-y).$$
$$(-x)(-y) = xy. \qquad x(-y) = -(xy).$$

Because of these laws involving negatives, the algebra of integers is different from the algebra of natural numbers, even though they share some common rules.

Other Algebras

We have made these brief comments about the natural number system and the system of integers for two purposes. One purpose is to show that there is more than one algebra or algebraic structure. Then it will not be a surprise when we encounter a new algebraic structure in the chapters on logic. The second purpose is to show what an algebra looks like. Then we shall be prepared to recognize this new structure as an algebra when we see it.*

* For an elementary introduction to algebraic structures, written for the layman, see *The New Mathematics*, by the same author, The John Day Company, New York, 1958.

CHAPTER 6

Calculating Machines

WHAT picture flashes through your mind as you read the title of this chapter? It is likely that you see an electrical desk calculator, with its rows of numbered buttons, and you hear the rhythmic sound it makes as its motor pushes levers and turns wheels. Or you see some long-forgotten newspaper photograph of a giant electronic brain that suggests a radio repairman's nightmare of a radio boiling over out of its case until it fills a whole room. It is not likely that you see simple, homely things like a pair of rulers, or the rows of beads on a baby's play-pen. But it is precisely these homely things that we shall talk about first, because they are both good examples of calculating machines.

A Simple Adding Machine

A pair of foot rulers can be used as an adding machine. The numbers from 1 to 12 are printed on the face of each foot ruler. Every number is next to a line, and it indicates the number of inches in the distance of that line from the left hand edge of the ruler. The number 0 is not printed on the ruler, but it can be understood to refer to the left hand edge itself. We can use the rulers to add any two of these numbers whose sum is not more than twelve. To add the numbers, place one ruler above the other so that the left edge of the upper ruler lies above one of the addends on the lower ruler. Then locate the other addend on the upper ruler. The sum of the two numbers will appear below it. The diagram shows the position of the rulers for adding 2 and 3.

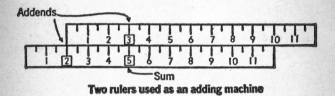

Two rulers used as an adding machine

The Abacus

The rows of beads on a play-pen are part of an *abacus*, an ancient calculating device that is still widely used throughout the world. In its simplest form, each row contains ten beads. In the first row, each bead stands for a unit. In the second row, each bead stands for ten. In the third row, each bead stands for one hundred, etc. The abacus is a place-value system for writing numbers by means of beads. To write the number 325, for example, first begin with all the beads at the left. Then move some beads to the right as follows: 5 beads on the first line to represent 5 units; 2 beads on the second line to represent 2 tens; 3 beads on the third line to represent 3 hundreds.

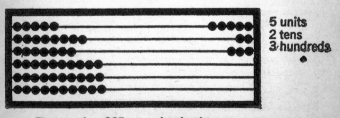

5 units
2 tens
3 hundreds

The number 325 on a simple abacus

To add 117 to this number, move one more bead to the right on the third line, and move one more bead to the right on the second line. We also have to move seven more beads to the right on the first line. We have to do this in two steps. First move as many as we can. After we move five beads, there are no more beads left to be moved. We still have to move two more, however. To provide beads for this purpose, we move the ten beads on the top line back and move another bead on the second line over to the right to take their place. This is an even exchange, since the bead on

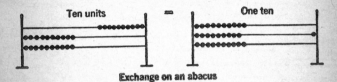

Exchange on an abacus

the second line stands for ten. Now we move two beads over on the top line, and the addition is complete. If we did this addition example with numerals written on paper, we would first add 5 and 7 to get 12. Then we would put down the 2 and carry 1 to the next column. The exchange of ten beads on the first line for one bead on the second line is equivalent to the *carry* step.

Although the abacus is only a toy in the United States, it is a practical calculator in the Soviet Union, China, Japan, and many other countries. The Japanese version of the abacus, called the *soroban,* is shown in the drawing below. A horizontal bar divides it into two parts. The beads below the bar represent, from right to left, units, tens, hun-

The number 162 on the Japanese soroban

dreds, etc. The beads above the bar represent five, fifty, five hundred, etc., respectively. Numbers are represented by moving the appropriate beads toward the bar from both sides. Experienced users of the soroban can calculate very quickly on it. Shortly after World War II, there was a calculating race between an American Army clerk, using an electrical desk calculator, and a Tokyo bank clerk using a soroban. The bank clerk won the race!

Two Types of Calculators

There are two major types of calculators in use today. They are distinguished by the manner in which they represent the numbers on which they perform calculations. One type is based on one of the ways in which we use numbers. The other type is based on the way we write numbers.

One of the important uses of numbers arises in the practical activity of measuring physical quantities. *Length* is an example of such a physical quantity. We measure a length by comparing it with a unit of length. The measure is then expressed as a number of units. In measurement, we use a number to represent a physical quantity. This process can be reversed. *We can use a physical quantity to represent a number.* Then, to perform arithmetic operations on numbers we can perform the corresponding operations on the physical quantities. This is what we were doing when we used two rulers as an adding machine. We represented each of the numbers by a length, and then we added the numbers by adding the lengths. Computers which represent numbers by physical quantities are called *analog computers*. The adding machine made of rulers is the simplest of analog computers. In other analog computers, numbers may be represented by such physical quantities as the amount of rotation of a wheel or the strength of an electric current.

When we write numbers in Arabic numerals, every number is represented by a sequence of digits. There are only ten digits in this system, 0, 1, 2, 3, 4, 5, 6, 7, 8, and 9. These ten symbols have no special qualifications for the job they do other than that they all look different. Any ten symbols that can be distinguished from each other can take their place. The symbols may be ink marks on paper, or sets of beads on a wire, or any physical object capable of appearing in ten distinct forms or of existing in ten distinct states. This opens up the possibility of using physical objects to represent digits. Then sequences of these physical objects can be used to represent numbers by representing their digits in the proper order. This is the underlying principle of the abacus. Each row of beads on the abacus can exist in ten states, viz., with no beads moved over, or with one bead moved over, or with two beads moved over, and so on. Each state represents a digit, and the sequence of rows of beads, each in a definite state, represents a number. Any computer that uses this principle is called a *digital computer*. The abacus is the simplest of digital computers. Since we move the beads of the abacus around by hand, it represents the lowest or hand-tool stage of evolution of digital computers. An electrical desk calculator is in the higher power-tool stage. The modern electronic calculators represent the most advanced or automatic-tool stage.

The Differential Analyzer

The best known of analog computers is the *differential analyzer* built at the Massachusetts Institute of Technology. In this machine, a number is represented as an amount of rotation of a wheel. Computations are made by combining the rotations of various wheels. There are two basic computing elements in the differential analyzer. One of them is a *differential gear,* like the gear assembly on the rear axle of an automobile. In the automobile the differential gear has the function of permitting the two rear wheels to turn

at different speeds when the car makes a turn. In the differential analyzer it has the job of computing the *average* of
two numbers. The other computing unit is an *integrator*,
which carries out mechanically one of the basic operations
of the calculus. The analyzer makes computations by a
sequence of steps in which it takes averages and performs
integrations, just as the Turing machine makes calculations
as a sequence of steps in which it writes or erases 1's and
X's.

As an example of analog computation, we describe how
a differential gear finds the average of two numbers. A
differential gear is shown in the drawing below. It is an
assembly of four gears, X, Y, Z, and W. Gears X and Y
have the same number of teeth and are attached to sleeves
on the axle of gear Z. Because of the sleeves, they can turn
independently around the axle. Gear W is mounted on an
axle across the cut-out section of gear Z. When gear Z
turns, it carries gear W around with it. Gears X and Y are
meshed with gear W as shown in the drawing. Suppose we
want to average two numbers x and y. To represent x we
turn gear X with a speed of x turns per second. To repre-

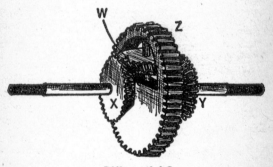

Differential Gear

sent y we turn gear Y with a speed of y turns per second in
the same direction as gear X. Then the speed of gear Z
will be $\dfrac{x+y}{2}$ turns per second. Let us see why.

Suppose first that x and y are equal numbers. Then gears X and Y turn with the same speed. In this case, gear W behaves like a rigid rod connecting gears X and Y. As gears X and Y turn, they push gear W, and in this way they make gear Z turn around with them at the same speed. However, if x and y are unequal numbers, so that gears X and Y turn at different speeds, then while gear W is being pushed it is also made to *turn* on its axle. Let us assume now that gear X is faster than gear Y, and let us denote by z the speed of gear Z. Imagine an observer who is on gear Z and turns with it. When he looks at gear X, he does not see all of its speed, because his own rotation with gear Z cancels part of it. He sees only the difference between the speed of gear X and the speed of gear Z. This difference is $x - z$. Similarly, when he observes gear Y, he sees only the difference between the speed of gear Y and the speed of gear Z. This difference is $z - y$. From his point of view, gear X passes him at the speed of $x - z$ and turns gear W as a result. Gear W then seems to be pushing gear Y, making it turn in a direction opposite to the turning of gear X. For every tooth on W that is pushed around by X, a tooth on the opposite side of W pushes Y. Therefore, as he sees it, the gears X and Y are turning at the same speed. That means that $x - z = z - y$. If we solve this simple equation for z, we find that $z = \dfrac{x + y}{2}$.

Once the differential gear has computed the average of two numbers, it is a simple matter to obtain their sum. If another gear with half as many teeth as gear Z is meshed directly with gear Z, it will turn twice as fast as gear Z does. So when the speed of gear Z is $\dfrac{x + y}{2}$, the speed of this smaller gear will be $x + y$. Note that this is the outcome only if gears X and Y are turning in the same direction. If we turn them in opposite directions, then the speed of gear Z will be $\dfrac{x - y}{2}$, and the speed of the smaller gear meshed with Z will be $x - y$. So a differential gear, with the help of just one more gear, can do addition and subtraction.

A Counting Machine

In a digital computer, a number is represented as a sequence of digits. If the numbers are expressed as Arabic numerals, the object which represents a single digit must be able to exist in ten distinct states, so that each state may stand for one of the digits from 0 to 9. An object that is frequently used for this purpose is a wheel whose circumference is divided into ten equal parts. The digits from 0 to 9 are printed on these parts in the proper order. Because of the circular arrangement, the 0 follows the 9. A viewing window near the wheel permits only one digit to be seen at a time. The ten "states" of the wheel are the ten positions to which the wheel may be turned so that different digits may be seen through the window. Several wheels like this, mounted side by side under one long window, can be used to display numbers with several digits. Combining the wheels with some gears can convert the set of wheels into a *counting machine*. One way of doing this is shown in the drawing. When the right hand wheel changes its state from 9 to 0, the cog over the gear on the left hand wheel pushes it and forces it to make one tenth of a turn. This makes the left hand wheel advance one step. That is, it changes its state, from whatever number it showed through the window to the next number on the wheel. The set of wheels is now equipped with a mechanism for *carrying*. In a hand-operated counting machine, a lever is pressed to register one unit. Every time the lever is pressed, the units wheel, which is on the far right, makes one tenth of a turn. If it starts with the 0 showing through the window, it advances one step at a time to 1, 2, 3, and so on, until it reaches 9. Then, the next time the lever is pressed, while the units wheel returns to 0, the tens wheel is advanced one step. In this way ten

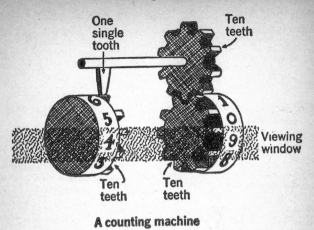

A counting machine

units on the units wheel are exchanged for a single ten on the tens wheel.

Counting devices of this type are frequently attached to machines that repeat the same operation over and over again. Then the device counts the number of times that the operation is performed. The *odometer* in an automobile is a counting machine used for counting the number of miles that the automobile travels. The first wheel of the odometer registers tenths of a mile. It is connected by means of a cable to a wheel of the car. When the wheel of the car has turned enough to move the car forward one tenth of a mile, the cable turns the first wheel of the odometer just enough to displace the digit that is under the viewing window, and move the next digit into place.

A Desk Calculator

To convert a counting machine into a hand-operated adding machine, all that is needed is an additional mechanical device for advancing each of the wheels by any chosen amount. In one type of adding machine, this device consists of a series of notched rods, one for each wheel of the counting machine. A row of buttons numbered from 0 to 9 is connected by levers to each rod. When a button is pressed down, the lever pushes the rod up until the number of teeth of the rod projecting beyond the wheel is equal to the number printed on the button. Then, when a hand lever is moved, the rod is pulled back. It engages the gear of the wheel as it moves, and advances it one step for each of the projecting teeth pulled back. In this way, the number on the button is added to the number previously registered on that wheel. Meanwhile, whenever the wheel completes a full turn, it *carries* one step over to the next wheel, so that the sum shows up as an Arabic numeral under the viewing window. When a sum has been completed, a lever is pressed to return all the wheels to the 0 state, so that the machine is ready to add a new set of numbers.

A machine that adds is easily adapted to do subtraction, multiplication, and division. Since it adds to the number on display through the viewing window by turning the wheels in one direction, it can subtract by turning the wheels in the opposite direction. It can multiply two numbers if it is equipped to register two numbers at a time. Then, as it keeps adding the multiplicand to itself on one register, it counts backwards from the multiplier to 1 on the other register. When it reaches 1, it has used the multiplicand as an addend a number of times equal to the multiplier. This is equivalent to multiplying by the multiplier. If it were set to multiply 4 × 5, for example, the pairs of numbers registered would be: 4, 5; 3, 10; 2, 15; 1, 20. When the multiplier has been reduced to 1, the number in the place of the multiplicand is the product. The machine can divide if it can be made to subtract a fixed number over and over again, and count the subtractions as it works. For example, to divide 35 by 11, the machine would start with 35 and keep subtracting 11, until the remainder is less than 11. If it displayed successive remainders and the count of the number of subtractions, the last count would be the quotient. In the division of 35 by 11, the successive pairs of numbers on display would be 24, 1; 13, 2; 2, 3. The final count of the subtractions is 3, so the quotient is 3.

One last modification is needed to speed up the process of calculation by the kind of machine we have been describing. The hand lever which is moved to carry out each step of addition or subtraction is replaced by an electric motor. When this is done, we have the basic elements of an electrical desk calculator. There are many such calculators available. They differ from each other in the details of mechanical design, but they all operate according to the same principles.

Change without Visible Motion

A great gain in speed of calculation is attained when moving parts such as levers and wheels are replaced by elements of an electrical circuit. Then the visible but slow motion of mechanical parts is replaced by the invisible but rapid motion of an electric current. The first step in designing a digital computer made of electrical elements would be to construct a device for representing digits, so that it can take over the job of the rotating wheel. If numbers are written as Arabic numerals, the device must be such that it can exist in any one of ten states. An example of such a device is a multiple switch that can route electric current into any one of ten separate lines. However, electrical elements, by their very nature, suggest a totally different approach to the problem of representing the digits of a number.

Switches, relays, and tubes are typical electrical elements. They have one simple and obvious characteristic in common. Each one of them may be either *on* or *off*. In other words each can exist in *two* states. This fact suggests that we use two states to represent digits, instead of straining to construct a device that has ten states. We need a ten-state device only when we write numbers as Arabic numerals. We can get by with a two-state device if we write numbers in the binary scale instead. The binary scale is the natural way of representing numbers by means of the state of electrical elements. That is why it is used in connection with electronic computers. The drawing below shows how a bank of four lamps can be used to represent the numbers from zero to nine. Each lamp represents one bit in the binary numeral for a number.

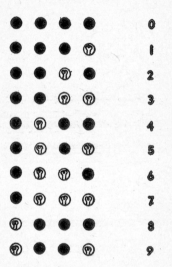

Numbers represented by lamps

Using binary numerals simplifies the problem of designing an electronic computer. But it also complicates the problem of using it. It compels us to translate numbers from the decimal scale to the binary scale before feeding them to the machine, and then translating the results of the machine's calculations back into the decimal scale. To avoid the extra steps of translation from one scale to another, some machines are designed on the basis of a compromise between the two scales. In these compromise machines, numbers are expressed by means of decimal digits, but each digit is written as four bits in the binary scale, as in the drawing on page 54. A two-digit number is expressed as two sets of four bits each. A three-digit number is expressed as three sets of four bits each, and so on. For example, if the word *OFF* is used to represent 0, and the word *ON* is used to represent 1, the decimal number 237 is represented by twelve bits as follows:

OFF OFF ON OFF   OFF OFF ON ON   OFF ON ON ON

This is so because OFF-OFF-ON-OFF represents the binary numeral 0010, which stands for *two;* OFF-OFF-ON-ON represents the binary numeral 0011, which stands for *three;* and OFF-ON-ON-ON represents the binary numeral 0111, which stands for *seven.*

In Chapter XI, where we describe some of the details of a typical electronic computer, we shall explain how numbers represented in this compromise form may be added or multiplied electrically.

CHAPTER 7

Words, Sentences, and Logic

Plain and Fancy Thinking

IN ORDER to design a machine that thinks, it is necessary to know the rules of thought. The study of the rules of thought is called *logic*. In this chapter we discover some of the principal ideas that occur in the study of logic. Then, in the next two chapters, we use these ideas to explore the rules of thought.

When you see the word "thinking," it may bring to your mind a picture of someone sitting in the pose of Rodin's statue of *The Thinker,* with his elbow on his knee and his chin on his hand, as he ponders the mysteries of the universe. Perhaps it suggests a lawyer threading his way through a complicated legal argument, or a mathematician writing out the proof of a theorem. In this age of specialization, we speak of some people as "thinkers" as if thinking were a specialized vocation engaged in only by a few. But no one has a monopoly on thinking. The plumber thinks when he decides how to cut and join pipes for a heating system. The housewife thinks when she plans a menu. A child thinks when he decides to climb a chair to reach a cookie on the table. The thinking of the philosopher, the lawyer and the mathematician is more intensive and more complicated than the common thinking of daily life, but it is built out of the same logical elements. All thinking, whether plain or fancy, follows the same rules.

Thoughts and Language

We express our thoughts in words. For this reason, the structure of thought is paralleled by the structure of language. We can get an idea of what is involved in thinking by examining the language we use. In fact, it will be enough to observe the language of a child as he learns to talk. Each stage in his language growth will introduce us to a major concept of logic.

Nouns and Classes

Let us accept without question the legend that the first word a baby learns is *Mama.* He soon learns his own name, say, *Peter,* and identifies *Daddy* and other members of the household. He also learns words like *spoon, cup, table,* and so on. Before long, he discovers that the words *Mama* and *table* are used in different ways. The word *Mama* is applied only to one object in his experience, the warm, gentle woman who feeds him, bathes him, dresses him, and hugs him. But the word *table* applies to several things. He may use it for the table in the kitchen, the table in the dining room, or the little table in his own bedroom. The word *table* is the name of a *class* of things, and is applied to any member of the class. Similarly, *spoon* and *cup* are class names, while *Peter* and *Daddy* refer to individuals only. In grammar, we distinguish between class names and the names of individuals by using different labels for them. We call a class name a *common noun.* We call an individual name a *proper noun.* To help us recognize the difference in writing, we capitalize proper nouns.

Underlying our use of common nouns, then, is the concept of a class. A class is any collection of objects that have some common property. The individual members of a class are referred to as *elements*. Any particular object may be an element of many classes. A dining room table, for example, may belong to the class of *wooden objects.* It also belongs to the class of *tables,* and to the class of *furniture.* Some classes overlap, or have common elements. The class of tables and the class of furniture have common elements. In fact, the class of tables lies wholly within the class of furniture. The class of furniture and the class of wooden objects also have common elements, but neither class lies wholly within the other. Not all wooden objects are articles of furniture, and not all pieces of furniture are made of wood. Some classes do not overlap at all. For example, the class of minerals and the class of animals have no common elements. No mineral is classified as an animal, and vice versa.

Sentences and Propositions

In a more advanced stage of a child's language growth, he begins to talk in whole sentences. Many of his sentences are statements or assertions. He may say, "The milk is hot," or "Peter is tired." He may seize his playmate's ball and say, "This ball is mine." An older child in a playful mood may string words together without rhyme or reason, to produce a sentence like, "The table sky jumps over the purple song." We observe immediately that we must distinguish between two kinds of sentences. Some sentences, like the first three, have a clear meaning. Other sentences, like the last one, have *no* meaning. The child sometimes makes up meaningless sentences to amuse himself or others. Lewis Carroll had the same purpose when he wrote:

> " 'Twas brillig, and the slithy toves
>   Did gyre and gimble in the wabe:
> All mimsy were the borogroves,
>   And the mome raths outgrabe."

Unfortunately some people write meaningless sentences while they think they are communicating meaning to the reader. While we may, if we wish, think of a meaningless sentence as a form of music, it is not a means of expressing thought. In the study of logic, we have to consider only sentences with meaning.

A statement that has meaning is called a *proposition*. Every proposition is either true or false. The truth or falsity of a proposition is called its *truth value*.

Propositional Forms

The statement, "The last note on the right on a piano keyboard has a higher pitch than middle C," is a proposition. If we replace the first ten words (the complete subject of the sentence) by a blank space, we obtain what is called a *propositional form:* "——————————— has a higher pitch than middle C." The propositional form is not a proposition. It is not even a sentence. It becomes a sentence, however, if we fill the blank space with some subject. Here, for example, are three sentences obtained by filling in the blank space with different subjects:

1) The second note from the right on a piano keyboard has a higher pitch than middle C.
2) The last note on the left on a piano keyboard has a higher pitch than middle C.
3) My hat has a higher pitch than middle C.

Notice that while all three are sentences, they aren't all propositions. Sentences 1 and 2 have meaning. The first one is true, and the second one is false. These are both propositions. But sentence 3 has no meaning. Therefore it is not a proposition. If we want to obtain a proposition from a propositional form, we are not free to fill the blank space with any subject at all. We must choose only subjects which yield a sentence that makes sense (whether it is true or false). A set of subjects that makes sense when put into a propositional form is called a *universe of discourse*. In this case, for example, we might choose as the universe of discourse the set of all notes on a piano keyboard.

A blank space is easy to show in writing, but hardly easy to express out loud. To be able to speak a propositional form as well as to write it, we take a cue from elementary algebra, and use a variable to serve as a place holder. If we use the variable X, then the propositional form is written in this way: X has a higher pitch than middle C. If X is replaced by any element in the universe of discourse, a meaningful sentence or proposition is obtained. For some of these elements, the proposition is true. The set of all such elements for which the proposition is true is a class within the universe of discourse. The propositional form, "X has a higher pitch than middle C," is called the *defining form* of that class.

Every class can be defined by means of a defining form. The procedure for defining a class is to specify first some universe of discourse within which the class may be found. Then set up a defining form which becomes a true proposition for elements of the universe of discourse that are in the class, and which becomes a false proposition for elements of the universe of discourse that are not in the class. The defining form serves as a kind of filter, sifting members of the class out of the universe of discourse. For example, to define a square, we might choose as the universe of discourse the set of all rectangles, and then use as the defining form, "X has equal sides."

Once a universe of discourse is specified, every class within it can be defined by means of an appropriate defining form. The procedure is also clearly reversible. Every defining form which makes sense in that universe of discourse defines a class within it. This fact shows that there is a close connection between the concept of *class* and the concept of *proposition*. It should not come as a surprise, then, to find that there is a close connection between the algebra of classes, which will be developed in Chapter VIII, and the algebra of propositions, which will be developed in Chapter IX.

Relations

Some of the words that a child learns very early denote *relations* between things. When he says, "The cup is on the table," the word *on* specifies a relation between the cup and the table. When he says, "Mr. Green is Johnny's daddy," he uses the word daddy (note the small d) to denote the relation "father of." In his early experiences with numbers, he learns of the relation "smaller than" that exists between certain numbers.

One of the problems that comes up in logic is to discover the properties possessed by relations, and to classify the relations according to their properties. Let us consider, for example, the relation *smaller than*. It is customary to represent it by the symbol $<$. Then the statement, "Two is smaller than three," can be written this way: $2 < 3$. It is a well-known fact about the *smaller than* relation that it has this property: If the first of three numbers is smaller than the second, and the second is smaller than the third, then the first is smaller than the third. This property is called the *transitive* property, because the *smaller than* relation passes right through the middle number to connect the first and third number. (*Transit* means goes through.)

Not all relations have the transitive property. For example, the relation *father of* does not have the transitive property. If John is the father of Fred, and Fred is the father of Henry, it is not true that John is the father of Henry.

Relations among Classes or Propositions

There are certain special relations that classes within a universe of discourse may have to each other. We have already encountered some of them. For example, two classes may have some elements in common. If they do, we shall say that they *intersect*. A particularly important case of intersection arises when one class lies wholly within another. For convenience, let us now use variables A, B, and C to denote classes within a certain universe of discourse. If A lies wholly within B, we shall say that A is a subclass of B. To denote the relation "is a subclass of" we shall use the symbol $\subset$. (Read $\subset$ as "is a subclass of" or "is included in.") Then the statement, "A is a subclass of B," can be written in this form: $A \subset B$. It is easy to see that if A is a subclass of B, and B is a subclass of C, then A is a subclass of C. Consequently, the relation $\subset$, like the relation $<$, has the transitive property. In fact the symbol for "is a subclass of" was deliberately made to resemble the symbol for "is smaller than" in order to remind us that the two relations have similar properties.

There are certain special relations that hold between some propositions. A particularly important one is the relation of *implication*. For example, the proposition, "It is raining," implies the proposition, "The street is wet." (That is, if the first proposition is true, the second one must also be true.) "The street is wet" implies that "Anyone walking on the street will get his shoes wet." From these two implications we obtain another one: "It is raining" implies that "Anyone walking on the street will get his shoes wet." We obtained this third implication by using the following well-known rule of logic: If one proposition implies a second proposition, and the second proposition implies a third proposition, then the first proposition implies the third proposition. In other words, the relation "implies" has the transitive property. To show it in abbreviated form, we shall use the symbol $\rightarrow$ for the relation "implies," and we shall use the letters p, q, and r as variables that may stand for propositions. Then we can state that the relation $\rightarrow$ is transitive in this way: If $p \rightarrow q$, and $q \rightarrow r$, then $p \rightarrow r$.

In the next two chapters we explore more relations among classes, and relations among propositions. We have already seen that the relation $\subset$, which connects some classes, and the relation $\rightarrow$, which connects some propositions, resembles the relation $<$, which connects some numbers. We shall find more such resemblances between the behavior of classes or propositions to the behavior of numbers. In fact, there will be enough resemblances to permit us to develop an algebra of classes and an algebra of propositions.

CHAPTER 8

Algebra of Classes

Classes in a Universe

PICK any collection of objects whatever as a universe of discourse. We shall call this collection the universe class, or, more briefly, the *universe*. By selecting elements within this universe in different ways, we can form classes that are included within the universe. They will all be subclasses of the universe class. The purpose of this chapter is to examine relationships among the set of all possible subclasses of the universe class.

We might, for example, choose as the universe class the set of all living people. We can define a variety of subclasses within this universe by means of defining forms. Here are some examples:

1. *X* is a resident of the United States.
2. *X* is a citizen of the United States.
3. *X* is a resident of New York City.
4. *X* is the author of this book.
5. *X* is President of the United States.
6. *X* is a living person.
7. *X* is dead.

The class specified by each defining form is the class of all those living persons for whom the defining form becomes a true statement when *X* is replaced by a member of the class. Notice that the classes defined by 1, 2, and 3 include some but not all members of the universe class. The class defined by 6, on the other hand, includes all members of the universe class. That is, the universe class is one of its own subclasses. The classes defined by 4 and 5 contain exactly one member each. A class that contains one and only one member is called a *unit class*. The class defined by 7 contains no members at all. We call it the *empty class*. We shall have to refer to the universe class and the empty class quite often, so we introduce special symbols for them. We shall use the symbol 1 to stand for the universe class, and the symbol 0 to stand for the empty class. The reason for this choice of symbols will soon be apparent.

A Small Universe

The relationships within a universe class are especially easy to see if the universe class contains only a few members. As an example, let us take as the universe class the set of three symbols, #, %, and $. We shall form all possible subclasses of this universe class. To specify a class, we shall put its members on display between a pair of braces, { }. For convenience in referring to these classes, we shall give each one a name. The universe class and the empty class already have names, 1 and 0. To name the other classes, we shall use capital letters such as *A*, *B*, and *C*, chosen from the beginning of the alphabet. For variables that may stand for any class we shall use capital letters, such as *X*, *Y*, and *Z*, chosen from the end of the alphabet. Here is a complete list of all the subclasses within this small universe, together with their names:

$$
\begin{aligned}
\text{The universe} \quad &= 1 = \{\#, \%, \$\} \\
A &= \{\#, \%\} \\
B &= \{\#, \$\} \\
C &= \{\%, \$\} \\
D &= \{\#\} \\
E &= \{\%\} \\
F &= \{\$\} \\
\text{The empty class} = 0 &= \{\ \}
\end{aligned}
$$

To form a subclass of any of the classes in this list, simply delete all, or some, or none of its members. If we begin with the class B, for example, and omit no elements we are left with $\{ \#, \$ \}$ or B. If we omit $\$$, we are left with $\{ \# \}$ or D. If we omit $\#$, we are left with $\{ \$ \}$ or F. If we omit both $\$$ and $\#$, we are left with $\{ \ \}$ or 0. So the subclasses of B are B, D, F, and 0. Then using the symbol $\subset$ for the relation "is a subclass of," we may say $B \subset B$, $D \subset B$, $F \subset B$, and $0 \subset B$. The subclasses of C are C, E, F, and 0. So we may say $C \subset C$, $E \subset C$, $F \subset C$, and $0 \subset C$.

The Subclass Relation

By using this small universe as a model, we can verify a few simple rules about the symbol $\subset$. It is not hard to see that these rules are true in any universe whatever:

The empty class is a subclass of every class in the universe. In symbols, the rule takes this form: $0 \subset X$, where X is a variable that may stand for any subclass of the universe class.

Since the only classes we are talking about are subclasses of the universe class, we may say that every class is a subclass of the universe. In symbols: $X \subset 1$.

Every class is a subclass of itself. In symbols: $X \subset X$.

We have already observed that the relation $\subset$ has the transitive property. In symbols: If $X \subset Y$, and $Y \subset Z$, then $X \subset Z$.

We shall call two classes equal if they have the same membership. From time to time, we shall have to compare two classes to see if they are equal. A simple test for equality of classes is provided by this rule: Two classes are equal if each of them is a subclass of the other. In symbols: If $X \subset Y$, and $Y \subset X$, then $X = Y$.

There are at least two classes in the universe that are not equal. For example, the universe class is not equal to the empty class, because the empty class contains no members, while the universe class does contain members. (This rule breaks down only in the exceptional case where the universe class is the empty class. But in this case, with an empty universe of discourse, we have nothing to talk about. So let us agree now not to consider this exceptional case at all.) In symbols, the rule takes this form: there is a class X and a class Y such that $X \neq Y$. (Read $\neq$ as "is *not* equal to.")

Venn Diagrams

We shall find it helpful in the rest of this chapter to draw diagrams to illustrate the relationships between classes. The special diagrams we use are called Venn diagrams, after John Venn, a British mathematician of the nineteenth century. In the Venn diagrams, the universe is represented by the points inside a rectangle. A subclass of the universe is represented by the points inside some area within the rectangle. The area used most often to represent a subclass is a circle. The first diagram below shows a subclass A within the universe. The second diagram shows another subclass B lying wholly within A. This illustrates the relationship $B \subset A$.

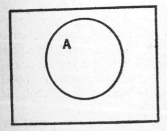
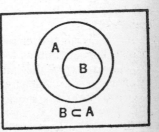

$B \subset A$

New Classes from Old

We now introduce some operations by which we can combine two classes to form a third class in the same universe. To make the meaning of each operation clear, we shall draw an appropriate Venn diagram that illustrates it. We shall also apply the operations in our model universe of three elements, #, %, and $.

The first operation we define is *addition* of classes, and it will be represented by means of a plus sign. If X and Y are classes in the universe 1, then $X + Y$ is the class made up of all those elements in the universe that are in X or in Y. (In logic this class is understood to include elements that are in both classes.) Note that the most significant idea here is expressed by the word *or*. In the Venn diagram below, if X is represented by the circle with vertical shading, and Y is represented by the circle with horizontal shading, then $X + Y$ is represented by the total shaded area enclosed within the thick black line.

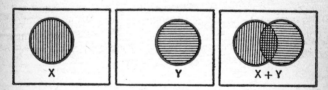

Addition of classes

In the universe $1 = \{ \#, \%, \$ \}$ (see page 65)
$B = \{ \#, \$ \}$, and $C = \{ \%, \$ \}$, So
$B + C = \{ \#, \%, \$ \}$. That is, $B + C = 1$.
$D = \{ \# \}$, and $E = \{ \% \}$. So $D + E = \{ \#, \% \} = A$.
$E = \{ \% \}$ and $F = \{ \$ \}$. So $E + F = \{ \%, \$ \} = C$.

If X and Y are classes in the same universe, $X + Y$ is called their *sum*. It is also sometimes called their *union*, because it is obtained by uniting within one class all the elements that are found in the two classes. The system of subclasses of a universe is closed under the operation +, because if X and Y are subclasses of the universe, so is $X + Y$.

Rules about Addition

Some simple rules governing the addition of classes follow immediately from the definition:

Uniting the elements of X and Y yields the same result as uniting the elements of Y and X. In symbols: $X + Y = Y + X$. (Commutative Law of Addition.) For example, if $B = \{\#, \$\}$ and $C = \{\%, \$\}$, $B + C$ contains all the elements of B, as well as the element $\%$ which is in C but not in B. $C + B$ contains all the elements of C, as well as the element $\#$ which is in B but not in C. In both cases, the total membership contains exactly the same elements, $\#$, $\%$, and $\$$. So $B + C = C + B$.

If X, Y and Z are classes, uniting X with the sum of Y and Z yields the same result as uniting the sum of X and Y with Z. In symbols: $X + (Y + Z) = (X + Y) + Z$. (Associative Law of Addition.) This rule is illustrated by the Venn diagrams below:

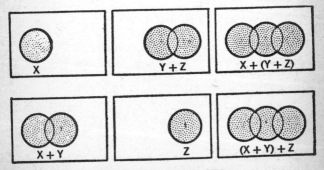

The associative law of addition

If any class is united with itself, the result is the same class all over again, because it includes all the elements of the original class, and no new elements. In symbols: $X + X = X$.

A class is unchanged if you unite it with the empty class, since the empty class contributes no additional elements. In symbols: $X + 0 = X$. (Law of 0.)

If any class is united with the universe, the result is the universe. This is clearly true because the union of any class with the universe must contain all elements in the universe, and cannot contain any others. In symbols: $X + 1 = 1$.

A class is wholly included in any union it forms with another class. In symbols: $X \subset X + Y$.

Notice that some of the rules governing addition of classes are like rules governing addition of numbers: the Commutative Law, the Associative Law, and the Law of 0. However, some of the rules for addition of classes like $X + X = X$, and $X + 1 = 1$, have no counterpart in the addition of numbers.

Multiplication of Classes

The second operation we define is *multiplication* of classes. As in the algebra of numbers, we shall represent multiplication by means of a dot, but this dot will often be omitted. If X and Y are classes in the universe 1, then XY is the class made up of all those elements that are in both X *and* Y. Note that the most significant idea here is

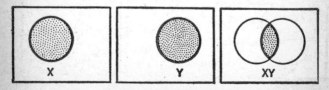

Multiplication of classes

expressed by the word *and*. The result of multiplying two classes is called their *product,* or their *intersection.* The Venn diagram for a product is shown on page 70.

In the universe $1 = \{\#, \%, \$\}$, $BC = \{\$\} = F$. There are no elements that belong to both D and E, so $DE = 0$.

The system of subclasses of a universe is closed under multiplication, because if X and Y are subclasses of the universe, then so is XY.

Rules about Multiplication

These rules governing multiplication of classes are easily verified:

The set of elements in both X and Y is the same as the set of elements in both Y and X. In symbols: $XY = YX$. (Commutative Law of Multiplication.)

If X, Y and Z are classes, multiplying X by the product of Y and Z yields the same result as multiplying the product of X and Y by Z. In symbols: $X(YZ) = (XY)Z$. (Associative Law of Multiplication.) This rule is illustrated by the Venn diagrams below.

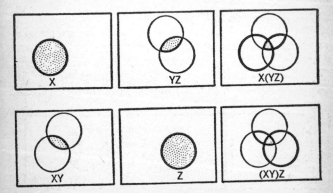

The associative law of multiplication

If X is any class, there are no elements that are in both the empty class and in X. Therefore multiplying any class by the empty class yields the empty class as the product. In symbois: $0X = 0$.

If X is any class, the elements that belong to the universe and to X are precisely the elements of X. So multiplying the universe by any class yields that same class as the product. In symbols: $1X = X$. (Law of 1.)

If any class is multiplied by itself, the same class is the product, because the elements in both X and X are obviously merely the elements in X. In symbols: $XX = X$.

If two classes X and Y are multiplied, the product is a subclass of either class. This is immediately obvious from the Venn diagram. In symbols: $XY \subset X$, and $XY \subset Y$.

Among these rules governing the multiplication of classes, there are some like the rules governing the multiplication of numbers: the Commutative Law, the Associative Law, and the Law of 1. However, there are also some rules, like $XX = X$, that do not apply to numbers at all.

The Distributive Laws

In the algebra of numbers, we had the distributive law: $X(Y + Z) = XY + XZ$. We can verify by means of Venn diagrams that this law holds for classes, too. The expression $X(Y + Z)$ means first unite Y and Z to form $Y + Z$, and then find the class of elements common to X and $Y + Z$. The expression $XY + XZ$ means first multiply X by Y and multiply X by Z. Then unite the two products. The two procedures are shown in these Venn diagrams below.

Comparing the two end results, we see that they are the same.

The law that $X(Y + Z) = XY + XZ$ may be put into

words as follows: To multiply a sum of two classes by a third class, it is just as good to multiply each of the two classes separately by that third class, and then add the products. It is interesting to see what becomes of this law if

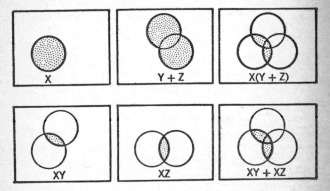

Multiplication is distributive with respect to addition

we interchange the words add and multiply, and interchange the words sum and product. Then, with a slight adjustment of language to conform to our customary word order, we get this statement: To add a third class to the product of two classes, it is just as good to add it to each of the two classes first, and then multiply the sums. In symbols, this statement says that $X + (YZ) = (X + Y) (X + Z)$. The original law says that multiplication is distributive with respect to addition. The new statement says that addition is distributive with respect to multiplication. The original law is true for both natural numbers and classes. Is the new statement also a law for natural numbers and classes?

To see if the new statement applies to numbers, let $X = 2$, $Y = 3$, and $Z = 4$. Then the statement says that $2 + (3 \cdot 4) = (2 + 3) (2 + 4)$, or $2 + 12 = 5 \cdot 6$. This assertion is obviously not true, so the new statement is *not* a law for natural numbers. However, it *is* a law for classes, as you can see from the Venn diagrams. So for classes, we have two distributive laws: Multiplication is distributive with respect to addition, and addition is distributive with respect to multiplication.

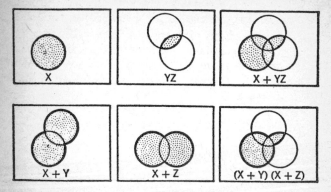

Addition is distributive with respect to multiplication

The Complement

We introduce a third operation of classes called *taking the complement*. If X is a class in the universe, the complement of X is the class obtained when you remove from the universe all the members of X. The operation of taking the complement is denoted by a bar drawn over the name of a class. Thus, the complement of X is written as $\bar{X}$. The operation is illustrated by the Venn diagram below.

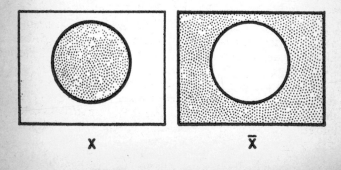

As an example of taking the complement, let us find the complement of B in the universe $1 = \{\#, \%, \$\}$. $B = \{\#, \$\}$. Therefore $\bar{B} = \{\%\} = E$. For a second example, let the universe be the class of all living people, and let X be the class of residents of the United States. Then $\bar{X}$ is the class of living people who do *not* reside in the United States. The bar denoting taking the complement serves the same function as the word *not* in ordinary speech. In fact, $\bar{X}$ may be read as "not X."

In any universe, it is obvious that the complement of the universe is the empty class and vice versa.

Rules about Complements

These rules follow directly from the definition of complement:

If you unite any class with its complement, you are putting into one class all the elements *in* the original class and all the elements *not in* the original class. The result obviously includes the whole universe. In symbols: $X + \bar{X} = 1$.

There are no elements that are in a class and also not in that class. So the product of a class and its complement is the empty class. In symbols: $X\bar{X} = 0$.

Since a class and its complement divide the universe between them, without any overlapping, then each is the complement of the other. Hence the complement of the complement of X is X itself. In symbols $(\bar{\bar{X}}) = X$. For example, saying that someone is *not* a *non*-resident of the United States is like saying that he *is* a resident of the United States.

There is a simple test by which complements can be recognized. Two classes are each other's complements if they do not overlap, and, together, they fill out the whole universe. In symbols: If $X + Y = 1$, and $XY = 0$, then $X = \bar{Y}$ and $Y = \bar{X}$.

Sums Versus Products

The fact that every class in a universe has a complement in that universe leads to an interesting pair of laws known as the laws of duality. These laws say that the complement of the sum of two classes is the product of their complements, and that the complement of the product of two

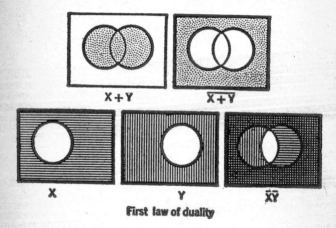

First law of duality

classes is the sum of their complements. In symbols: $(\overline{X + Y}) = \overline{XY}$, and $(\overline{XY}) = \overline{X} + \overline{Y}$.

The first of these laws is verified in the Venn diagrams above. In the first line of diagrams, we first add X and Y, and then take the complement of the sum. In the second line of diagrams, we first take the complement of X and Y and then multiply these complements. $\overline{X}$ is shown by horizontal shading. $\overline{Y}$ is shown by vertical shading. If the two diagrams are superposed, the product $\overline{X} \cdot \overline{Y}$ is the area that has both horizontal and vertical shading. Inspection of the last diagram on each line shows that the results are equal.

Venn diagrams can be used in the same way to verify the second law of duality.

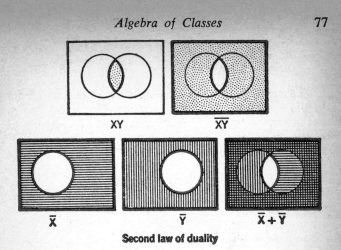

Second law of duality

Subclass Redefined

We have introduced a special symbol $\subset$ for the concept "is a subclass of." However, we can do without this symbol, because the same concept can be expressed by means of a sum or a product of classes. The Venn diagram below shows the situation when X is a subclass of Y. It is clear in this situation that the part of X and Y that is common to both is precisely X. So, if $X \subset Y$, then $XY = X$. On the other hand, if $XY = X$, it means that

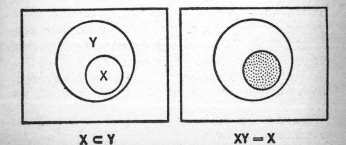

X is the common part of X and Y, so that X is wholly included in Y, or $X \subset Y$. Hence the statement $X \subset Y$ is completely equivalent to the statement $XY = X$, and either statement may be replaced by the other. It is easily seen that the statement $X \subset Y$ is also equivalent to the statement $X + Y = Y$. If X lies wholly within Y, uniting X and Y does not enlarge the class Y at all. So the union of X and Y in this case is precisely Y. Conversely, if the union of X and Y is precisely Y, it means that X has contributed to the union only elements that are in Y, hence X lies wholly within Y.

Some Rules Imply Others

The rules about classes that we have observed so far are not entirely independent of each other. Some of them can be derived from others. This fact suggests that the algebra of classes be organized into a deductive system analogous to that of geometry. In high school geometry we are taught many rules about geometric figures. But they are not presented as isolated facts. They are organized into a system in this way: A small set of rules, known as *axioms*, is separated from the rest in order to serve as the foundation of the system. Then all the other rules are derived from the axioms by logical reasoning. The derived rules are known as *theorems*. No verbal definitions are given of the terms used in the axioms. The meaning of these terms consists solely of what the axioms say about them. For example, we do not try to define the words *point* and *line* in geometry. But we know from the axioms that there is one and only one line through any two points. This assertion is part of the meaning of the words *point* and *line*. However, when new terms, not already mentioned in the axioms, are introduced in the system, they are carefully defined first.

We can follow the same procedure with the rules of the

algebra of classes. We can select from these rules a core set of rules that may serve as axioms, from which we can derive all the other rules as theorems. There are many different ways of selecting the rules that will serve as axioms. One particular choice of the axioms is given below.

Axioms for the Algebra of Classes

Here is a set of axioms for the algebra of classes. The undefined terms used in these axioms are "class," "plus" and "times." The usual symbols are used to represent "plus" and "times."

I. If X and Y are classes, there is a class Z such that $X + Y = Z$.

II. If X and Y are classes, there is a class W such that $XY = W$.

III. There exists a class 0 such that, if X is any class, $X + 0 = X$.

IV. There exists a class 1 such that, if X is any class, $1X = X$.

V. If X and Y are classes, $X + Y = Y + X$.

VI. If X and Y are classes, $XY = YX$.

VII. If X, Y and Z are classes, $X + YZ = (X + Y)(X + Z)$.

VIII. If X, Y and Z are classes, $X(Y + Z) = XY + XZ$.

IX. If X is a class, there exists a class $\bar{X}$ such that $X + \bar{X} = 1$, and $X\bar{X} = 0$.

X. There exist classes X and Y such that $X \neq Y$.

Axioms I and II merely assert that any two classes have a sum and a product. Axioms III and IV are the Law of 0 and the Law of 1, respectively. Axioms V and VI are the commutative laws of addition and multiplication. Axioms VII and VIII are the two distributive laws. Axiom IX asserts that every class has a complement. Axiom X guarantees that the system includes classes that are not empty.

Notice that the associative laws for addition and multiplication are not included among the axioms. They can be derived as theorems from these ten axioms. Notice, too, that the concept of *subclass* is not included among the undefined terms. We can, if we wish, define this concept by using the terms that do appear in the axioms. For example, we might introduce the following definition: $X \subset Y$ shall mean that $XY = X$.

One of the very important rules of logic is the rule that the relation $\subset$ is transitive. That is, if $X \subset Y$, and $Y \subset Z$, then $X \subset Z$. This rule is not an axiom, so it must be a theorem. That is, we should be able to *prove* it with the help of the axioms and other theorems. The proof turns out to be quite simple: If $X \subset Y$, and $Y \subset Z$, then by the definition of $\subset$, $XY = X$, and $XZ = Y$. The latter statement means that Y can be replaced by YZ. Making this substitution in the statement $XY = X$, we get $X(YZ) = X$. The associative law of multiplication says that we may replace $X(YZ)$ by $(XY)Z$. Making this substitution, we get the statement that $(XY)Z = X$. But, since $XY = X$, we may replace XY by X. The resulting statement, $XZ = X$, is equivalent to the statement that $X \subset Z$.

Axiom IX asserts that every class has a complement. It seems to leave open the possibility that a class may have more than one complement. However, all the axioms taken together exclude this possibility. It can be proved as a theorem that every class has only one complement having the properties listed in Axiom IX. Consequently, any time we come across two classes X and Y such that $X + Y = 1$, and $XY = 0$, we can conclude at once that $X = \bar{Y}$ and $Y = \bar{X}$. (That is, each is the complement of the other.)

All of the rules that we have listed about addition and multiplication of classes that are not in the list of axioms are theorems that can be proved. In what follows we shall assume that they have been proved.

Abstract Boolean Algebra

We obtained the rules which we have called Axioms I to X by first taking some fixed universe class, and then observing relationships among the subclasses of that universe class. Our daily experience with classes and subclasses is the mother which has given birth to these axioms. But now, like any live child, this set of axioms begins to lead an independent existence. We cut the umbilical cord which ties the axioms to their mother by forgetting that the axioms refer to subclasses of a universe class. We think of them as referring to some collection of objects whose properties, as far as we are interested in them, are only those asserted by the axioms, and by theorems that can be derived from the axioms. The infant system, thus given independent status, is called Abstract Boolean Algebra, a branch of pure mathematics named after the British logician George Boole, who was the first to construct an algebra of logic. To make the separation from the concept of class absolutely clear, we replace the word class wherever it appears in Axioms I to X by the expression, "element of the system."

When we separate the axioms from the class concept from which we derived them in the first place, it may look as though we are robbing them of their content. Actually, we are enriching them, and giving ourselves a tool of greater power.

There are *many different systems* for which the axioms of Boolean Algebra are true statements. So far we have become acquainted only with systems that consist of subclasses of a universe class. In later chapters, we shall be introduced to some others. By disregarding for the time being any specific interpretations of Boolean Algebra, and developing it in abstract form, we guarantee that the theorems that we derive apply to *all* systems which satisfy the axioms. Thus, the theorems we derive will apply to the algebra of classes of this chapter. But they will also apply to the algebra of propositions of the next chapter, and to the algebra of switching circuits described in Chapter X.

Examples of Boolean Algebras

The set of all subclasses of some universe class is a Boolean algebra. By choosing universe classes of different sizes, we can get examples of many different Boolean algebras. For example, if the universe class is the set of three elements #, %, and $, then it has eight subclasses, 1, *A, B, C, D, E, F,* and 0, as defined on page 65. These eight elements, related to each other by the operations of addition, multiplication, and taking the complement, constitute a Boolean algebra. The relationships within this system can be given explicitly in the form of tables as follows:

Addition Table

+	1	A	B	C	D	E	F	0
1	1	1	1	1	1	1	1	1
A	1	A	1	1	A	A	1	A
B	1	1	B	1	B	1	B	B
C	1	1	1	C	1	C	C	C
D	1	A	B	1	D	A	B	D
E	1	A	1	C	A	E	C	E
F	1	1	B	C	B	C	F	F
0	1	A	B	C	D	E	F	0

Multiplication Table

·	1	A	B	C	D	E	F	0
1	1	A	B	C	D	E	F	0
A	A	A	D	E	D	E	0	0
B	B	D	B	F	D	0	F	0
C	C	E	F	C	0	E	F	0
D	D	D	D	0	D	0	0	0
E	E	E	0	E	0	E	0	0
F	F	0	F	F	0	0	F	0
0	0	0	0	0	0	0	0	0

Table of Complements

X	X̄
1	0
A	F
B	E
C	D
D	C
E	B
F	A
0	1

If the universe class is the set of two symbols, @ and ¢, then it has these subclasses:

$$1 = \{@, ¢\} \qquad A = \{@\} \qquad B = \{¢\} \qquad 0 = \{\ \ \}$$

These four elements constitute a Boolean algebra whose internal relationships are expressed in these tables:

Addition Table +	1	A	B	0		Multiplication Table ·	1	A	B	0		Table of Complements X	X̄
1	1	1	1	1		1	1	A	B	0		1	0
A	1	A	1	A		A	A	A	0	0		A	B
B	1	1	B	B		B	B	0	B	0		B	A
0	1	A	B	0		0	0	0	0	0		0	1

If the universe class is a unit class (containing only one member) then it has only two subclasses, 1 and 0, the universe class and the empty class. These two elements together constitute a Boolean algebra whose complete structure is revealed in these tables:

Addition Table +	1	0		Multiplication Table ·	1	0		Table of Complements X	X̄
1	1	1.		1	1	0		1	0
0	1	0		0	0	0		0	1

The Boolean algebra with only two elements is called a two-valued algebra. It is the simplest possible example of a Boolean algebra. It is also a very important one, as we shall see in the next chapter.

Some Theorems Proved

Proving a theorem in Boolean algebra is a purely mathematical exercise. To show what some further theorems are like, and to demonstrate the techniques of proof, we shall now carry out a few proofs in detail.

First we prove that if X and Y are elements of a Boolean algebra, then $X(X + Y) = X$. We prove it by building up a sequence of expressions in which $X(X + Y)$ is the first expression and X is the last expression. We show at the same time that each expression is equal to the one that follows it in the sequence. Each equality is justified by an axiom or theorem that we know already. The chain of equalities will assure us that the first expression, $X(X + Y)$, is equal to the last expression, X, in the sequence:

$$X(X + Y) = (X + 0)(X + Y), \quad \text{since by axiom, I, } X \text{ can be replaced by } X + 0,$$
$$= X + (0 \cdot Y) \quad , \quad \text{by axiom XII,}$$
$$= X + 0 \quad , \quad \text{since } 0 \cdot Y = 0,$$
$$= X \quad , \quad \text{by axiom III.}$$

As an example of the meaning of this theorem, let us apply it to the case where X is the class of people who have blue eyes, and Y is the class of people who have hair on their heads. Then reading the multiplication sign as *and,* and the plus sign as *or,* we find that the theorem makes this assertion: The class of people who have blue eyes and who either have blue eyes or have hair on their heads is identical with the class of people who have blue eyes.

In a similar manner, we prove that $X + XY = X$:

$$X + XY = 1 \cdot X + XY \quad \text{by axiom IV,}$$
$$= X \cdot 1 + XY \quad \text{by axiom VI,}$$
$$= X(1 + Y) \quad \text{by axiom VIII,}$$
$$= X \cdot 1 \quad \text{since } 1 + Y = 1,$$
$$= 1 \cdot X \quad \text{by axiom VI,}$$
$$= X \quad \text{by axiom IV.}$$

From this theorem we get the assertion that the class of people who either have blue eyes or have blue eyes and also have hair on their heads is identical with the class of people who have blue eyes.

A third theorem that is easily proved asserts that $XY + X\overline{Y} = X$:

$$\begin{aligned} XY + X\overline{Y} &= X(Y + \overline{Y}) && \text{by axiom VIII,} \\ &= X \cdot 1 && \text{by axiom IX,} \\ &= 1 \cdot X && \text{by axiom VI,} \\ &= X && \text{by axiom IV.} \end{aligned}$$

If 1 is the class of all people, and Y is the class of all people who have hair on their heads, then $\overline{Y}$ is the class of all bald people. Then the third theorem asserts that the class of people who either have blue eyes and have hair on their heads or have blue eyes and are bald is the same as the class of people who have blue eyes.

As a fourth example, we prove that $(X + Y)(X + \overline{Y}) = X$:

$$\begin{aligned} (X + Y)(X + \overline{Y}) &= X + (Y\overline{Y}) && \text{by axiom VII,} \\ &= X + 0 && \text{by axiom IX,} \\ &= X && \text{by axiom III.} \end{aligned}$$

Interpreting X and Y in the same way as we have above, we learn from this theorem that the class of people of whom it is true that they either have blue eyes or have hair on their heads while it is also true that they either have blue eyes or are bald is identical with the class of people who have blue eyes.

Equivalent Expressions

Each of the theorems just proved asserts that two expressions are equivalent. One of the expressions is complicated, while the other one is simple. In the last theorem, for instance, we assert that the complicated expression, $(X + Y)(X + \bar{Y})$, is equivalent to the simple expression, X. This is a good thing to know, because it entitles us to replace the complicated expression by the simpler one. If X and Y are classes, as in the interpretation we used four times above, then the theorem permits us to replace a complicated description of a class by a much shorter and simpler description of the same class. Sometimes a clause in a contract is a complicated description of a class of circumstances. If the clause is expressed symbolically, it is often possible to simplify the clause by means of Boolean algebra.

In Chapter X we shall deal with situations in which the variables used in Boolean algebra stand for switches. Then the theorems such as those we have proved give us ways of simplifying a complicated switching circuit. When Boolean algebra is used for this purpose it pays dividends in money saved through economy of design.

The Law of Duality

To underscore the practical importance of Boolean algebra as a means of simplifying circuit designs, we now prove algebraically some theorems that we shall use in Chapter XI, when we discuss the design of electronic computers. The first of these theorems is the law of duality. The other two are consequences of this law.

We shall prove the law of duality that asserts that $\overline{(X + Y)} = \bar{X}\bar{Y}$. Expressed in words, this law says that $\bar{X}\bar{Y}$ is the complement of $X + Y$. To prove that this statement is true, all we need do is show that the sum of $X + Y$ and $\bar{X}\bar{Y}$ is 1, while their product is 0. (See page 75.)

To show that the sum of $X + Y$ and $\bar{X}\bar{Y}$ is 1, we begin with the true statement, $X + \bar{X} = 1$. Since we have proved that $X + XY = X$, we can replace X by $X + XY$. Since $\overline{X} = 1 \cdot \overline{X} = \overline{X} \cdot 1$, we can replace $\overline{X}$ by $\overline{X} \cdot 1$. Then we have: $(X + XY) + \overline{X} \cdot 1 = 1$. Since $Y + \overline{Y} = 1$, we may replace the 1 on the left hand side of the equation by $Y + \overline{Y}$. Now we have: $(X + XY) + \overline{X}(Y + \overline{Y}) = 1$. Because the distributive laws, the commutative laws and the associative laws hold in Boolean algebra, we can manipulate the left hand side exactly as we do in high school algebra. Then we get this sequence of equations:

$$X + XY + \overline{X}Y + \overline{X}\overline{Y} = 1$$
$$X + (X + \overline{X})Y + \overline{X}\overline{Y} = 1$$
$$X + 1 \cdot Y + \overline{X}\overline{Y} = 1$$
$$X + Y + \overline{X}\overline{Y} = 1$$

The last equation is the result we set out to get.

To show that the product of $X + Y$ and $\overline{X}\overline{Y}$ is equal to 0, multiply them, and then simplify as follows:

$$
\begin{aligned}
(X + Y)\overline{X}\overline{Y} &= X(\overline{X}\overline{Y}) + Y(\overline{X}\overline{Y}) \\
&= X(\overline{X}\overline{Y}) + Y(\overline{Y}\overline{X}) \\
&= (X\overline{X})\overline{Y} + (Y\overline{Y})\overline{X} \\
&= 0 \cdot \overline{Y} + 0 \quad \overline{X} = 0 + 0 = 0.
\end{aligned}
$$

The second law of duality, which asserts that $\overline{X} + \overline{Y} = \overline{XY}$, can be proved by analogous argument.

We now use the law of duality to help us prove that if $C = AB$, then $\overline{A}B + A\overline{B} = (A + B)\overline{C}$:

$$
\begin{aligned}
\overline{A}B + A\overline{B} &= \overline{A}B + 0 + 0 + A\overline{B} \\
&= \overline{A}B + \overline{B}B + A\overline{A} + A\overline{B} \\
&= B(\overline{A} + \overline{B}) + A(\overline{A} + \overline{B}) \\
&= B(\overline{AB}) + A(\overline{AB}) \\
&= B\overline{C} + A\overline{C} \\
&= (B + A)\overline{C} = (A + B)\overline{C}.
\end{aligned}
$$

As a second consequence of the law of duality, we prove that $\overline{\bar{A}B + A\bar{B}} = AB + \bar{A}\bar{B}$. The law of duality says that the complement of a sum of two classes is the product of their complements. Then $\overline{\bar{A}B + A\bar{B}}$, which is the complement of the sum of $\bar{A}B$ and $A\bar{B}$, is equal to the product of the complement of $\bar{A}B$ and the complement of $A\bar{B}$. But, by the law of duality, the complement of a product of two classes is equal to the sum of their complements. So the complement of $\bar{A}B$ is equal to $A + \bar{B}$, and the complement of $A\bar{B}$ is equal to $\bar{A} + B$. Summarizing these observations, and then simplifying, we get this sequence of equalities:

$$
\begin{aligned}
\overline{\bar{A}B + A\bar{B}} &= (\overline{\bar{A}B})(\overline{A\bar{B}}) \\
&= (A + \bar{B})(\bar{A} + B) \\
&= A\bar{A} + AB + \bar{B}\bar{A} + \bar{B}B \\
&= 0 + AB + \bar{A}\bar{B} + 0 \\
&= AB + \bar{A}\bar{B}.
\end{aligned}
$$

A Census Problem

There are many practical situations in which we must deal with classes related to each other in complex ways. When the classes are described in words, it may be difficult to unravel the relationships among them. However, if Boolean algebra is used, expressing the relationships and solving relevant problems becomes a routine mathematical exercise. To show how Boolean algebra provides us with techniques for solving logical problems, we now apply it to three puzzle problems not much different from some of the problems that may arise in insurance, commerce, or industry.

The first problem we tackle is a census problem. In a high school with 100 students, a count was taken of the number of students taking science courses. The clerk who made the survey reported that there were 21 students taking biology, 40 students taking chemistry, 50 students taking physics, 11 students taking chemistry and physics, 9 students taking biology and physics, 20 students taking biology and chemistry, and 5 students taking biology, chemistry, and physics. After the principal of the school had studied the report, he threw it out and reprimanded the clerk. Why?

To see why, let us check the figures in the report for consistency. Let B = the class of students taking biology, C = the class of students taking chemistry, and P = the class of students taking physics. Then $\bar{B}$ = the class of students not taking biology, $\bar{C}$ = the class of students not taking chemistry, and $\bar{P}$ = the class of students not taking physics. As usual, 1 stands for the universe class, which, in this case, is the class of all students in the school. If X is a class, let $n(X)$ denote the number of members of the class. Then the report of the clerk may be summarized as follows:

$$
\begin{aligned}
n(1) &= 100. & n(CP) &= 11. \\
n(B) &= 21. & n(BP) &= 9. \\
n(C) &= 40. & n(BC) &= 20. \\
n(P) &= 50. & n(BCP) &= 5.
\end{aligned}
$$

We know that $B + \bar{B} = 1$. Multiplying by CP, we get $CP(B + \bar{B}) = (CP) \cdot 1$. Therefore, $CPB + CP\bar{B} = CP$. This equation expresses a decomposition of the class CP into two classes, CPB, and $CP\bar{B}$. Moreover, these two classes do not overlap, since $(CPB) \cdot (CP\bar{B}) = CCPP(B\bar{B}) = CP \cdot 0 = 0 =$ the empty class. Consequently, $n(CPB) + n(CP\bar{B}) = n(CP)$. But according to the survey report, $n(CPB)$, which is equal to $n(BCP)$, $= 5$, and $n(CP) = 11$. So $5 + n(CP\bar{B}) = 11$. We conclude then, that $n(CP\bar{B}) = 6$. Similarly, multiplying $C + \bar{C} = 1$ by BP, we get $BPC +$

$BP\bar{C} = BP$, and $n(BPC) + n(BP\bar{C}) = n(BP)$. Hence $5 + n(BC\bar{P}) = 20$, and $n(BC\bar{P}) = 15$. Now multiply the equation $(P + \bar{P})(C + \bar{C}) = 1$ by B. We get $B(P + \bar{P})(C + \bar{C}) = B$. Expanding the product on the left hand side of this equation, we get $BPC + BP\bar{C} + B\bar{P}C + B\bar{P}\bar{C} = B$. This equation expresses a decomposition of the class B into four classes. It is easy to see that no two of them overlap, since the product of any two of these classes is 0. Therefore it is necessary that $n(BPC) + n(BP\bar{C}) + n(B\bar{P}C) + n(B\bar{P}\bar{C}) = n(B)$. This equation requires that $5 + 4 + 15 + n(B\bar{P}\bar{C}) = 21$, which is impossible no matter how small the class $B\bar{P}\bar{C}$ may be. Therefore the figures in the clerk's report are inconsistent, and his survey was not accurate.

A Lewis Carroll Puzzle

Lewis Carroll, who is best known as the author of *Alice in Wonderland,* was a mathematician and logician. He made up many amusing logical problems for use as exercises in his textbook on *Symbolic Logic.* The next puzzle we solve is one of these exercises.

The problem is to find out what conclusion is a logical consequence of these ten propositions:

(1) The only animals in this house are cats;
(2) Every animal is suitable for a pet, that loves to gaze at the moon;
(3) When I detest an animal, I avoid it;
(4) No animals are carnivorous, unless they prowl at night;
(5) No cat fails to kill mice;
(6) No animals ever take to me, except what are in this house;

(7) Kangaroos are not suitable for pets;

(8) None but carnivora kill mice;

(9) I detest animals that do not take to me;

(10) Animals that prowl at night always love to gaze at the moon.

To solve this problem by Boolean algebra, we first introduce symbols for various classes:

Let 1 = the universe class = the class of all animals

A = the class of animals avoided by me

B = the class of carnivora

C = the class of cats

D = the class of animals detested by me

E = the class of animals in this house

H = the class of kangaroos

K = the class of animals that kill mice

L = the class of animals that love to gaze at the moon

M = the class of animals that prowl at night

N = the class of animals that are suitable for pets

R = the class of animals that take to me

Expressed in terms of these symbols, the ten propositions take this form:

(1) $EC = E$ (6) $RE = R$

(2) $LN = L$ (7) $H\bar{N} = H$

(3) $DA = D$ (8) $KB = K$

(4) $BM = B$ (9) $\bar{R}D = \bar{R}$

(5) $CK = C$ (10) $ML = M$

Now we develop a chain of equations as follows: Multiply equation (1) by R, to get $R(EC) = RE$. Using the associative law of multiplication, this can be rewritten as $(RE)C = RE$. By equation (6), RE may be replaced by R. So we get as equation (11), $RC = R$. Multiply equation (5) by R, and use the associative law, to get $(RC)K = RC$.

By equation (11), RC may be replaced by R. So we get as equation (12), $RK = R$. Multiply equation (8) by R, and use the associative law, to get $(RK)B = RK$. By equation (12), RK may be replaced by R. So we get as equation (13), $RB = R$. Multiply equation (4) by R, and use the associative law, to get $(RB)M = RB$. By equation (13), RB may be replaced by R. So we get as equation (14), $RM = R$. Multiply equation (10) by R, and use the associative law, to get $(RM)L = RM$. By equation (14), RM may be replaced by R. So we get as equation (15), $RL = R$. Multiply equation (2) by R, and use the associative law, to get $(RL)N = RL$. By equation (15), RL may be replaced by R. So we get as equation (16), $RN = R$. Multiply equation (7) by R. This gives us $R(H\bar{N}) = RH$. By equation (16), we may replace the R on the left by RN, to get $(RN)(H\bar{N}) = RH$. Using the associative and commutative laws of multiplication to rearrange the order and regroup the factors on the left, we get $(N\bar{N})(RH) = RH$. But $N\bar{N} = 0$, so we get $0(RH) = RH$, and hence $RH = 0$. We know that $R + \bar{R} = 1$. If we multiply this equation by H, we get $HR + H\bar{R} = H$. But $HR = RH = 0$, so it follows that $H\bar{R} = H$, and we call this equation (17). Multiply equation (9) by H, and use the associative law, to get $(H\bar{R})D = H\bar{R}$. By equation (17), we may replace $H\bar{R}$ by H. So we get as equation (18), $HD = H$. Multiply equation (3) by H, and use the associative law, to get $(HD)A = HD$. By equation (18), we may replace HD by H. Our final result is that $HA = H$. This is equivalent to the statement that $H \subset A$. The conclusion from propositions (1) to (10), therefore, is the proposition, *I always avoid kangaroos.*

Who Is the Engineer?

The third puzzle that we solve by means of Boolean alegbra is a brain twister that is well known to puzzle fans. Here is one of the many versions of it. For convenience, we number the separate statements that are made.

(1) Smith, Jones and Robinson are the conductor, brakeman, and the engineer on a train, but not necessarily in that order.

(2) There are three passengers on the train named Mr. Smith, Mr. Jones, and Mr. Robinson. We shall use the title *Mister* only when we refer to one of these passengers.

(3) The conductor lives in Manhattan.

(4) The conductor's namesake (the passenger who has the same name as the conductor) lives in Philadelphia.

(5) Mr. Jones earns $10,000 per year.

(6) Mr. Robinson lives in Queens.

(7) One of the three passengers is the conductor's next-door neighbor.

(8) The conductor earns in cash each year exactly one third of the salary of his next-door neighbor.

(9) Smith beats the brakeman at billiards.

The problem is, who is the engineer?

In the solution given below, after defining the symbols that are used, we give only a sequence of equations. The reader should be able to justify each equation by referring to information already known and to some relevant axioms or theorems. (Keep in mind that if X is a subclass of Y, $XY = X$, and that if X and Y have no common members, $XY = 0$.)

Let S = the unit class whose member is Smith
$\quad J$ = the unit class whose member is Jones
$\quad R$ = the unit class whose member is Robinson
$\quad C$ = the unit class whose member is the conductor
$\quad B$ = the unit class whose member is the brakeman
$\quad E$ = the unit class whose member is the engineer
$\quad C'$ = the unit class whose member is the conductor's namesake
$\quad S'$ = the unit class whose member is Mr. Smith
$\quad J'$ = the unit class whose member is Mr. Jones
$\quad R'$ = the unit class whose member is Mr. Robinson
$\quad T$ = the class of all people earning \$10,000 per year
$\quad M$ = the class of all people living in Manhattan
$\quad P$ = the class of all people living in Philadelphia
$\quad Q$ = the class of all people living in Queens
$\quad C''$ = the unit class whose member is the conductor's next-door neighbor

$S + J + R = C + B + E.$

$SJ = 0$, $SR = 0$, and $JR = 0.$

$CM = C.$ Therefore $CP = 0$ and $CQ = 0.$

$C'P = C'.$ Therefore $C'M = 0$ and $C'Q = 0.$

$R'Q = R'.$ Therefore $R'M = 0$, and $R'P = 0.$

$J'T = J'.$ $SB = 0.$

$C''M = C''.$ Therefore $C''P = 0$, and $C''Q = 0.$

$C''(S' + J' + R') = C''.$ $C''T = 0.$

$C''(S' + J'T + R') = C''.$

$C''S' + C''J'T + C''R' = C''.$

Therefore $C''S' + C''R' = C''.$

$M(C''S' + C''R') = MC''.$

$MC''S' + MC''R' = MC''.$

Therefore $C''S' = C''$, hence $C'' = S'$, and $S'P = 0.$

$C'(S' + J' + R') = C'.$

$C'S' + C'J' + C'R' = C'.$

$P(C'S' + C'J' + C'R') = PC'.$

$C'(S'P) + (C'P)J' + C'(R'P) = PC'.$

Therefore $C'J' = C'$, hence $C' = J'$, and $C = J$.

But if $C = J$, $SC = SJ = 0$.

$S(C + B + E) = S$.

$SC + SB + SE = S$. Therefore $SE = S$, and $S = E$.

That is, *Smith is the engineer.*

CHAPTER 9

Algebra of Propositions

Propositions about Propositions

EVERY proposition is either true or false. The typical job of a scientist is to determine whether certain propositions are true or false. The propositions always concern the subject matter of his science. The biologist tries to separate the true from the false among propositions about plants and animals and their relations to each other and the environment. The chemist tries to separate the true from the false among propositions about chemical elements and their compounds. The physicist tries to separate the true from the false among propositions about matter and energy.

The logician, too, seeks the truth value of propositions about his subject matter. An important part of the science of logic is concerned with propositions, and their relations to each other. So the logician tries to separate the true from the false among *propositions about propositions*.

Here is a typical proposition that may come up in the study of logic: If it is true that if it is raining, then the ground is wet, and if it is true that if the ground is wet, then your shoes get wet, then it is also true that if it is raining, then your shoes get wet. This is a rather complicated proposition built up out of simpler propositions. The simpler propositions are: It is raining; the ground is wet; your shoes get wet. They are joined together in the complicated proposition by the words "if . . . then" and the word "and." The latter are called *connectives*. The set of words "if . . . then" can be replaced by the word "implies." Thus, the part of the proposition that says, ". . . if it is raining, then the ground is wet," can be replaced by, "*It is raining* implies that *the ground is wet*." In order to reveal the structure of the complicated proposition more clearly, let us use the letter p to stand for the proposition "It is raining." Let q stand for "The ground is wet." Let r stand for "Your shoes get wet." Then the proposition says "If p implies q, and q implies r, then p implies r." You will recognize that this proposition merely asserts the transitive property of the relation "implies," so that it is true, no matter what propositions p, q, and r stand for. The truth of this proposition depends only on its form. One of the major goals of the logician is to discover propositions of precisely this kind. Since, for his purposes, p, q, and r may stand for any propositions whatever, it is better for him to make his assertions in terms of such variables, rather than about specific propositions.

Symbols for Truth Values

Following the lead of the logician, we shall use small letters like p, q, and r as variables that stand for propositions, just as in elementary algebra we use letters like x, y and z as variables that stand for numbers. As long as we shall be using symbols for propositions, we may as well use symbols to stand for their truth values. Let us agree to use the symbol 1 for *true*, and the symbol 0 for *false*. Let us agree, too, that whenever a small letter stands for a proposition, the corresponding capital letter stands for its truth value. Thus, if p stands for a proposition, then P stands for its truth value. While p may stand for any proposition whatever, P may take on only two values, 1 and 0. If p is the proposition, "All men are mortal," then $P = 1$. If p is the proposition, "The area of a circle equals twice the square of its radius," then $P = 0$.

Symbols for Connectives

The connectives "if . . . then" and "and" enable us to form new, compound propositions from old propositions. Other connectives that serve the same purpose are the words, "or," "not," and "if and only if." We now give the meaning of each of these connectives, and introduce a convenient symbol for it.

Or. Let p and q be propositions. Then the proposition *p or q* is the proposition that asserts that at least one of the propositions p and q is true. We shall use a plus sign to stand for *or*, so *p or q* will be written as $p + q$. For example, if p stands for the proposition "it is raining," and q stands for the proposition "the ground is wet," then $p + q$ stands for the proposition, "Either it is raining, or the ground is wet, or it is raining and the ground is wet." The proposition $p + q$ is called the *disjunction* of p and q.

And. The proposition *p and q* is the proposition that asserts that both p and q are true. We shall use a multiplication sign (usually omitted) to stand for *and*, so that *p and q* will be written as pq. If p stands for "it is raining," and q stands for "the ground is wet," then pq stands for, "It is raining and the ground is wet." The proposition pq is called the *conjunction* of p and q.

Not. The proposition *not p* is the proposition that asserts that p is not true. We shall use the symbol $\sim$ for *not,* so that *not p* will be written as $\sim p$. If p stands for "it is raining," then $\sim p$ stands for, "It is not true that it is raining," or, more briefly, "It is not raining." The proposition $\sim p$ is called the *negation* of p.

If . . . then. The proposition *if p, then q* is the proposition that asserts that if p is false, q may be true or false, but if p is true, then q is true. We shall use a single-headed arrow to stand for *if . . . then,* so that *if p, then q* will be written as $p \rightarrow q$. The proposition $p \rightarrow q$ is called the *conditional* of p and q.

If and only if. The proposition *p if and only if q* is the proposition that asserts that p and q are either both true or both false. We shall use a double-headed arrow to stand for *if and only if*, so that *p if and only if q* will be written as $p \longleftrightarrow q$. The proposition $p \longleftrightarrow q$ is called the *biconditional of p* and *q*.

Truth Tables

The expression $p + q$ is not a proposition. It is only a propositional form. It becomes a proposition when *p* and *q* are replaced by specific propositions. The truth value of the proposition that results depends on the truth values of the propositions that replace *p* and *q*. Let us write $P + Q$ for the truth value of $p + q$. By definition, $p + q$ is true if either *p* or *q* or both are true. Otherwise $p + q$ is false. Therefore, $P + Q = 1$ if $P = 1$, or $Q = 1$, or $P = Q = 1$. Otherwise, $P + Q = 0$. These facts may be conveniently summarized in the following *truth table*, which shows the truth value for $p + q$ for all possible combinations of truth values for *p* and *q*:

P	Q	$P + Q$
1 (*p* is true)	1 (*q* is true)	1 (*p or q* is true)
1 (*p* is true)	0 (*q* is false)	1 (*p or q* is true)
0 (*p* is false)	1 (*q* is true)	1 (*p or q* is true)
0 (*p* is false)	0 (*q* is false)	0 (*p or q* is false)

Let us write PQ for the truth value of pq, $\sim P$ for the truth value of $\sim p$, $P \rightarrow Q$ for the truth value of $p \rightarrow q$, and $P \longleftrightarrow Q$ for the truth value of $p \longleftrightarrow q$. The truth tables for these propositional forms are easily constructed on the basis of the definitions given above.

P	Q	PQ
1	1	1
1	0	0
0	1	0
0	0	0

P	$\sim P$
1	0
0	1

P	Q	$P \rightarrow Q$
1	1	1
1	0	0
0	1	1
0	0	1

P	Q	$P \leftrightarrow Q$
1	1	1
1	0	0
0	1	0
0	0	1

Using these five basic truth tables, we can construct the truth tables for more complicated propositional forms that use more than one connective. For example, to find all possible truth values of $(\sim p) + q$, corresponding to all combinations of truth values of p and q, we use the truth tables for $\sim p$, and for $p + q$. List the combinations of values for P and Q in the first two columns. In the third column, list the value of $\sim P$ that corresponds to each value of P. When $P = 1$, $\sim P = 0$, and vice versa. Then, in the fourth column, list the values of $(\sim P) + Q$ that correspond to the combinations of values of $\sim P$ and Q. $P + Q = 0$ only when $P = Q = 0$. $P + Q = 1$ in all other cases. Therefore, $(\sim P) + Q = 0$ only when $\sim P = Q = 0$. Otherwise $(\sim P) + Q = 1$.

P	Q	$\sim P$	$(\sim P) + Q$
1	1	0	1
1	0	0	0
0	1	1	1
0	0	1	1

Equivalent Propositional Forms

In the preceding table, we used the third column only to help us calculate the entries in the fourth column. Now that it has served its purpose, we may disregard it. The complete truth table for $(\sim p) + q$ is given by columns 1, 2, and 4. Comparing these with the three columns in the truth table for $p \to q$, we see that the truth table for $p \to q$ is exactly the same as the truth table for $(\sim p) + q$. When two propositional forms have the same truth table, we say they are *equivalent*. Equivalent forms are either true together, or false together. Hence if X and Y are equivalent, $X \longleftrightarrow Y$. Therefore the symbol $\longleftrightarrow$ may be read as "is equivalent to."

To calculate all possible truth values of $\sim (\sim p)$, prepare a table with three columns, as shown below. In the first column, put all possible truth values of p. In the second column, put the corresponding truth values of $\sim p$. They are the opposite of the truth values of p. That is, when $p = 0$, $\sim p = 1$, and vice versa. In the third column, put the truth values of $\sim (\sim p)$. They are the opposite of the truth values of $\sim p$. Now compare the third column with the first column. They are exactly the same. In other words, p and $\sim (\sim p)$ have the same truth tables. Therefore p is equivalent to $\sim (\sim p)$. That is, $p \longleftrightarrow \sim (\sim p)$. This is the familiar rule of the "double negative."

P	$\sim P$	$\sim(\sim P)$
1	0	1
0	1	0

To calculate all possible truth values of $(p \to q) \cdot (q \to p)$, which we read as "$p$ implies q, and q implies p," prepare a table with five columns. In the first two columns put all possible combinations of truth values of the two propositions p and q. In the third column, put the corresponding truth values of $p \to q$. $P \to Q$ is 0 when $P = 1$ and $Q = 0$. Otherwise it is 1. In the fourth column, put the corresponding truth values of $q \to p$. $Q \to P$ is 0 when $Q = 1$ and $P = 0$. Otherwise it is 1. In the fifth column, put the corresponding truth values of $(p \to q) (q \to p)$. The value is 1 when the value appearing in columns 3 and 4 is 1. In all other cases, the value is 0.

P	Q	$P \to Q$	$Q \to P$	$(P \to Q)(Q \to P)$
1	1	1	1	1
1	0	0	1	0
0	1	1	0	0
0	0	1	1	1

If we compare the first, second and fifth columns of this table with the table for $p \longleftrightarrow q$, we see that $p \longleftrightarrow q$ is equivalent to $(p \to q) (q \to p)$. That is why $p \longleftrightarrow q$ is called the biconditional.

As a practice exercise, show that the propositional form $pq \longleftrightarrow p$ is equivalent to $p \to q$.

Reducing the Number of Connectives

When two propositional forms are equivalent, they have the same truth values no matter what propositions are substituted for the variables that appear in the forms. To express this fact, we put an "equals" sign between the expressions for their truth values. Thus, since p is equivalent to $\sim (\sim p)$, we say $P = \sim (\sim P)$. Since $p \to q$ is equivalent to $(\sim p) + q$, we say $P \to Q = (\sim P) + Q$. Since $p \longleftrightarrow q$ is equivalent to $(p \to q) (q \to p)$, we say $P \longleftrightarrow Q = (P \to Q) (Q \to P)$. Moreover, when two propositional forms always have the same truth values, it means that they have the same truth tables, and must be equivalent. So a statement that two propositional forms are equivalent is interchangeable with the statement that the expressions for their truth values are equal.

In the expressions for truth values that we have examined, five different connectives appear. It is now possible for us to reduce the number to three. Since $P \rightarrow Q = (\sim P) + Q$, we can always replace $P \rightarrow Q$ by $(\sim P) + Q$. In this way we replace an expression using the connective $\rightarrow$ by an expression using the connectives $\sim$ and $+$. Since $P \longleftrightarrow Q = (P \rightarrow Q)(Q \rightarrow P)$, then, making the appropriate substitutions, we have $P \longleftrightarrow Q = [(\sim P) + Q] \cdot [(\sim Q) + P]$. So any expression using the connective $\longleftrightarrow$ can be replaced by an expression using the connectives $\sim$, $\cdot$ and $+$. By means of these substitutions, all expressions using our five original connectives are transformed into expressions using only the three connectives, *not, and* and *or.*

The Algebra of Propositions

The words *not, and* and *or* have come up before in another context. In Chapter VIII, where we explored the algebra of classes, the word *not* was the key word in defining the operation of taking the complement of a class. The word *and* was the key word in the operation we called multiplication. The word *or* was the key word in the operation we called addition. Complementation, multiplication, and addition are the three basic operations of the Boolean algebra of classes. This suggests the possibility of having an algebra of propositions. We already have at hand all the materials needed for constructing such an algebra. As the system of elements that make up the algebra we shall use the *truth values* of propositions. For basic operations in the algebra, we use the connectives *not, and* and *or,* denoted by the symbols $\sim$, $\cdot$, and $+$. We already have tables for these three operations in the form of truth tables:

P	Q	$P + Q$
1	1	1
1	0	1
0	1	1
0	0	0

P	Q	PQ
1	1	1
1	0	0
0	1	0
0	0	0

P	$\sim P$
1	0
0	1

The first two tables can be recast in another form in which the values of P are written at the left hand side, and the values of Q are written at the top. This is the form usually used for addition and multiplication tables:

$+$	1	0
1	1	1
0	1	0

$\cdot$	1	0
1	1	0
0	0	0

P	$\sim P$
1	0
0	1

If we compare these tables with those on page 83, we see that they are precisely the tables for a two-valued Boolean algebra, with disjunction taking the place of addition, conjunction taking the place of multiplication, and negation taking the place of complementation. Consequently, the *algebra of propositions is a Boolean algebra.* This means that all the axioms and theorems of Boolean algebra are true statements about the truth values of propositions. It is understood, of course, that in making such statements, we must replace every expression like $\overline{X}$ by the analogous expression $\sim X$.

Now that we know that the algebra of propositions is a Boolean algebra, we have a way of identifying equivalent propositional forms without constructing their truth tables. Two propositional forms are equivalent, if we can transform the expression for the truth value of one into the expression for the truth value of the other by the laws of Boolean algebra. For example, one of the distributive laws says that $P(Q + R) = PQ + PR$. Therefore $p(q + r)$ and $pq + pr$ must have the same truth table. This fact is verified directly in the truth tables below. Notice that we need eight lines in each of these truth tables to take into account the eight possible combinations of truth values of the three propositions p, q, and r.

P	Q	R	Q + R	P(Q + R)
1	1	1	1	1
1	1	0	1	1
1	0	1	1	1
1	0	0	0	0
0	1	1	1	0
0	1	0	1	0
0	0	1	1	0
0	0	0	0	0

P	Q	R	PQ	PR	PQ + PR
1	1	1	1	1	1
1	1	0	1	0	1
1	0	1	0	1	1
1	0	0	0	0	0
0	1	1	0	0	0
0	1	0	0	0	0
0	0	1	0	0	0
0	0	0	0	0	0

The law of duality says that $\sim (P + Q) = (\sim P)(\sim Q)$. As a practice exercise, verify that $\sim(p + q)$ and $(\sim p)(\sim q)$ have the same truth tables.

Tautologies

There are some propositional forms that always have the truth value 1 no matter what propositions are substituted for the variables that appear in the forms. Such forms are easily recognized by the fact that only 1's appear in the last column of their truth tables. We call these forms *tautologies*. If we join two equivalent propositional forms by the connective $\longleftrightarrow$, the resulting form is a tautology. This fact is verified directly in the truth table below for the propositional form $(p \rightarrow q) \longleftrightarrow (pq \longleftrightarrow p)$. In this table, an entry in the fifth column is 1 only when the corresponding entries in the first and fourth column are the same. (See the definition of $\longleftrightarrow$ on page 99.) An entry in the sixth column is 1 only when the corresponding entries in the third and fifth columns are the same.

P	Q	$P \rightarrow Q$	PQ	$PQ \leftrightarrow P$	$(P \rightarrow Q) \leftrightarrow (PQ \leftrightarrow P)$
1	1	1	1	1	1
1	0	0	0	0	1
0	1	1	0	1	1
0	0	1	0	1	1

Valid and Invalid Reasoning

Tautologies play an important part in deductive reasoning. A deductive argument is made up of a string of assertions in which we say that if certain propositions are true, then some other proposition is also true as a consequence. Each of these assertions is itself a proposition. If we replace the propositions within it by variables, the result is a propositional form. The reasoning is logical, and we say the argument is *valid,* if and only if each of the propositional forms obtained is a tautology, For example, let us consider the argument written out on pages 96 and 97. As we pointed out there, the structure of the argument is embodied in the propositional form, *if p implies q, and q implies r, then p implies r.* Using the symbol $\rightarrow$ for *implies,* we can write the argument more briefly in this form: if $p \to q$, and $q \to r$, then $p \to r$. We can abbreviate it even further by writing $\to$ for *if . . . then*, and $\cdot$ for *and*. In purely symbolic form, the argument looks like this: $(p \to q) (q \to r) \to (p \to r)$. The truth table for this form shows that it is a tautology:

P	Q	R	$P \to Q$	$Q \to R$	$(P \to Q)(Q \to R)$	$P \to R$	$(P \to Q)(Q \to R)$ $\to (P \to R)$
1	1	1	1	1	1	1	1
1	1	0	1	0	0	0	1
1	0	1	0	1	0	1	1
1	0	0	0	1	0	0	1
0	1	1	1	1	1	1	1
0	1	0	1	0	0	1	1
0	0	1	1	1	1	1	1
0	0	0	1	1	1	1	1

When the form of an argument is not a tautology, the argument is fallacious, and really does not prove what it claims to prove. It is not always easy to recognize a fallacious argument when it is expressed in words. But it can always be exposed by constructing the truth table of the underlying propositional form. As an example, let us analyze an argument that is frequently heard in the United States. The argument runs as follows: If a man is a communist, then he criticizes the government's foreign policy. This man criticizes the government's foreign policy. Therefore he is a communist. The propositional form underlying this argument is: If $(p \to q)$ and q, then p. Expressing it all in symbols, we have $(p \to q) q \to p$. The truth table for this propositional form, constructed below, has a 0 in the last column, so the form is not a tautology. Hence the argument is fallacious.

P	Q	$P \to Q$	$(P \to Q)Q$	$(P \to Q) Q \to P$
1	1	1	1	1
1	0	0	0	1
0	1	1	1	0
0	0	1	0	1

Another way of expressing the same argument is this: $p \rightarrow q$ is equivalent to $q \rightarrow p$. People are tempted to accept this as a true statement because of the superficial resemblance between the two conditionals. However, the truth tables below show that these forms are not equivalent.

P	Q	$P \rightarrow Q$
1	1	1
1	0	0
0	1	1
0	0	1

P	Q	$Q \rightarrow P$
1	1	1
1	0	1
0	1	0
0	0	1

The form $q \rightarrow p$ is called the converse of $p \rightarrow q$. While the converse of $p \rightarrow q$ is not equivalent to it, there is another propositional form that is. The form $(\sim q) \rightarrow (\sim p)$, which is known as the *contrapositive* of $p \rightarrow q$, is equivalent to $p \rightarrow q$. As an exercise, verify this fact by constructing their truth tables.

A Form for a Truth Table

A truth table can be constructed for any given propositional form. The process can also be reversed. Given any truth table, it is possible to find a propositional form that has that truth table. There is a simple procedure for constructing the form. The best way to explain the procedure is to demonstrate it in connection with a specific problem.

Problem: Construct a three-variable propositional form that has the truth table appearing on page 109.

Procedure: First we construct eight forms, each corresponding to one of the lines in the table. Each

P	Q	R	Truth Value of Required Form
1	1	1	1
1	1	0	1
1	0	1	0
1	0	0	1
0	1	1	0
0	1	0	1
0	0	1	0
0	0	0	1

form is the product (conjunction) of three factors. The first factor is p or $\sim p$, depending on whether $P = 1$ or 0. The second factor is q or $\sim q$, depending on whether $Q = 1$ or 0. The third factor is r or $\sim r$, depending on whether $R = 1$ or 0. Thus the form corresponding to the first line is pqr; the form for the second line is $pq\,(\sim r)$; the form for the third line is $p\,(\sim q)r$; etc. We get the required form by taking the sum (disjunction) of some of these forms. We use only those forms that correspond to a line where the value 1 appears in the last column of the table. The required form for this table is: $pqr + pq(\sim r) + p(\sim q)\,(\sim r) + (\sim p)\,q\,(\sim r) + (\sim p)\,(\sim q)\,(\sim r)$.

We have seen that it is possible for different forms to have the same truth table. So a given table belongs, in general, to many forms. The procedure described above gives only one of them. However, other equivalent forms can be obtained from it by using the rules of Boolean algebra. First write the expression for the truth value of the form. This simply means rewrite it with capital letters instead of small letters. Transform this expression into a new one according to the rules of Boolean algebra. Then get the form that belongs to the new expression by simply rewriting it with small letters. The practical purpose of all this work would be to get a simpler form than the original one. For example, the truth value for the form we constructed for the table is $PQR + PQ(\sim R) + P(\sim Q)(\sim R) + (\sim P)Q(\sim R) + (\sim P)(\sim Q)(\sim R)$. By the rules of Boolean algebra, this expression is equal to:

$$PQ(R + \sim R) + P(\sim Q)(\sim R) \\ + (\sim P)(\sim R)(Q + \sim Q).$$

But $R + \sim R = 1$, and $Q + \sim Q = 1$, so the expression is equal to $PQ \cdot 1 + P(\sim Q)(\sim R) + (\sim P)(\sim R)1$, which in turn is equal to $PQ + P(\sim Q)(\sim R) + (\sim P)(\sim R)$. This gives us the simpler propositional form $pq + p(\sim q)(\sim r) + (\sim p)(\sim r)$ as another solution to the problem.

In the search for equivalent propositional forms, we can take a short-cut by manipulating the propositional forms themselves instead of the expressions for their truth values. This is legitimate because it merely means skipping the steps in which we change from small letters to capital letters, and then back again to small letters. When the short-cut is used, we would say $p + \sim p = 1$, although, strictly speaking, the correct statement is that $P + \sim P = 1$.

The technique for constructing a propositional form for a given truth table has important practical applications. In Chapter XI we shall have occasion to use it for designing some basic components of an electronic computer. Meanwhile, we shall use it now to solve a well-known logical puzzle.

Puzzle: A logician once visited a country inhabited by two tribes, the Saints and the Sinners. The Saints and the Sinners look alike, dress alike, and have the same speech pattern, so that they cannot be distinguished by any outward signs. However, they differ in one important respect. The Saints always tell the truth, while the Sinners always lie. Once, while the logician was traveling on foot to the city Metropolis, he came to a fork in the road. There were no road signs to indicate which branch of the road led to the city. However, there was a native standing at the fork at the time. The logician, of course, did not know whether he was a Saint or a Sinner, so he could not count on a truthful answer to any question he might ask. Nevertheless, he asked the native a single question, and found out from the answer which branch of the road he should take. What was the question?

A solution to the puzzle can be worked out as follows. Since there are two branches that the logician must choose from, his question should permit only two answers. This requirement is met if his question calls for *yes* or *no* as an answer. He should frame the question in such a way that the answer will be *yes* if the left branch is the road to the city, and will be *no* if the right branch is the road to the city, whether the native tells the truth, or not. To construct such a question, first denote by *p* the statement, "The left branch is the road to Metropolis," and denote by *q* the statement, "You are a Saint." Now construct a table with four columns. In the first two columns list all possible combinations of truth values to *p* and *q*. In the third column list the answer the logician wants to get to his question. It will depend on the truth value of *p*. Express the answer in code by writing 1 for *yes* and 0 for *no*. In the fourth column, put down what appears in the third column on lines where $Q = 1$. Where $Q = 0$, make the entry in the fourth column the opposite of the entry in the third column. The fourth column will give the truth values of an unknown compound propositional form. Here is the table:

P	Q	*Answer Wanted*	*Unknown Form*
1	1	1	1
1	0	1	0
0	1	0	0
0	0	0	1

A propositional form that has the truth values shown in the last column is $pq + (\sim p)(\sim q)$. If the logician asks "Is $pq + (\sim p)(\sim q)$ true?", the answer, no matter what the circumstances shown in columns 1 and 2, will be the one indicated in column 3. So, the appropriate question, expressed in words, is this: Is it true that either the left branch is the road to Metropolis and you are a Saint, or the left branch is not the road to Metropolis and you are a Sinner?

Boolean Algebra in Medicine

We close this chapter on the algebra of propositions by describing one of its most interesting applications. We show how Boolean algebra can be used to make a medical diagnosis.

When a doctor examines a patient, he looks for certain symptoms. His observations take the form of propositions: the patient has this symptom; he doesn't have that symptom; etc. The doctor also has medical knowledge. His knowledge is a collection of propositions about how symptoms and diseases are related. His diagnosis is a logical deduction from the two sets of propositions.

Let us assume that there are two symptoms s and t, each of which is either present or absent. Let us denote by s the proposition, *the patient has symptom s*. Then $\sim s$ denotes the proposition, *the patient does not have symptom s*. Let t denote the proposition, *the patient has symptom t*. Then $\sim t$ means *the patient does not have symptom t*.

Let us assume that there are two diseases, c and d. Denote by c the proposition, *the patient has disease c*. Denote by d the proposition, *the patient has disease d*. Assume that the state of medical knowledge about these diseases is embodied in these propositions:

1) If the patient has disease d, he must have symptom s.
2) If the patient has disease c and not disease d, he must have symptom t.

3) If the patient has disease d and not disease c, he cannot have symptom t.

4) If the patient has symptom s or t or both, then he must have either disease c or disease d or both.

What is the diagnosis if the patient has symptom t but does not have symptom s?

The first step in solving this problem is to express propositions 1 to 4 in symbolic form:

1) $d \rightarrow s$.   2) $c(\sim d) \rightarrow t$.   3) $d(\sim c) \rightarrow \sim t$.
4) $s + t \rightarrow c + d$.

On page 102, we mentioned that the form $p \rightarrow q$ is equivalent to the form $pq \longleftrightarrow p$. So the four propositions may be expressed just as well in this way:

1) $ds \longleftrightarrow d$.   2) $c(\sim d)t \longleftrightarrow c(\sim d)$.
3) $d(\sim c)(\sim t) \longleftrightarrow d(\sim c)$.   4) $(s+t)(c+d) \longleftrightarrow (s+t)$.

Equivalent propositions have equal truth values. So the last four propositions lead to these equations about truth values:

I) $DS = D$.
II) $C(\sim D)T = C(\sim D)$.
III) $D(\sim C)(\sim T) = D(\sim C)$.
IV) $(S+T)(C+D) = S+T$.

From now on, we work only with truth values. Multiplying equation I by $\sim S$, we get $DS(\sim S) = D(\sim S)$. But $S(\sim S) = 0$. Therefore $D(\sim S) = 0$. Similarly, from equation II we get $C(\sim D)(\sim T) = 0$, and from equation III we get $D(\sim C)T = 0$. From equation IV we get $(S+T)[\sim(C+D)] = 0$.

We know that $S + \sim S = 1$, and $T + \sim T = 1$. Multiplying these two equations we get $(S + \sim S)(T + \sim T) = 1$. Expanding the left hand member, we get: $ST + S(\sim T) + (\sim S)T + (\sim S)(\sim T) = 1$. Similarly, from $C + \sim C = 1$, and $D + \sim D = 1$, we get $CD + C(\sim D) +$

$(\sim C)D + (\sim C)\ (\sim D) = 1$. Multiplying the two expanded equations, we get:

$$[ST + S(\sim T) + (\sim S)T + (\sim S)(\sim T)] \cdot$$
$$[CD + C(\sim D) + (\sim C)D + (\sim C)(\sim D)] = 1.$$

This equation, in expanded form, asserts:

$$STCD + STC(\sim D) + ST(\sim C)D + ST(\sim C)(\sim D) +$$
$$S(\sim T)CD + S(\sim T)C(\sim D) + S(\sim T)(\sim C)D +$$
$$S(\sim T)(\sim C)(\sim D) + (\sim S)TCD + (\sim S)TC(\sim D) +$$
$$(\sim S)T(\sim C)D + (\sim S)T(\sim C)(\sim D) + (\sim S)(\sim T)$$
$$CD + (\sim S)(\sim T)C(\sim D) + (\sim S)(\sim T)(\sim C)D +$$
$$(\sim S)(\sim T)(\sim C)(\sim D) = 1.$$

Because $D(\sim S) = 0$, the 9th, 11th, 13th and 15th terms on the left hand side are equal to 0. Because $C(\sim D)\ (\sim T) = 0$, the 6th and the 14th terms are equal to 0. Because $D(\sim C)T = 0$, the third term is 0. So all these terms drop out of the equation, and we get:

$$STCD + STC(\sim D) + ST(\sim C)(\sim D) + S(\sim T)CD +$$
$$S(\sim T)(\sim C)D + S(\sim T)(\sim C)(\sim D) + (\sim S)TC(\sim D)$$
$$+ (\sim S)T(\sim C)(\sim D) + (\sim S)(\sim T)(\sim C)(\sim D) = 1.$$

We can simplify this equation further by making use of the equation $(S + T)\ [\sim(C + D)] = 0$ which we had derived from IV. By the law of duality $\sim(C + D) = (\sim C)(\sim D)$. So we have

$(S + T)(\sim C)(\sim D) = 0$. Hence $S(\sim C)(\sim D) + T(\sim C)(\sim D) = 0$.

The addition table for the two-valued Boolean algebra shows that the sum of two terms is 0 only if each term is itself 0. Therefore $S(\sim C)\ (\sim D) = 0$, and $T(\sim C)\ (\sim D) = 0$. So three more terms drop out of the equation, and we have:

$$STCD + STC(\sim D) + S(\sim T)CD + S(\sim T)(\sim C)D +$$
$$(\sim S)TC(\sim D) + (\sim S)(\sim T)(\sim C)(\sim D) = 1.$$

Using the distributive law to rewrite terms 1 and 2, and also terms 3 and 4, we get:

$$STC(D + \sim D) + S(\sim T)D(C + \sim C) + (\sim S)TC(\sim D)$$
$$+ (\sim S)(\sim T)(\sim C)(\sim D) = 1.$$ Since $D + \sim D = 1$, and $C + \sim C = 1$, we finally get: $STC + S(\sim T)D +$
$(\sim S)TC(\sim D) + (\sim S)(\sim T)(\sim C)(\sim D) = 1.$

This last equation summarizes the state of medical knowledge concerning the relationship between diseases c and d and symptoms s and t. Let us call it equation *MK*.

If the patient has symptom t, but not s, then $T = 1$, $\sim T = 0$, $S = 0$, and $\sim S = 1$. Making these substitutions into equation *MK*, we get:

$$0 \cdot 1 \cdot C + 0 \cdot 0 \cdot D + 1 \cdot 1 \cdot C(\sim D) + 1 \cdot 0 \cdot (\sim C)(\sim D) = 1.$$

This reduces to $C(\sim D) = 1$. This is true if and only if $C = 1$ and $\sim D = 1$. Therefore the diagnosis is: The patient has disease c, but not disease d.

Suppose the patient has symptom s, but not t. What is the diagnosis then? Under these circumstances, $S = 1$, $\sim S = 0$, $T = 0$, and $\sim T = 1$. Making these substitutions into equation *MK*, we get:

$$1 \cdot 0 \cdot C + 1 \cdot 1 \cdot D + 0 \cdot 0 \cdot C(\sim D) + 0 \cdot 1(\sim C)(\sim D) = 1.$$

This reduces to $D = 1$. Therefore the diagnosis is: The patient has disease d. However, the diagnosis is incomplete, because it does not say whether or not the patient also has disease c. The medical knowledge expressed in equation *MK* is inadequate for settling this question.

CHAPTER 10

Switching Circuits

An Algebra of Switches

IN THE diagram below we show an electrical appliance in a line joined to the terminals of an electrical power supply. The switch S is used to control the current through the appliance. When the switch is closed, the current is on. When the switch is open, the current is off.

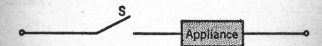

The two possible states of a switch, closed or open, are analogous to the two possible truth values of a proposition, true or false. The resemblance prompts us to introduce symbols to represent these states. Let 1 stand for the state of being closed, and let 0 stand for the state of being open.

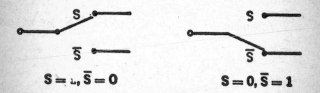

$$S = 1, \overline{S} = 0 \qquad\qquad S = 0, \overline{S} = 1$$

Pursuing the analogy further, we can introduce operations on switches to correspond to the operations we can perform on propositions. 1) We can couple another switch

$\bar{S}$ to switch S in such a way that $\bar{S}$ is open whenever S is closed, and vice versa. The linkage of the states of these switches is then shown in this table:

S	$\bar{S}$
1	0
0	1

This table is like the truth table for the negation of a propositional form. Let us call switch $\bar{S}$ the complement of switch S.

2) We can control the current in the appliance by a combination of two switches in parallel. If the two switches are called S and T, let us designate the parallel combination by $S + T$. It behaves like a single switch that may be open or closed. If S and T are both closed, current flows through the appliance, so $S + T$ is closed. $S + T$ is also closed if S is closed and T is open, or if S is open and T is closed. If

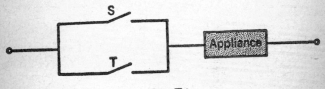

S + T

both S and T are open, then no current flows through the appliance. In this case, $S + T$ is open. The way the state of $S + T$ depends on the states of S and T is shown in this table:

S	T	$S + T$
1	1	1
1	0	1
0	1	1
0	0	0

This table is like the truth table for the disjunction of two propositions.

3) Two switches S and T can be put into the circuit in series. Let us designate the series combination by ST. It, too, behaves like a single switch. ST is closed if and only

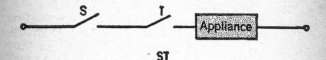

if both S and T are closed. The way the state of ST depends on the states of S and T is shown in this table:

S	T	ST
1	1	1
1	0	0
0	1	0
0	0	0

This table is like the truth table for the conjunction of two propositions.

The three tables show that the resemblance between switches and the truth values of propositions is not accidental. Switches, with the three operations defined above, constitute a two-valued Boolean algebra. Hence switching circuits can be analyzed by algebraic methods. This fact was first discovered by Claude E. Shannon in 1938.

Designing a Circuit

An immediate consequence of Shannon's discovery is that it is possible to use the techniques of Boolean algebra for designing a switching circuit that must satisfy special requirements. The procedure is to set up a "truth table" showing the characteristics we want the circuit to have. Then, using the methods of the last chapter, we can get a formula for the circuit. In the formula, every plus sign represents a parallel connection, every multiplication sign represents a series connection, and every bar over the name of a switch represents taking its complement.

As an example, let us solve the following common switching problem: A light for a flight of stairs is to be controlled by two switches. One of them, S, is upstairs. The other one, T, is downstairs. We want to be able to turn the light on or off by using either switch. Let X stand for the desired switching circuit. Each switch has two states that we designate by 1 and 0. Assume that the light is on, and hence $X = 1$, when each switch is in the state 1. Changing the state of either switch should turn the light off. Hence $X = 0$ when $S = 1$ and $T = 0$, or when $S = 0$ and $T = 1$. Another change in state of a single switch should turn the light on again. Hence $X = 1$ when $S = T = 0$. The truth table for X therefore has this form:

S	T	X
1	1	1
1	0	0
0	1	0
0	0	1

Applying the procedure described on page 109, we find $X = ST + \bar{S}\bar{T}$. The circuit described by this formula is shown in the diagram below:

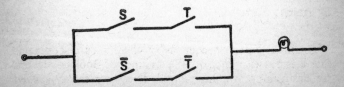

The diagram above does not show the linkage between S and $\bar{S}$ and between T and $\bar{T}$. There is another diagram for the same circuit that does:

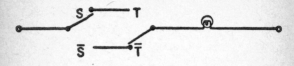

Simplifying a Circuit

Boolean algebra gives the engineer a powerful tool for simplifying a circuit. After a circuit is represented symbolically by an algebraic expression, the rules of Boolean algebra can be used to find equivalent expressions. Each of these equivalent expressions represents a circuit that can take the place of the original one. For example, let us try to simplify the circuit shown in the diagram below.

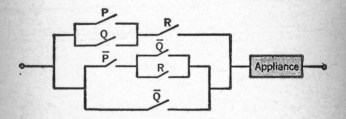

The expression for this circuit is
$(P + Q)R + [\bar{P}(\bar{Q} + R) + \bar{Q}]$. This expression can be transformed as follows:

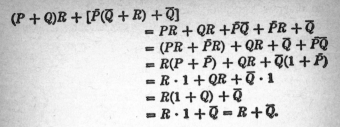

$$(P + Q)R + [\bar{P}(\bar{Q} + R) + \bar{Q}]$$
$$= PR + QR + \bar{P}\bar{Q} + \bar{P}R + \bar{Q}$$
$$= (PR + \bar{P}R) + QR + \bar{Q} + \bar{P}\bar{Q}$$
$$= R(P + \bar{P}) + QR + \bar{Q}(1 + \bar{P})$$
$$= R \cdot 1 + QR + \bar{Q} \cdot 1$$
$$= R(1 + Q) + \bar{Q}$$
$$= R \cdot 1 + \bar{Q} = R + \bar{Q}.$$

Notice that, in carrying out these transformations, we used certain rules, such as the distributive law, the associative laws, the commutative laws, and the law of 1, that are common to Boolean algebra and the algebra of numbers. But we also used some special rules of Boolean algebra, such as $X + \bar{X} = 1$, and $1 + X = 1$. The results of the algebraic computation show that the original circuit can be replaced by the following much simpler one:

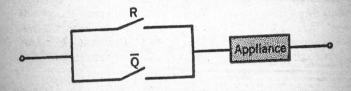

Circuits and Logic

Switching circuits and propositions have the same algebra. It is the two-valued Boolean algebra. Because of this fact, any expression in the algebra may be given two different interpretations. It may be interpreted as a compound switch built out of elementary switches, or it may be interpreted as a compound proposition built out of elementary propositions. For example, the expression $s\,t$ represents equally well the conjunction of two propositions s and t, or a series combination of two switches s and t. Because of this double interpretation that is possible, the algebraic expressions set up a correspondence between the elements of the system of switching circuits and the elements of the system of propositional forms. We have used this correspondence in one direction by employing symbolic logic to solve circuit problems. We can also use it in the opposite direction by employing circuits to solve logical problems. For example, the truth table of a compound propositional form can be represented by a switching circuit. If we use a meter as the appliance in the circuit, then it will indicate automatically the truth value of the form for each choice of truth values for the variables in it. To show that a variable s is given the truth value 1, simply close the corresponding switch s. To show that the variable s is being given the truth value 0, leave the switch s open. The truth value of the compound proposition will be 1 if and only if the meter shows the presence of current. The circuits needed for

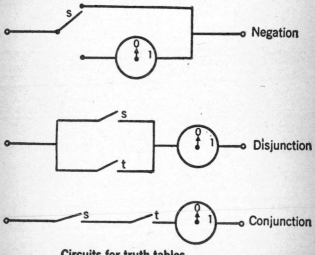

Circuits for truth tables

negation, disjunction, and conjunction are immediately obvious, and are shown above. But if switching circuits can solve logical problems, it means that we can use them to do some of our thinking. This is the reason why switching circuits, or their electronic equivalents, are the materials from which the control systems of thinking machines are built.

CHAPTER 11

Electronic Computers

Gates

A SWITCH is an electrical gate placed across the path of an electric current. When the switch is closed, the gate is open, and current can pass through. When the switch is open, the gate is closed and the current is stopped. The parallel and series combinations of switches described in the preceding chapter are gates of a special kind. Two switches in parallel form what is called an *or* gate, because they permit current to flow through only if one *or* the other switch is closed. Two switches in series form what is called an *and* gate, because they permit current to flow through only if one switch *and* the other switch are closed.

We have talked about the opening and closing of switches without considering how they are opened and closed. One way of opening and closing switches is to operate them electrically, in the device known as a *relay*. In a relay, the moving arm of a switch is adjacent to the iron core of an electromagnet. When current flows through the coil of the electromagnet, the core is magnetized and pulls the switch closed. When the current stops, the core ceases being a magnet. Then the arm of the switch is released, and a spring pulls it back, so that the switch is opened. The effect of the relay is that a current in one circuit is used to control the current in another circuit. Let us call the current in the electromagnet the *input,* and the current in the line containing the switch the *output*. Denote a flow of current by 1, and the absence of current by 0. Then the behavior of a single relay-operated switch can be

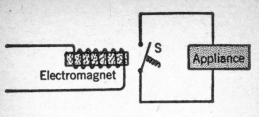

A relay

described in these terms: If the input is 1, the output is 1; while if the input is 0, the output is 0.

If two switches *A* and *B* are relay-operated, and are in parallel to form an *or* gate, the behavior of the *or* gate can be described in these terms: If the input to either *A or B* is 1, then the output is 1. Otherwise the output is 0. Here is another way of stating this fact: The *or* gate produces the output by *adding* the inputs according to the rules of the two-valued Boolean algebra.

If *A* and *B* are in series to form an *and* gate, the behavior of the *and* gate may be described as follows: If the input to *A and B* is 1, then the output is 1. Otherwise the output is 0. Here is an equivalent formulation of this statement: The *and* gate produces the output by *multiplying* the inputs according to the rules of the two-valued Boolean algebra.

A relay can also be wired so that the switch it operates is opened when the arm is pulled by the electromagnet, and is closed when the arm is released. In this case, an input of 1 produces an output of 0, and vice versa. A relay operating in this way is called an *inverter*. The behavior of an *inverter,* too, can be described in the language of Boolean algebra: The output of an *inverter* is the *complement* of the input.

The *or* gate, the *and* gate, and the *inverter* are the electrical analogues of union, intersection, and complementation of classes, and of disjunction, conjunction, and negation of propositions. They are the hardware embodiment of the logical concepts denoted by the words *or, and,* and *not.*

With these gates supplying the basic operations of addition, multiplication, and complementation, currents become the elements of a Boolean algebra.

Electronic Gates

There are electronic components made of combinations of tubes, resistors, etc., that serve the same functions as the relay-operated gates. They, too, will be referred to by the names *or gate, and gate,* and *inverter.* A simplified schematic diagram for each of these components is shown below. We shall not discuss how they work, because such a discussion involves electronic details that go beyond the

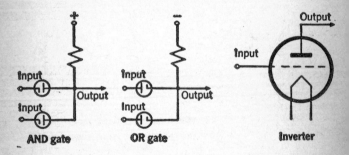

AND gate   OR gate   Inverter

scope of this book. However, we are interested here in how they are used. Our first goal in this chapter is to see how appropriate combinations of these electronic components can be put together to form an electronic computer capable of doing such things as adding or multiplying numbers.

In diagrams of the logical organization of an electronic computer, a special symbol is used for each of these three electronic components. These symbols are shown below alongside diagrams of the analogous switching circuits. (In the switching diagrams, for the sake of simplicity, the electromagnet that operates each switch is omitted.) The *and* gate and the *or* gate both have two inputs and one output. Using Boolean algebra notation, if the inputs are A and B, then the output of the *and* gate is AB, and the output of the *or* gate is $A + B$. The inverter has one input, A, and its output is $\bar{A}$.

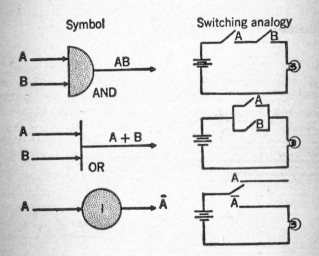

Symbol	Switching analogy

Numbers Written by Currents

The current in a wire may be either *on* or *off*. This two-valued nature of the state of the current permits it to be used to represent a bit in a binary numeral. If we use a separate wire for each bit, then the whole numeral can be expressed by the state of the currents in them. For example, suppose we have four wires side by side, from left to right, with the state of the current in these wires as follows: on—off—on—off. Then these states represent the binary numeral 1010, which stands for the number *ten*.

When we use decimal numerals, we refer to the position

of the first digit on the right as the *units* column. The second digit is in the *tens* column, the third digit is in the *hundreds* column, and so on. Similarly, we shall refer to positions from right to left in a binary numeral as the *units* column, the *twos* column, the *fours* column, etc.

Designing an Electronic Adding Machine

We are now ready to deal with the problem of designing an electronic circuit that is capable of doing addition of numbers. Let us begin by observing the procedure of a person who adds two numbers written in binary notation. First he writes the numbers one under the other. Then he adds the columns, one at a time, starting with the units column. The addition of the units column differs in an important way from the addition of every other column. In the units column, there are only *two* bits to add. In every other column there are *three* bits to add. Two of them are the bits that appear in the addends in that column. The third bit is the *carry* from the addition in the column to the right. This carry may be a 1 or a 0. (The carry is 0 when the sum of the bits added is 0 or 1. The carry is 1 when the sum is 10 or 11.) So, to carry out addition electronically, we need two different kinds of devices. We need one that can add *two* bits and then produce separately the bit that is put down in the sum and the bit that is to be carried. Such a device is called a *half adder*. We also need a device that can add *three* bits, and produce separately the bit for the sum and the carry. This device is known as a *full adder*. A half adder would suffice to add the bits in the units column. A full adder would be needed for each of the other columns.

The Half Adder

A half adder has two inputs. These are the bits in the units column of the addends. Let us call these bits A and B. The half adder also has two outputs, the bit that goes into the sum, and the bit that is carried. Let us call these S and C respectively. The values of S and C for different values of A and B are shown in the table below:

A	B	S	C
1	1	0	1
1	0	1	0
0	1	1	0
0	0	0	0

What we really have here is a truth table for S and C. Using the procedure described on page 109, we can get from these truth tables a formula for S and a formula for C:

$$S = \bar{A}B + A\bar{B}; \qquad C = AB.$$

These formulas give us instructions for making a circuit that will work as a half adder. Every bar in the formulas indicates the use of an inverter. Every multiplication sign indicates the use of an *and* gate. Every plus sign indicates the use of an *or* gate. To produce the output S, we proceed as follows: Use an inverter to change A into $\bar{A}$. Use an inverter to change B into $\bar{B}$. Use an *and* gate to multiply $\bar{A}$ and B, producing the product $\bar{A}B$. Use an *and* gate to multiply A and $\bar{B}$, producing the product $A\bar{B}$. Then use an *or* gate to add $\bar{A}B$ and $A\bar{B}$, producing S. To produce the output C, we need only an *and* gate to multiply A and B. The circuit for the half adder is shown in the diagram below.

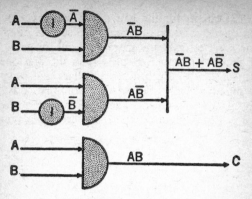

Circuit for half adder

The formulas for S and C given above are not the only ones that fit the truth tables for S and C. There are others that we can get by manipulating these formulas according to the rules of Boolean algebra. Each set of formulas obtained in this way is the design for another circuit that can do the work of a half adder. For example, on page 87 we showed that the expression $\bar{A}B + A\bar{B}$ is equivalent to $(A + B)\bar{C}$. So another formula for S is $S = (A + B)\bar{C}$. This formula gives us another circuit for producing S. In this circuit, an inverter is used to produce $\bar{C}$ from C. An *or* gate is used to add A and B. Then an *and* gate is used to multiply $A + B$ by $\bar{C}$. The new circuit for the half adder is shown below.

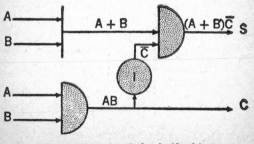

Simplified circuit for half adder

The first circuit for the half adder used two inverters, three *and* gates, and one *or* gate. The second circuit uses only one inverter, two *and* gates, and one *or* gate. So the second circuit is cheaper to make than the first one. This shows that Boolean algebra has a dollars and cents value for the manufacturers of electronic computers. By using Boolean algebra, they can sometimes replace a circuit by one that is simpler and cheaper and serves the same purpose.

The Full Adder

A full adder has three inputs. Two of them are the bits of the addends that appear in the column being added. Let us call them A and B. The third one is the carry from the addition of the next column to the right. Let us call this bit C. The full adder has two outputs, the bit that goes into the sum, and the bit that is carried. Let us call these S and D respectively. The values of S and D for different values of $A, B,$ and C are shown in this table:

A	B	C	S	D
1	1	1	1	1
1	1	0	0	1
1	0	1	0	1
1	0	0	1	0
0	1	1	0	1
0	1	0	1	0
0	0	1	1	0
0	0	0	0	0

From this table, using the procedure of page 109, we get these formulas for S and D: $S = ABC + A\overline{B}\overline{C} + \overline{A}B\overline{C} +$

$\overline{A}\overline{B}C.$ $D = ABC + AB\overline{C} + A\overline{B}C + \overline{A}BC.$ Now, using the rules of Boolean algebra, we modify these formulas as follows:

$$S = ABC + A\overline{B}\overline{C} + \overline{A}B\overline{C} + \overline{A}\overline{B}C$$
$$= (ABC + \overline{A}\overline{B}C) + (\overline{A}B\overline{C} + A\overline{B}\overline{C})$$
$$= (AB + \overline{A}\overline{B})C + (\overline{A}B + A\overline{B})\overline{C}$$

On page 88 we found that $AB + \overline{A}\overline{B} = \overline{\overline{A}B + A\overline{B}}$. Substituting the latter expression for $AB + \overline{A}\overline{B}$, we get

$$S = (\overline{\overline{A}B + A\overline{B}})C + (\overline{A}B + A\overline{B})\overline{C}.$$

This may look like a more complicated expression for S, but it has an important advantage over the earlier one. It expresses S in terms of $\overline{A}B + A\overline{B}$ and C. The former is the *sum* output of a half adder operating on A and B, while the latter is the *carry* output from the addition of the preceding column. This version of the formula permits us to incorporate a half adder as a unit in the design of a full adder.

$$D = ABC + AB\overline{C} + A\overline{B}C + \overline{A}BC$$
$$= (\overline{A}BC + A\overline{B}C) + (ABC + AB\overline{C})$$
$$= (\overline{A}B + A\overline{B})C + AB(C + \overline{C})$$
$$= (\overline{A}B + A\overline{B})C + AB(1)$$

So $D = (\overline{A}B + A\overline{B})C + AB.$

This formula for D expresses it in terms of $\overline{A}B + A\overline{B}$, AB, and C. The first of these is the *sum* output of a half adder operating on A and B. The second is the *carry* output of the same half adder. The third is the *carry* output from the addition of the preceding column. So we can also use a half

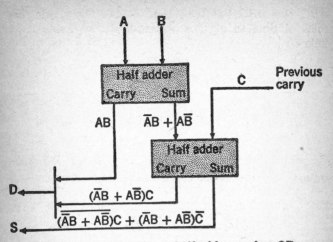

Full adder made with two half adders and an OR

adder as a unit in the part of the circuit that produces *D*. Taking our cue from these formulas, we can build a full adder out of two half adders, as shown in the diagram.

A Calculator with a Heart Beat

Just as there are many ways of putting *and* gates, *or* gates, and *inverters* together to form a half adder, there are many ways of putting half adders and adders together to form a calculator. To give a specific example, we shall examine some of the details of the design of a particular machine, the Naval Ordnance Research Calculator (known by its initials as NORC), built for the Navy by the International Business Machines Corporation.

A special feature of the NORC is that it has a "heart" beat. Electrical pulses, generated electronically, beat a regular rhythm throughout the machine. The pulses are generated at the rate of one million per second. There are other pulses that are fed into the machine to represent numbers, instructions, and so on. When the pulses are passed on from one part of the machine to another, they move in step with the rhythm of the heart beat.

The Dynamic Pulse Unit

Another feature of the NORC is its use of a special component known as a Dynamic Pulse Unit, or DPU. A DPU has an input terminal through which it may receive an electrical pulse, and an output terminal through which it may send one out. The chief function of the DPU is to introduce a delay of a microsecond (one millionth of a

Symbol for a dynamic pulse unit

second) between the input pulse and the output pulse. If it receives a pulse at the moment of one heart beat, it sends one out at the moment of the next heart beat. Otherwise it doesn't send out any pulse at all. The NORC contains about 1500 DPU's.

At each heart beat, a DPU receives a signal through its input terminal. This signal is either the presence or the absence of a pulse. At the next heart beat, it passes on this same signal to its output terminal. There are multitudes of electronic switches in the NORC. By opening or closing the switches in various combinations, different pathways are opened up along which the signal may be routed. A signal can be stored for any number of microseconds in a DPU. To store a signal in a DPU, it is fed into the input terminal of the DPU at the moment of a heart beat. Then, immediately, the output terminal is connected to the input terminal of the same DPU. So, when the DPU transmits the pulse at the next heart beat, it transmits the pulse to itself. In this way the pulse is renewed over and over again every microsecond, until it is switched into some other component. A DPU whose output is joined to its input is said to be in the *circulate* condition.

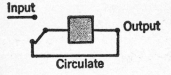

Temporary storage in a DPU

Numbers in the NORC

To write numbers, the NORC uses the compromise system described on page 54. It expresses numbers in terms of decimal digits, but each digit is represented by four bits. The four bits for a digit are expressed as signals along four separate wires. A thirteen-digit number would require 52 bits to represent it. These are accompanied by 12 other bits that serve these additional purposes: 8 bits, standing for 2 digits, indicate the position of the decimal point in the number; 4 bits, standing for one digit, indicate the algebraic sign. So 64 bits altogether represent the number. Two more bits are used for checking purposes. The total of 66 bits constitutes what is called a *number word*.

The position of the decimal point is indicated by means of a simple code. The digit 0, in this code, means that the decimal point is in standard position, that is, to the right of the first digit in the number. A code number between 1 and 30 inclusive indicates that the decimal point is that number of places to the right of standard position. For example, the code number 5 means that the decimal point is five places to the right of standard position. A code number between

70 and 99 inclusive indicates that the decimal point is to the left of standard position. To find out how many places to the left it is, you must subtract the code number from 100. For example, if the code number is 97, the decimal point is three places to the left of standard position.

To show the algebraic sign of the number, the digits 0 and 1 are used. The digit 0 indicates a positive number, and the digit 1 indicates a negative number. Whenever a number is written, the code number for the sign is placed to the left of the digits of the number. The code number for the position of the decimal point is placed to the left of the code number for the sign. According to this scheme, for example, the sequence 08/0/567 123 806 542 9 would represent the number + 567,123,806.5429.

The NORC Memory

The memory or storage unit of the NORC is a set of tubes like the picture tubes of a television set. The face of each tube is thought of as being divided into little squares. Each square is a *location*. A single bit can be stored in each location. This is done by aiming the electron gun of the tube at the location or at a spot near it. The electron gun sends out a stream of electrons. If the stream strikes the location, it knocks electrons out of the glass there. Electronic engineers call this *digging a hole*. If the stream strikes a spot near a location in which a hole has been dug, it restores the missing electrons. This is called *filling the hole*. The stream is made to *dig* a hole in order to store a 0. It is made to fill the hole in order to store a 1.

There is a conducting surface outside each storage tube, near its face. This surface is used for reading the bits that are stored in the tube. To read the bit stored at a location, the electron stream is aimed at it. If the bit is a 1, there is no hole at that location. The stream now digs a hole there. The digging causes a pulse of current to appear in a wire connected to the conducting surface. So a 1 stored at the location is read as a pulse in the wire. If the bit stored at the location is a 0, there is a hole there. Then the electron stream does no digging there, because the hole is already dug. As a result no pulse appears in the wire from the conducting surface. So a 0 stored at the location is read as the absence of a pulse in the wire.

Taking a Number from Storage

The 64 bits that represent a number can be stored at 64 locations in the storage unit. This combination of bit locations is a *word* location. To take a number out of storage, the wire from each bit location is switched to the input terminal of a separate DPU. At the next heart beat, each bit enters a DPU. Then the DPU's are switched to *circulate*. The number is now stored in the set of 64 DPU's until it is needed. This set of DPU's, used together as a unit, is called a *register*. When two numbers are to be added, each is first stored in a register. Then the numbers are fed from the two registers into the adding unit. In what follows we disregard decimal points and algebraic signs, and consider only the addition of natural numbers.

Moving a Number

Once a number is stored in a register, the machine can make the number move. To make it move, it first arranges the digits of the number in a line. This is done by switching the DPU's so that they form four lines, as shown in the diagram below. Each set of four DPU's that are in a vertical column contains the bits that represent a single digit. The column on the extreme right contains the units digit, the next column contains the tens digit, and so on. In other words, the arrangement of the digits along the four lines matches exactly our usual way of writing a decimal numeral.

Now suppose each of the four lines is lengthened by joining more DPU's to its right hand end. At the first heart beat after that, each DPU passes its bit on to the DPU to its right. The four bits that represent a digit therefore move in unison, one place to the right. At the next heart beat, they

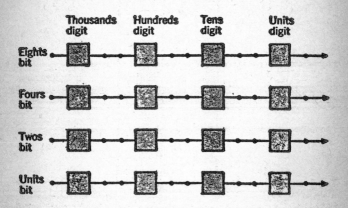

move to the right again. The four rows of bits march to the right, in step with the rhythm of the heart beat, like a column of soldiers on parade.

How the NORC Adds Numbers

To add two numbers, first each is stored in a register. Then their digits are lined up, as described above, and they are moved into an adding unit, one digit at a time. At the moment of a heart beat, the units digits enter the adding unit. The adding unit adds the digits and obtains two digits, one for the sum, and one to carry. At the next heart beat, it passes the sum digit on to the left end of a register, and passes the carry digit on to itself. The carry digit enters the adder at the same time that the tens digits enter. In

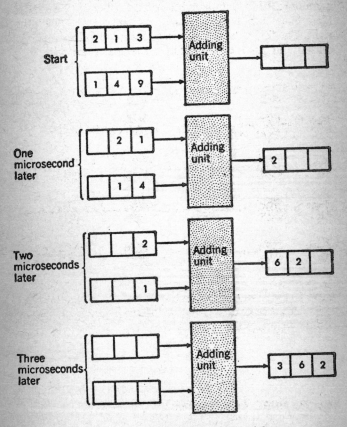

Adding three-digit numbers

this way the adding unit carries from the units column to the tens column just as we do when we add with pencil and paper. Beat by beat, the digits of the two numbers march into the adding unit, and the digits of the sum march out at the other end.

Now let us peek inside the adding unit to see how it produces the sum and carry digits. When two digits enter the adding unit, each digit makes its entrance in the guise of a four-bit binary numeral. We saw on page 128 that two such numerals can be added by a combination of one half adder and three full adders. We can provide for a carry digit that may be 0 or 1 by replacing the half adder

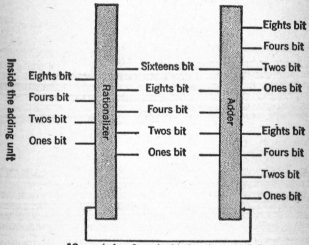

Inside the adding unit

Rationalizer

Eights bit
Fours bit
Twos bit
Ones bit

Sixteens bit
Eights bit
Fours bit
Twos bit
Ones bit

Adder

Eights bit
Fours bit
Twos bit
Ones bit

Eights bit
Fours bit
Twos bit
Ones bit

10, carried as 1, and added to the next digit

by a full adder. So a battery of four full adders can take care of the addition of two digits and the carry from the previous addition. Let us use the word *adder* as a brief designation for this battery of full adders. Its output is sometimes a number that is higher than fifteen, and may even be as high as nineteen $(9 + 9 + 1)$. To write a number this high requires five bits. So the sum appears at first as a five-bit numeral. If the sum is ten or higher, it is necessary to decompose the number into two parts. One part is the sum digit that is to be passed on to the register that receives the answer. The other part is the ten which is exchanged for a 1 to be carried. This job of decomposing the sum is carried out by a special unit called a *rationalizer*. The complete adding unit includes a rationalizer as well as an adder.

How the NORC Multiplies

To see how the NORC multiplies numbers, let us first examine the common paper and pencil method of doing multiplication. If we want to multiply 327 by 415, first we multiply 327 by the digits 4, 1, and 5 separately. We

$$\begin{array}{r} 327 \\ \times\ 415 \\ \hline 1635 \\ 327 \\ 1308 \\ \hline 135705 \end{array}$$

Common method of multiplying

write the products one under the other, with successive products shifted one place to the left. Then we add these products. To be prepared to multiply *any* two numbers, we need only know how to 1) multiply by any digit from 0 to 9, 2) arrange the appropriate partial products correctly, and 3) add them. The NORC multiplies numbers in essentially the same way. However, its method differs from the common one in two respects. In the common method of multiplication, we multiply the multiplicand by only those digits that appear in the multiplier. Moreover, we multiply by one digit at a time. The NORC multiplies by all the digits from 0 to 9, and does all these ten multiplications at the same time. Then it *selects* for addition only those products that correspond to digits of the multiplier. So the work of the NORC is made up of four parts: 1) multiply by the digits, 2) select the appropriate products, 3) arrange them, and 4) add them. Let us examine the details of each of these parts.

Multiplying. Multiplying by 1 requires no effort at all, since the product is the same as the multiplicand. To multiply by 2, we make use of a fact we observed on page 35: You can multiply a binary numeral by 2 by shifting each bit one place to the left. The NORC does it in this way: The digits of the multiplicand are lined up in a register, and are then fed, one at a time, into a rationalizer. But the bits that represent the digits are not put into the usual input terminals. Instead they are shifted one place to the left. The units bit is put into the twos terminal, the twos bit is put into the fours terminal, and so on. This automatically doubles each digit. Meanwhile, the rationalizer decomposes the result into a single digit and a carry. The single digit emerges from the output of the rationalizer. The carry is joined to the units input

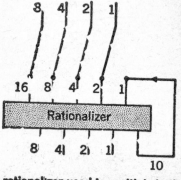

A rationalizer used to multiply by 2

terminal of the rationalizer. Then it is combined with double the next digit that enters the rationalizer. In this way the modified rationalizer doubles a number by doubling its digits, one after another, and carrying where necessary, just as we do in mental multiplication.

To multiply a number by 3, the NORC is guided by the distributive law: $3N = (2 + 1) N = 2N + 1N$. It multiplies a number by 3 by doubling the number and then adding the result to the original number. To multiply a number by 4, it doubles the number, and then doubles the result.

To multiply a number by 5, the NORC multiplies it by ten, and then divides by two. As we saw on page 35, you can multiply a decimal number by ten by moving each digit one place to the left. In the NORC, the digits of a number are lined up in a register, and then are fed into the calculating units one digit at a time. The first digit to enter is the units digit. Then the tens digit enters, and so on. There is a special time reserved for the entry of each digit. If the entry digits are all delayed for the interval between two successive heart beats, then the units digit enters at the time reserved for the tens digit, the tens digit enters at the time reserved for the hundreds digit, and so

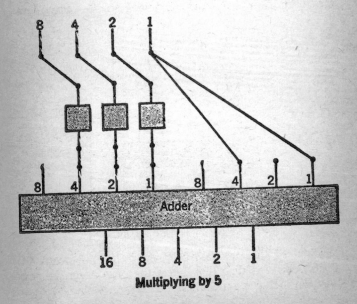

Multiplying by 5

on. It is as if all the digits had been shifted one place to the left in the register. The result is that the number has been multiplied by ten. Dividing by two is the opposite of multiplying by two, and is accomplished by shifting one place to the right the bits that represent each digit. The NORC applies these two techniques simultaneously on the twos bit, the fours bit, and the eights bit of each digit, as they are fed into an adder. To multiply the units bit by 5, it simply feeds it into both the units and fours terminal, so that a one is converted into one plus four. The connections for multiplying a number by 5 are shown in the diagram.

To multiply a number by 6, the NORC first multiplies it by 3, and then doubles the result. To multiply a number by 7, it multiplies the number separately by 5 and 2, and

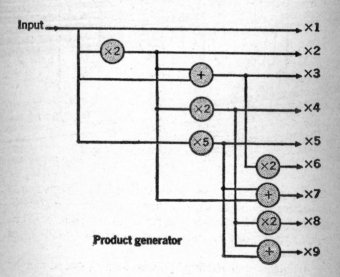

Product generator

then adds the products. To multiply by 8, it doubles the result of multiplying by 4. To multiply by 9, it first multiplies by 4 and 5 separately, and then adds the products.

All the multiplications are carried out in one unit called

the *product generator*. A diagram of the product generator
is shown above.

Selecting. As all nine products emerge from the genera-

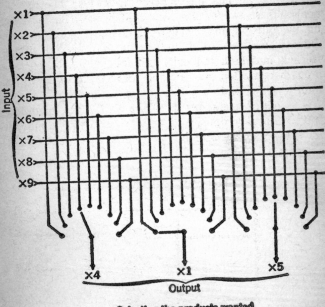

Selecting the products wanted

tor, they are fed to a set of selector switches. Each switch
is set for one of the digits of the multiplier. If the multiplier digit is 0, the switch is set to an *off* position. Thus
each switch picks out only one of the products and passes
it on as its own output.

Arranging and Adding. This is done at one stroke by
feeding the outputs of the selector switches into components joined in series as shown in the diagram. The
product by the digit furthest to the left is fed into a DPU,
while the rest are fed into adding units. Each of these units
introduces a delay of one microsecond. The delay has the

effect of shifting successive partial products one place to the left at the same time that they are being added.

Putting all these complex connections together, we get

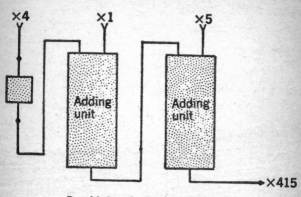

Combining the partial products

the NORC *multiplier*. When two numbers are multiplied, they are fed from registers into the multiplier. Five microseconds after the multiplicand begins moving into the multiplier, the product begins to emerge into another register.

Numbers for Places

Suppose a number is stored in the NORC's memory, and we want the machine to transfer this number from storage to a register. Then we must instruct the machine to connect a register to certain storage locations. The instructions must describe the locations in a language that the machine can "understand." This language takes the form of numbers. A number is assigned to each location, just as we assign street numbers and house numbers to the locations at which we live. The number assigned to a location is called its *address*. The machine is wired so that when the address of a location is fed into the machine as part of its instructions, the appropriate switches are closed to join a register to this location.

Numbers for Instructions

The instructions given to the NORC also tell it what to do. It may be told to add two numbers, or to multiply them, etc. These instructions, too, must be given in a language that the machine can understand. A number code is used for this purpose, too. For example, if two numbers drawn from storage are called *A* and *B*, the instruction number 20 means, "Find $A + B$ and store the result." The instruction number 23 means, "Find $A - B$, change the sign of the answer, and store the result."

By means of this code, all instructions to the machine can be written out as a sequence of digits. Sixteen digits, or 64 bits, are used. Two additional bits are used for checking purposes. The total of 64 bits is called an *instruction word*. Here is part of an instruction word, and its translation into English:

Instruction: . . . 20/0168/0341/0649
Meaning: Take the number in storage location 168, add to it the number in storage location 341, and store the result in storage location 649.

An important consequence of using a number code for instructions is that *instructions* can be stored in the machine's memory unit. This makes it possible to tell the machine to perform certain operations, and then go to a certain storage address to find out what to do next.

Input and Output

To put information into storage, it is first entered on a punch card. This is done on a machine that has a keyboard resembling that of a typewriter. When the operator strikes the appropriate keys, holes are punched in a card to express the information in the punch card code. From the punch card, the information is transferred to magnetic tape.

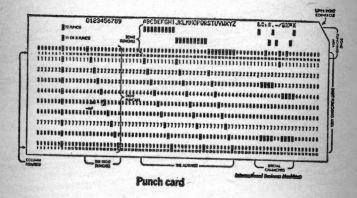

Punch card

It is recorded electrically on the tape in the form of bits. Each bit takes the form of the presence or the absence of a magnetized spot on the tape, just as each bit in the memory tube takes the form of the presence or absence of a charged spot. From the tape, the information is transferred into a register, and from the register, it is fed into storage. To get the output of the machine in printed form, this procedure is reversed. Information is moved from storage to a register, and from there to a tape. From the tape it is transferred to a punch card, from which it can be read off by a printer.

The machine has one more avenue of contact with its operator. There is a console with switches and indicators.

By means of the switches, the operator can give and modify instructions. Through the indicators, she sees what the machine is doing at each step.

Speed

Because it works to the rhythm of its heart beat, the NORC works very fast. It can add two thirteen-digit numbers in fifteen microseconds. At this speed, it can do in one second as many calculations as a man working with pencil and paper can do in a week. As a result, calculations that are "impossible" if done by hand, simply because they would take too long to be practical, become practical, and hence possible, if done by machine.

CHAPTER 12

Thinking Machines and the Brain

Machines That Behave Like Brains

AUTOMATIC calculating machines have been called thinking machines because they behave in many ways like a brain. They can carry out numerical calculations. These range in difficulty and complexity from simple counting to solving differential equations. They can receive and follow instructions. They have memories, in which they can store information for future use. Because they are equipped with *and, or* and *not* components, they can carry out the logical operations we call deductive reasoning.

The combination of all these qualities gives the machines another brain-like property. They can make comparisons, and then, on the basis of what they observe, choose among alternative courses of action. A checker-playing machine, for example, can calculate ahead, for several moves, the consequences of each move it may make. Then, using fixed rules that are part of its instructions, it evaluates the different possible moves, and chooses the one that is "best" according to its built-in standards of judgment.

A recent improvement has been the design of machines that can learn from their experience. One of these is the machine that plays checkers. In its first games, it is guided by its original instructions. As it plays, it stores a record of all its moves in its memory. Then, after a certain number of games have been played, it evaluates its moves in terms of their actual consequences. Then it modifies its own instructions to take its past experience into account. Tactics that did not work out so well are discarded. Tactics that led most often to victory are given greater emphasis. By repeatedly revising its instructions the machine steadily perfects its game.

The Brain Is Like a Machine

Since it seems to make sense to compare a calculating machine to the brain, it is natural to try to turn the comparison around. Is the brain like a calculating machine? We find that in some respects it is. A digital calculating machine is a complex electrical network built up out of a large number of units. The most basic unit is the vacuum tube, or its modern substitute, the transistor. There are also other units built out of the basic units. These include such components as DPU's, *and* gates, *or* gates, and inverters. The brain is also a complex electrical network built up out of a large number of units. The basic unit in the brain is the *nerve cell*. The behavior of many nerve cells is something like that of a DPU. If they are stimulated by a nerve impulse from another cell, they send out a nerve impulse of their own. Some nerve cells will act when stimulated by any one of several other cells. These cells behave like *or* gates. Others will act only when stimulated by all of a group of other cells. These behave like *and* gates. In these aspects of its behavior, the brain seems to work like a digital computer. However, it is possible, too, that the action of a nerve cell depends on the spatial arrangement of the cells that are joined to it, and the position of a cell that sends it an impulse. Nerve impulses, and chemical and physical stimuli to nerve cells seem to add up to a total stimulus. In this respect, the behavior of the brain is like that of an analog computer. So the brain, to the extent that it is like a calculating machine, seems to be one of mixed type, part digital and part analog.

Brain Versus Machine

How do the brain and the machine compare in complexity and efficiency as pieces of thinking apparatus? We can get a crude answer to this question from certain known facts about the brain and machines. We can use as an index of relative complexity the ratio of the number of unit actions that can be performed by equal volumes of each in equal times. This can be calculated from the ratio of the volumes of the basic units in each, and the ratio of their speeds. A neuron is about one billion times smaller than the basic unit of a calculating machine, and it is about one hundred thousand times slower in its action. Dividing these two figures gives us the desired index. Nerve tissue is about ten thousand times more efficient than electronic hardware.

An aspect of the brain's greater complexity is the great size of its memory capacity. A large modern computer has a memory capacity of one million bits. The memory capacity of the brain has been estimated at 280 billion billion bits. So the brain's memory capacity is 280 million million times as great as that of any existing machine.

The Brain's Memory Unit

In order to give an electronic computer adequate memory capacity, engineers have found it necessary to give the computer a separate memory unit. In order to make this unit efficient, they have found it necessary to build it out of components that are different from the basic active units in the logic and arithmetic sections of the machine. In the NORC, for example, the basic memory unit is a charge on the face of a television tube, rather than a DPU. These facts suggest an interesting series of questions about the brain. Does the brain have a separate memory unit? If it does, where is it? What are the basic units of which it is composed? Experience with electronic computers suggests the possible direction in which answers to these questions may be found. Because the brain has such a great memory capacity, it seems reasonable to assume that, as in the case of machines, the basic memory unit is different from the basic active unit, the nerve cell. For example, the basic stuff of which the memory is composed might be the connections between the nerve cells, rather than the cells themselves. This and other suggestions are being investigated by students of the nervous system.

Toward Better Understanding

Comparisons between the brain and electronic computers are not idle speculations. They are a necessary part of the scientific study of both. These comparisons have already shown themselves to be useful. When the late John von Neumann and his co-workers were designing the computer known as the JONIAC, they deliberately tried to imitate in it some of the known characteristics of the brain. On the other hand, investigators studying the functioning of the brain follow lines of investigation suggested by our knowledge about computers. Neurology and the theory of computers are separate branches of science. But they run parallel to each other to a certain extent, and advances in one field stimulate advances in the other. One of the truly exciting prospects arising from this relationship is that, the more we develop computers, the better we shall understand them. And the better we understand our computers, the better we shall understand ourselves.

Bibliography

Adler, Irving, *Magic House of Numbers*, The John Day Company, New York, N. Y.; The New American Library, New York, N. Y. For a simple introduction to the binary scale.

Adler, Irving, *The New Mathematics*, The John Day Company, New York, N. Y.; The New American Library, New York, N. Y. A popular introduction to algebraic structures.

Boole, George, *An Investigation of the Laws of Thought*, Dover Publications, Inc., New York, N. Y. The pioneer work on Boolean algebra. Mainly of historical interest.

Carroll, Lewis, *Symbolic Logic and the Game of Logic*, Dover Publications, Inc., New York, N. Y. Has a large collection of amusing, logical problems.

Eckert, W. J., and Jones, Rebecca, *Faster, Faster*, McGraw-Hill Book Company, New York, N. Y. A popular description of the NORC.

Gorn, Saul, and Manheimer, Wallace, *The Electronic Brain and What It Can Do*, Science Research Associates, Inc., Chicago, Ill. A fine popular pamphlet.

Langer, Susanne K., *An Introduction to Symbolic Logic*, Dover Publications, Inc., New York, N. Y. An excellent textbook.

Von Neumann, John, *The Computer and the Brain*, Yale University Press, New Haven, Conn. Notes for a popular lecture.

Index

157

SIGNET and MENTOR Books of Related Interest

"If she sl
who would help her?"

"Who was there anywhere who could help her? John Holbrook perhaps. In his quiet way he had a sort of strength and conviction. They might have listened to John. But he was far away in the wilderness of Massachusetts. Nat Eaton? He was halfway down the river and banished from town as well. William? Why of course! William could help her . . .

"The thought steadied her. She thought of him coming to champion her, confident, unruffled, those wide dependable shoulders like a fortress between her and the angry face of Goodwife Cruff. Dear dependable William! Perhaps he would come tonight. Kit drew a deep breath, and sitting on the floor, her knees drawn tight against her chest, she waited for William."

"Superior"
—*Best Sellers*

The
WITCH
of Blackbird Pond

Elizabeth George Speare

A DELL BOOK

Published by
DELL PUBLISHING CO., INC.
1 Dag Hammarskjold Plaza
New York, New York 10017

For information contact Houghton Mifflin Company,
Boston, Mass.
Dell ® TM 681510, Dell Publishing Co., Inc.
Reprinted by arrangement with
Houghton Mifflin Company
Boston, Massachusetts

Printed in the United States of America
First Dell printing—April 1971
Second Dell printing—August 1971
Third Dell printing—October 1971
Fourth Dell printing—March 1972
Fifth Dell printing—July 1972
Sixth Dell printing—September 1972
Seventh Dell printing—January 1973

The
WITCH
of Blackbird Pond

CHAPTER ONE

ON A MORNING in mid-April, 1687, the brigantine *Dolphin* left the open sea, sailed briskly across the Sound to the wide mouth of the Connecticut River and into Saybrook harbor. Kit Tyler had been on the forecastle deck since daybreak, standing close to the rail, staring hungrily at the first sight of land for five weeks.

"There's Connecticut Colony," a voice spoke in her ear. "You've come a long way to see it."

She looked up, surprised and flattered. On the whole long voyage the captain's son had spoken scarcely a dozen words to her. She had noticed him often, his thin wiry figure swinging easily hand over hand up the rigging, his sandy, sun-bleached head bent over a coil of rope. Nathaniel Eaton, first mate, but his mother called him Nat. Now, seeing him so close beside her, she was surprised that, for all he looked so slight, the top of her head barely reached his shoulder.

"How does it look to you?" he questioned.

Kit hesitated. She didn't want to admit how disappointing she found this first glimpse of America. The bleak line of shore surrounding the gray harbor was a disheartening contrast to the shimmering green and white that fringed the turquoise bay of Barbados

7

which was her home. The earthen wall of the fortification that faced the river was bare and ugly, and the houses beyond were no more than plain wooden boxes.

"Is that Wethersfield?" she inquired instead.

"Oh, no, Wethersfield is some way up the river. This is the port of Saybrook. Home to us Eatons. There's my father's shipyard, just beyond the dock."

She could just make out the row of unimpressive shacks and the flash of raw new lumber. Her smile was admiring from pure relief. At least this grim place was not her destination, and surely the colony at Wethersfield would prove more inviting.

"We've made good time this year," Nat went on. "It's been a fair passage, hasn't it?"

"Oh, yes," she sparkled. "Though I'm glad now 'tis over."

"Aye," he agreed. "I never know myself which is best, the setting out or the coming back to harbor. Ever been on a ship before?"

"Just the little pinnaces in the islands. I've sailed on those all my life."

He nodded. "That's where you learned to keep your balance."

So he had noticed! To her pride, she had proved to be a natural sailor. Certainly she had not spent the voyage groaning and retching like some of the passengers.

"You're not afraid of the wind and the salt, anyway. At least, you haven't spent much time below."

"Not if I could help it," she laughed. Did he think anyone would stay in that stuffy cabin by choice? Would she ever have had the courage to sail at all had she known, before she booked passage, that the sugar and molasses in the hold had been paid for by a load of Connecticut horses, and that all the winds of the Atlantic could never blow the ship clean of that unbearable stench? "That's what I minded most about the storm," she added, "four days shut away down there with the deadlights up."

"Were you scared?"

"Scared to death. Especially when the ship stood right on end, and the water leaked under the cabin door. But now I wouldn't have missed it for anything. 'Twas the most exciting thing I ever knew."

His face lighted with admiration, but all for the ship. "She's a stout one, the *Dolphin*," he said. "She's come through many a worse blow than that." His eyes dwelt fondly on the topsails.

"What is happening?" Kit asked, noting the sudden activity along the deck. Four husky sailors in blue jackets and bright kerchiefs had hurried forward to man the capstan bars. Captain Eaton, in his good blue coat, was shouting orders from the quarterdeck. "Are we stopping here?"

"There are passengers to go ashore," Nat explained. "And we need food and water for the trip upriver. But we've missed the tide, and the wind is blowing too hard from the west for us to make the landing. We're going to anchor out here and take the longboat in to shore. That means I'd better look to the oars." He swung away, moving lightly and confidently; there was a bounce in his step that matched the laughter in his eyes.

With dismay, Kit saw the captain's wife among the passengers preparing to disembark. Must she say goodbye so soon to Mistress Eaton? They had shared the bond of being the only two women aboard the *Dolphin* and the older woman had been sociable and

9

kindly. Now, catching Kit's eye, she came hurrying along the deck.

"Are you leaving the ship, Mistress Eaton?" Kit greeted her wistfully.

"Aye, didn't I tell you I'd be leaving you at Saybrook? But don't look so sad, child. 'Tis not far to Wethersfield, and we'll be meeting again."

"But I thought the *Dolphin* was your home!"

"In the wintertime it is, when we sail to the West Indies. But I was born in Saybrook, and in the spring I get to hankering for my house and garden. Besides, I'd never let on to my husband, but the summer trips are tedious, just back and forth up and down the river. I stay at home and tend my vegetables and my spinning like a proper housewife. Then, come November, when he sails for Barbados again, I'm ready enough to go with him. 'Tis a good life, and one of the best things about it is coming home in the springtime."

Kit glanced again at the forbidding shore. She could see nothing about it to put such a twinkle of anticipation in anyone's eye. Could there be some charm that was not visible from out here in the harbor? She spoke on a sudden impulse.

"Would there be room in the boat for me to ride to shore with you?" she begged. "I know it's silly, but there is America so close to me for the first time in my life—I can't bear not to set my foot upon it!"

"What a child you are, Kit," smiled Mrs. Eaton. "Sometimes 'tis hard to believe you are sixteen." She appealed to her husband. The captain scowled at the girl's wind-reddened cheeks and shining eyes, and then shrugged consent. As Kit gathered her heavy skirts about her and clambered down the swaying rope ladder, the men in the longboat good-naturedly

10

shoved their bundles closer to make room for her. Her spirits bobbed like the whitecaps in the harbor as the boat pulled away from the black hull of the *Dolphin*.

As the prow scraped the landing piles, Nat leaped ashore and caught the hawser. He reached to help his mother, then stretched a sure hand to swing Kit over the boat's edge.

With a bound she was over the side and had set foot on America. She stood taking deep breaths of the salt, fish-tainted air, and looked about for someone to share her excitement. She was quite forgotten. A throng of men and boys on the wharf had noisily closed in on the three Eatons, and she could hear a busy catching up of the past months' news. The other passengers had hurried along the wharf to the dirt road beyond. Only three shabbily-dressed women lingered near her, and because she could not contain her eagerness, Kit smiled and would have spoken, but she was abruptly repulsed by their sharply curious eyes. One hand moved guiltily to her tangled brown curls. She must look a sight! No gloves, no cover for her hair, and her face rough and red from weeks of salt wind. But how ill-mannered of them to stare so! She pulled up the hood of her scarlet cloak and turned away. Embarrassment was a new sensation for Kit. No one on the island had ever presumed to stare like that at Sir Francis Tyler's granddaughter.

To make matters worse, America was behaving strangely underfoot. As she stepped forward, the wharf tilted upward, and she felt curiously light-headed. Just in time a hand grasped her elbow.

"Steady there!" a voice warned. "You haven't got your land legs yet." Nat's blue eyes laughed down at her.

11

"It will wear off in a short time," his mother assured her. "Katherine, dear, I do hate to let you go on alone. You're sure your aunt will be waiting for you at Wethersfield? They say there's a Goodwife Cruff going aboard, and I'll tell her to keep an eye on you." With a quick clasp of Kit's hand she was gone and Nat, shouldering her trunk in one easy motion, followed her along the narrow dirt road. Which one of those queer little boxlike houses did they call home? Kit wondered.

She turned to watch the sailors stowing provisions into the longboat. She already regretted this impulsive trip ashore. There was no welcome for her at this chill Saybrook landing. She was grateful when at last the captain assembled the return group and she could climb back into the longboat. Four new passengers were embarking for the trip up the river, a shabby, dour-looking man and wife and their scrawny little girl clutching a wooden toy, and a tall, angular young man with a pale narrow face and shoulder-length fair hair under a wide-brimmed black hat. Captain Eaton took his place aft without attempting any introduction. The men readied their oars. Then Nathaniel, coming back down the road on a run, slipped the rope from the mooring and as they pulled away from the wharf leaped nimbly to his place with the crew.

They were halfway across the harbor when a wail of anguish broke from the child. Before anyone could stop her the little girl had flung herself to her knees and teetered dangerously over the edge of the boat. Her mother leaned forward, grasped the woolen jumper and jerked her back, smacking her down with a sharp cuff.

"Ma! The dolly's gone!" the child wailed. "The dolly Grandpa made for me!"

Kit could see the little wooden doll, its arms sticking stiffly into the air, bobbing helplessly in the water a few feet away.

"Shame on you!" the woman scolded. "After the work he went to. All that fuss for a toy, and then the minute you get one you throw it away!"

"I was holding her up to see the ship! Please get her back, Ma! Please! I'll never drop it again!"

The toy was drifting farther and farther from the boat, like a useless twig in the current. No one in the boat made a move, or paid the slightest attention. Kit could not keep silent.

"Turn back, Captain," she ordered impulsively. " 'Twill be an easy thing to catch."

The captain did not even glance in her direction. Kit was not used to being ignored, and her temper flared. When a thin whimper from the child was silenced by a vicious cuff, her anger boiled over. Without a second's deliberation she acted. Kicking off her buckled shoes and dropping the woolen cloak, she plunged headlong over the side of the boat.

The shock of cold, totally unexpected, almost knocked her senseless. As her head came to the surface she could not catch her breath at all. But after a dazed second she sighted the bobbing piece of wood and instinctively struck out after it in vigorous strokes that set her blood moving again. She had the doll in her hand before her numbed mind realized that there had been a second splash, and as she turned back she saw that Nathaniel was in the water beside her, thrashing with a clumsy paddling motion. She could not help laughing as she passed him, and with a feeling of triumph she beat him to

13

the boat. The captain leaned to drag her back over the side, and Nathaniel scrambled in behind her without any assistance.

"Such water!" she gasped. "I never dreamed water could be so cold!"

She shook back her wet hair, her cheeks glowing. But her laughter died away at sight of all their faces. Shock and horror and unmistakable anger stared back at her. Even Nathaniel's young face was dark with rage.

"You must be daft," the woman hissed. "To jump into the river and ruin those clothes!"

Kit tossed her head. "Bother the clothes! They'll dry. Besides, I have plenty of others."

"Then you might have a thought for somebody else!" snapped Nat, slapping the water out of his dripping breeches. "These are the only clothes I have."

Kit's eyes flashed. "Why did you jump in anyway? You needn't have bothered."

"You can be sure I wouldn't have," he retorted, "had I any idea you could swim."

Her eyes widened. "Swim?" she echoed scornfully. "Why my grandfather taught me to swim as soon as I could walk."

The others stared at her in suspicion. As though she had sprouted a tail and fins right before their eyes. What was the matter with these people? Not another word was uttered as the men pulled harder on their oars. A solid cloud of disapproval settled over the dripping girl, more chilling than the April breeze. Her high spirits plunged. She had made herself ridiculous. How many times had her grandfather cautioned her to think before she flew off the handle? She drew her knees and elbows tight under the red cloak and clenched her teeth to keep them from chattering. Water dripped off her matted hair and ran in icy trickles down her neck. Then, glancing defiantly from one hostile face to another, Kit found a small measure of comfort. The young man in the black hat was looking at her gravely, and all at once his lips twisted in spite of himself. A smile filled his eyes with such warmth and sympathy that a lump rose in Kit's throat, and she glanced away. Then she saw that the child, silently clutching her sodden doll, was staring at her with a gaze of pure worship.

Two hours later, dressed in a fresh green silk, Kit was spreading the wet dress and the woolen cloak to dry on the sun-warmed planking of the deck when her glance was caught by the wide black hat, and she looked up to see the new passenger coming toward her.

"If you will give me leave," he said, with stiff courtesy, removing the hat to reveal a high fine forehead, "I would like to introduce myself. I am John Holbrook, bound for Wethersfield, which I learn is your destination as well."

Kit had not forgotten that comforting smile. "I am Katherine Tyler," she answered forthrightly. "I am on the way to Wethersfield to live with my aunt, Mistress Wood."

"Is Matthew Wood your uncle then? His name is well known along the river."

"Yes, but I have never seen him, nor my aunt either. I do not even know very much about her, just that she was my mother's sister back in England, and that she was very beautiful."

The young man looked puzzled. "I have never met your aunt," he said politely. "I came to look for you now because I felt I should ask your pardon for the

15

way we all behaved toward you this morning. After all, it was only a kind thing you meant to do, to get the toy back for the child."

" 'Twas a very foolish thing, I realize now," she admitted. "I am forever doing foolish things. Even so, I can't understand why it should make everyone so angry."

He considered this gravely. "You took us aback, that is all. We were all sure you would drown before our eyes. It was astonishing to see you swimming."

"But can't you swim?"

He flushed. "I cannot swim a stroke, nor could anyone else on this ship, I warrant, except Nat who was born on the water. Where in England could they have taught you a thing like that?"

"Not England. I was born on Barbados."

"Barbados!" He stared. "The heathen island in the West Indies?"

" 'Tis no heathen island. 'Tis as civilized as England, with a famous town and fine streets and shops. My grandfather was one of the first plantation owners, with a grant from the King."

"You are not a Puritan then?"

"Puritan? You mean a Roundhead? One of those traitors who murdered King Charles?"

A spark of protest flashed across his mild gray eyes. He started to speak, then thought better of it, and asked gently, "You are going to stay here in Connecticut?"

Under his serious gaze Kit was suddenly uneasy. She had had enough questioning. "Do you live in Wethersfield yourself?" she turned the tables. The young man shook his head.

"My home is in Saybrook, but I am going to

Wethersfield to study under the Reverend Bulkeley. In another year I hope to be ready to take a church of my own."

A clergyman! She might have guessed it. His very smile had a touch of solemnness. But even as she thought it, she was surprised by the humor that quirked his fine straight lips.

"I mistrust you will be a surprise to the good people of Wethersfield," he said mildly. "What will they make of you, I wonder?"

Kit started. Had he guessed? There was no one who could possibly have told him. She had kept her secret even from the captain's wife. Before she could ask what he meant, she was diverted by the sight of Nat Eaton swinging along the deck in their direction. His thin clothing had dried on him, but the friendly grin of that morning had been replaced by an aloof and mocking smile that showed only too well that his morning's ducking had not been forgotten.

"My father sent me to find you, Mistress Tyler." One couldn't have guessed, by his tone, that he had ever addressed her before. "Since my mother has left the ship he thinks it best that you eat at board with Goodwife Cruff and her family."

Kit wrinkled up her nose. "Ugh," she exclaimed, "that sour face of hers will curdle my food."

Nat laughed shortly. " 'Tis certain she expects you will curdle hers," he answered. "She has been insisting to my father that you are a witch. She says no respectable woman could keep afloat in the water like that."

"How dare she!" Kit flared, indignant as much at his tone as at the dread word he uttered so carelessly.

"Don't you know about the water trial?" Nat's

eyes deliberately taunted her. " 'Tis a sure test. I've seen it myself. A true witch will always float. The innocent ones just sink like a stone."

He was obviously paying her back for the morning's humiliation. But she was surprised to see that John Holbrook was not at all amused. His solemn young face was even more grave than before.

"That is not a thing to be laughed at," he said. "Is the woman serious, Nat?"

Nat shrugged. "She'd worked up quite a gale," he admitted. "But my father has smoothed her down. He knows Barbados. He explained that the sea is always warm and that even respectable people sometimes swim in it. All the same, Mistress Katherine," he added, with a quizzical look, "now that you're in Connecticut I'd advise you to forget that you ever learned."

"No danger," Kit shuddered. "I wouldn't go near your freezing river again for the world."

She had made them both laugh, but underneath her nonchalance, Kit felt uneasy. In spite of his mocking tone, Nat had unmistakably warned her, just as she knew now that John Holbrook had been about to warn her. There was something strange about this country of America, something that they all seemed to share and understand and she did not. She was only partially reassured when John said, with another of those surprising flashes of gentle humor, "I shall sit with you at supper, if I may. Just to make sure that no one's food gets curdled."

CHAPTER TWO

It took nine days for the *Dolphin* to make the forty-three mile voyage from Saybrook to Wethersfield. As though the ship were bewitched, from the moment they left Saybrook everything went wrong. With the narrowing of the river the fresh sea breeze dropped behind, and by sunset it died away altogether. The sails sagged limp and soundless, and the *Dolphin* rolled sickeningly in midstream. On one or two evenings a temporary breeze raised their hopes and sent the ship ahead a few miles, only to die away again. In the morning Kit could scarcely tell that they had moved. The dense brown forest on either side never seemed to vary, and ahead there was only a new bend in the river to tantalize her.

"How can you stand it?" she fumed to a redheaded sailor who was taking advantage of the windless hours to give the carved dolphin at the prow a fresh coat of paint. "Doesn't the wind ever blow on this river?"

"Mighty seldom, ma'am," he responded with indifferent good humor. "You get used to it. We'll spend most of the summer waiting for a breeze, going or coming."

"How often do you go up this river?"

"Every few weeks. We make a run, say to Boston

or New Orleans, fill up the hold, and then back to Hartford."

She could see why Mistress Eaton chose to stay at home in Saybrook. "Does it always take as long as this?"

"Call this long?" the sailor replied, swinging far out to daub the curving tail of the dolphin. "Why, ma'am, I've known it to take as many days to get from here to Hartford as to go all the way to Jamaica. But I'm in no hurry. The *Dolphin*'s home to me, and I'm satisfied, wind or no wind."

Kit was ready to fly to pieces with frustration. How could she eke out the patience that had been scarcely enough to see her through a few remaining hours? And how could she force herself to endure another meal at the same board with Goodwife Cruff and her cowed shadow of a husband? Never a civil word had been spoken by either one of them. Plainly they considered the becalmed ship all her doing. And it spoiled her appetite just to watch that miserable little wraith of a child Prudence, not even allowed to sit at board with them, but kept behind her mother where she had to eat standing up the stingy portion they handed back to her. Once or twice she had seen the father furtively slip the child an extra morsel from his plate, but he was plainly too spineless to stand up for her against his shrew of a wife.

A more unpromising child she had never seen, Kit thought, yet she couldn't get Prudence out of her mind. There was some spark in that small frame that refused to be quenched. Late one afternoon Kit had come upon the little girl standing alone by the rail, and seeing the child's wistful, adoring gaze, had moved closer. As they stood side by side a crane rose slowly from the beach, with a graceful lift of its great wings, and they followed its flight, a leisurely line of white against the dark trees. The child had gasped, tilting back her head, her peaked little face aglow with wonder and delight. But in that instant a harsh call from the hatchway sent her scurrying. With a pang Kit realized that not once since they boarded the ship had she glimpsed the wooden doll. Had her own rash performance only served to cheat the child of the one toy she possessed?

They were certainly not good at forgetting, these New Englanders. Captain Eaton treated her with punctilious caution. Nat remained aloof, absorbed in a totally male world of rigging and canvas. On such a small ship it was remarkable how he managed to avoid her. The few times she happened to be directly in his path he tossed her an indifferent grin and his quizzical blue eyes flicked past and dismissed her.

If it weren't for John Holbrook I couldn't bear it, she thought. He's the only one on this ship who doesn't seem to begrudge my existence. He doesn't mind the delay, either. I believe he's actually grateful for it.

She looked with envy at where he sat, propped against a bulkhead, lost in a bulky brown volume. What could there be in those books of his? There he sat, hour after hour, so intent that often his lips moved, and two spots of color burned in his pale cheeks, as though some secret excitement sprang from the pages. Sometimes he forgot meals entirely. Only when he had wrung the last dregs of light from the sunset, and the shadows reached across the water and fell upon his book, would he reluctantly raise his head and become aware of the ship again.

When that moment came, Kit made sure that his eyes, blinking half blindly from his book, would focus

21

on her gay, silk-clad figure nearby. John would smile, mark his place with deliberation, and come to join her. In the soft half-darkness his stiff manners gradually relaxed into a boyish eagerness. Slowly Kit pieced together the details of what seemed to her an appallingly dull history.

"I suppose it was foolish for a tanner's son even to think about Harvard," John told her. "It was six miles to the school, and my father never could spare me for more than a month or so out of the year. He wanted me to learn, though. He never minded how long I burned the candles at night."

"You mean you worked all day and studied at night? Was it worth it?"

"Of course it was worth it," he answered, surprised at her question. "I was set on college. I finished all the requirements in Latin. I know the *Accidence* almost by heart."

"But you're not going to Harvard?"

He shook his head. "Up till this spring I kept hoping I could save money enough. I planned to walk over the foot trails through Connecticut and across Massachusetts. Well, the Lord didn't see fit to provide the money, but now He has opened another way for me. Reverend Bulkeley of Wethersfield has agreed to take me as a pupil. He is a very famous scholar, in medicine as well as theology. I couldn't have found a more learned teacher, even at Harvard."

Such frank talk about money embarrassed Kit. Her grandfather had seldom mentioned such a thing. She herself had rarely so much as held a coin in her hand, and for sixteen years she had never questioned the costly and beautiful things that surrounded her. In the last few months, to be sure, she had had a terrifying glimpse of what it might mean to live

22

without money, but it seemed shameful to speak of it. Instead she tried to tell him of her own childhood, and it was as though they each spoke a totally different language. She saw that John was scandalized at the way she had grown up on the island, running free as the wind in a world filled with sunshine. The green palms, the warm turquoise ocean rolling in to white beaches meant nothing to him. Didn't her parents give her work to do? he insisted.

"I don't remember my parents at all," she told him. "My father was born on the island and was sent to England to school. He met my mother there and brought her back to Barbados with him. They had only three years together. They were both drowned on a pleasure trip to Antigua, and Grandfather and I were left alone."

"Were there no women to care for you?"

"Oh, slaves of course. I had a black nursemaid. But I never needed anyone but Grandfather. He was —" There were no words to explain Grandfather. In the twilight the memory of him was very sharp, the soft pink skin aging on his fine cheekbones, the thin aristocratic nose, the eyes, so shrewd and yet so loving. She dared not trust her voice.

"It must have been hard to lose him," said John gently. "I am so glad you have an aunt to come to."

"She was my mother's only sister," said Kit, the tight pain easing a little. "Grandfather says my mother talked about her the livelong day and never got over being homesick for her. Her name is Rachel, and she was charming and gay, and they said she could have had her pick of any man in her father's regiment. But instead she fell in love with a Puritan and ran away to America without her father's blessing. She wrote to my mother from Wethersfield, and

23

she has written a letter to me every year of my life."

"She is going to be very happy to see you."

"I've tried so hard to imagine Aunt Rachel," mused Kit. "Grandfather said that my mother was thin and plain, like me. But Aunt Rachel was beautiful. Her hair and eyes will be dark, I suppose, like mine. But what will her voice be like? My mother remembered that she was always laughing."

John Holbrook looked earnestly at the girl beside him. "That was a great many years ago," he reminded her. "Don't forget, your aunt has been away from England for a long time."

Kit was aware again of that intangible warning that she could not interpret. Every day of this delay made it harder for her to shake off her uneasiness.

On the seventh morning Captain Eaton resorted to a curious device which John Holbrook called "walking up the river." Two sailors in a small boat went some distance ahead bearing a long rope fastened to a small anchor. Rowing as far as the rope would stretch, they dropped the anchor. On the deck of the ship the crew lined up, ten hearty men bared to the waist, each grasping the rope, and began a rhythmical march from one end of the ship to the other. As one man reached the end, he dropped the rope, and raced back to grasp it again at the end of the line. Painfully, almost imperceptibly, the *Dolphin* inched forward through the water. In an hour's time they had reached the anchor and the rowboat went ahead a second time. Over and over, hour after hour, the men moved, hauling the ship by the sheer force of straining muscle and gasping breath. Sweat poured down their arms and shoulders.

The agonizing slowness was harder to endure than no motion at all. Kit shuddered away from the sight of those lunging bodies. A hot spring sun beat down without relief. She twitched her own shoulders fretfully under the silk that stuck clammily against her skin. In the heat the stench of horses steamed up from the depths of the hold as though the animals were still there. This morning the cook had refused to spare her enough water even for a decent bath. It was almost too much to bear when she heard a splash directly below her and saw that Nat and two of the other young men had taken advantage of a wait for the rowboat and were thrashing about like porpoises in the river.

Nat looked up and caught her wistful eye. "Jump in, why don't you?" he taunted.

"You warned me never to do it again," Kit replied incautiously.

"Do you need an excuse? I'll shout for help and go under. You couldn't just stand there and watch me drown, could you?"

"Yes, I could," Kit laughed in spite of herself. "and I would, too."

"Then you can stay there and frizzle," responded Nat. As he paddled toward the ladder Kit watched him with both envy and relief. He had sounded as friendly and easy as on that first morning in Saybrook harbor.

As though to prove that the constraint between them was broken, in the next wait for the rowboat Nat strolled over to join her where she stood watching.

"I'll wager you're wishing you'd never left Barbados," he said. " 'Twas unfair of me to tease you."

"How I envied you," she exclaimed. "To get into that water and away from this filthy ship even for a moment!"

In a split second a squall darkened Nat's blue eyes. "Filthy—the *Dolphin?*"

"Oh," she laughed impatiently, "I know you're forever scrubbing. But that stable smell! I'll never get it out of my hair as long as I live!"

Nat's indignation found vent in scorn. "Maybe you think it would smell prettier with a hold full of human bodies, half of them rotting in their chains before anyone knew they were dead!"

Kit recoiled, as much from his angry tone as from the repulsive words. "What are you talking about? People—down in the hold?"

"I suppose you never knew about slaves on Barbados?"

"Of course I knew. We own—we used to own—more than a hundred. How else could you work a plantation?"

"How did you think they got there? Did you fancy they traveled from Africa in private cabins like yours?"

She had never thought about it at all. "But don't you have slaves in America?"

"Yes, to our shame! Mostly down Virginia way. But there are plenty of fine folk like you here in New England who'll pay a fat price for black flesh without asking any questions how it got here. If my father would consent to bring back just one load of slaves we would have had our new ketch by this summer. But we Eatons, we're almighty proud that our ship has a good honest stink of horses!"

Nat was gone again. What a touchy temper he had! She hadn't meant to insult his precious ship. Why did he deliberately turn everything to her disadvantage? He had been just on the point of making friends. Now the trip would probably be over before she could speak to him again. And why should she care—a rude, freckle faced sailor who took more notice of a strip of canvas than of a brocaded gown? At least John Holbrook knew how to speak with respect.

But even John Holbrook did not approve of her completely. She was forever astonishing him. Last night, for instance, she had reached impulsively for the volume he held, opened it at the marked page, and squinting curiously at the words in the wan light, had read aloud:

"We are in the first place to apprehend that there is a time fixed and stated by God for the Devil to enjoy a dominion over our sinful and therefore woful world. Toward the end of his time the descent of the Devil in Wrath upon the World will produce more woful effects than what have been in former Ages. The death pangs of the Devil will make him to be more of a Devil than ever he was—"

"Goodness!" Kit wrinkled up her nose. "Is this what you read all day long?" She looked up to find John staring at her.

"You can read that?" he questioned, with the same amazement he had shown when she had proved she could swim. "How did you learn to read when you say you just ran wild like a savage and never did any work?"

"Do you call reading work? I don't even remember how I learned. When it was too hot to play, Grandfather would take me into his library where it was dark and cool, and read to me out loud from his books, and later I would sit beside him and read to myself while he studied."

"What sort of books?" John's voice was incredulous.

"Oh, history, and poetry, and plays."

"Plays!"

"Yes, the plays were the best. Wonderful ones by Dryden and Shakespeare and Otway."

"Your grandfather allowed a girl to read such things?"

"They were beautiful, those plays! Have you never read them?"

John's pale cheeks reddened. "There are no such books in Saybrook. In Boston, perhaps. But the proper use of reading is to improve our sinful nature, and to fill our minds with God's holy word."

Kit stared at him. She pictured Grandfather, the blue-veined hands caressing the leather bindings, and she knew that he had not cherished his books with any thought of improving his sinful nature. She could imagine the twinkle that would have danced in his eyes at those solemn words. All the same, the reproof in John Holbrook's voice left her discomforted. Somehow she felt that John was always drawing back, uneasy at this friendship that was growing between them. And she herself was often repelled by the hard uprightness that lay just under his gentle voice and looks. She saw now that she could not tell him about the books she had loved any more than she could make him see the palm trees swaying under a brilliant blue sky.

Early the next morning a contrary breeze came whistling along the river. The *Dolphin* sprang to life, scudded the last few miles, and bumped against the wharf at Wethersfield landing. The shore, muffled in thick scarves of drifting mist, looked scarcely different from the miles of unbroken forest that they had seen for the past week.

Sailors began vigorously to roll out the great casks of molasses and pile them along the wharf. Two of the men lowered over the side the seven small leather trunks that held all of Kit's belongings and piled them, one beside the other, on the wet planking. Kit clambered down the ladder and stood for the second time on the alien shore that was to be her home.

Her heart sank. This was Wethersfield! Just a narrow sandy stretch of shoreline, a few piles sunk in the river with rough planking for a platform. Out of the mist jutted a row of cavernous wooden structures that must be warehouses, and beyond that the dense, dripping green of fields and woods. No town, not a house, only a few men and boys and two yapping dogs who had come to meet the boat. With something like panic Kit watched Goodwife Cruff descend the ladder and stride ahead of her husband along the wharf. Prudence, dragging at her mother's hand, gazed back imploringly as they passed.

"Ma," she ventured timidly, "the pretty lady got off here at Wethersfield!"

Kit summoned the boldness to speak to her. "Yes, Prudence," she called clearly. "And I hope that I will see you often."

Goodwife Cruff halted and glared at Kit. "I'll thank you to let my child alone!" she spat out. "We do not welcome strangers in this town, and you be the kind we like least." Jerking Prudence nearly off her feet, she marched firmly up the dirt road and disappeared in the fog.

Even John Holbrook's farewells were abstracted. A formal bow, a polite wish for her pleasant arrival, and he, too, strode eagerly into the fog in quest of his new teacher. Then Kit saw Captain Eaton approaching and knew that the moment had come when the truth would have to be told.

"There must be some mistake," the captain began. "We signaled yesterday that we would reach Wethersfield at dawn. I expected that your aunt and uncle would be here to meet you no matter how early it might be."

Kit swallowed and gathered her courage. "Captain Eaton," she said boldly, "my uncle and aunt can hardly be blamed for not meeting me. You see—well, to be honest, they do not even know that I am coming."

The captain's jaw tightened. "You gave me to understand that they had sent for you to come."

Kit lifted her head proudly. "I told you that they wanted me," she corrected him. "Mistress Wood is my mother's sister. Naturally she would always want me to come."

"Even assuming that to be true, how could you be sure they were still in Connecticut?"

"My Aunt Rachel's last letter came only six months ago."

He scowled with annoyance. "You know very well that I should never have taken you on board had I known this. Now I shall have to take the time to find where your uncle lives and deliver you. But understand, I take no responsibility for your coming."

Kit's head went higher. "I am entirely responsible for my own coming," she assured him haughtily.

"Fair enough," the captain responded grimly. "Look here, Nat," he turned back. "See if two hands can be spared to carry this baggage."

Kit's cheeks went scarlet. Why should Nat, who had carefully been somewhere else during the whole of the last nine days, have to be so handy at just this moment? Now whatever befell he was going to be there to witness it, with those mocking blue eyes and that maddening cool amusement. What if Aunt Rachel—but there was no time for doubt now. Between trying to hold up her head confidently and at the same time find a place to set down her dainty kid shoes between the slimy ruts and the mud puddles, Kit had all she could tend to.

CHAPTER THREE

ALONG WITH her pretty shoes, Kit's spirits sank lower at each step. She had clutched at a hope that the dark fringe of dripping trees might somehow be concealing the town she had anticipated. But as they plodded along the dirt road past wide stumpy fields, her last hopes died. There was no fine town of Wethersfield. There was a mere settlement, far more lonely and dreary than Saybrook.

A man in a leather coat and breeches led a cow along the road. He stopped to stare at them, and even the cow looked astonished. Captain Eaton took advantage of the meeting to ask directions.

"High Street," the man said, pointing his jagged stick. "Matthew Wood's place is the third house beyond the Common."

High Street indeed! No more than a cow path! Kit's shoes were wet through, and the soaked ruffles of her gown slapped against her ankles. She would naturally have lifted her skirts free of the uncut grass, but a new self-consciousness restrained her. She was aware at every step of the young man who strode behind her with a trunk balanced easily on each shoulder.

She relaxed slightly at the first glimpse of her uncle's house. At least it looked solid and respectable, compared to the cabins they had passed. Two and a half stories it stood, gracefully proportioned, with leaded glass windows and clapboards weathered to a silvery gray.

The captain lifted the iron knocker and let it fall with a thud that echoed in the pit of the girl's stomach. For a moment she could not breathe at all. Then the door opened and a thin, gray-haired woman stood on the threshold. She was quite plainly a servant, and Kit was impatient when the captain removed his hat and spoke with courtesy.

"Do I have the honor of addressing—?"

The woman did not even hear him. Her look had flashed past to the girl who stood just behind, and her face had suddenly gone white. One hand reached to clutch the doorpost.

"Margaret!" The word was no more than a whisper. For a moment the two women stared at each other. Then realization swept over Kit.

"No, Aunt Rachel!" she cried. "Don't look like that! It is Kit! I am Margaret's daughter."

"Kit? You mean—can it possibly be Katherine Tyler? For a moment I thought—oh, my dear child, how wonderful!"

All at once such a warmth and happiness swept over her pale face that Kit too was startled. Yes, this strange woman was indeed Aunt Rachel, and once, a long time ago, she must have been very beautiful.

Captain Eaton cleared his throat. "Well," he observed, "I am relieved that this has turned out well

32

after all. What will you have me do with the baggage, ma'am?"

Rachel Wood's eyes focused for the first time on the three trunk bearers. "Goodness," she gasped, "do all these belong to you, child? You can just set them there, I suppose, and I'll ask my husband about them. Can I offer you and your men some breakfast, sir?"

"Thank you, we can't spare any more time. Good day, young lady. I'll tell my wife I saw you safely here."

"I'm sorry to have caused you trouble," Kit said sincerely. "And I do thank you, all of you."

Two of the three sailors had already started back along the road, but Nat still stood beside the trunks and looked down at her. As their eyes met, something flashed between them, a question that was suddenly weighted with regret. But the instant was gone before she could grasp it, and the mocking light had sprung again into his eyes.

"Remember," he said softly. "Only the guilty ones stay afloat." And then he was gone.

The doorway of Matthew Wood's house led into a shallow hallway from which a narrow flight of stairs climbed steeply. Through a second door Kit stepped into the welcome of the great kitchen. In a fireplace that filled half one side of the room a bright fire crackled, throwing glancing patterns of light on creamy plaster walls. There was a gleam of rubbed wood and burnished pewter.

"Matthew! Girls!" cried her aunt. "Something wonderful has happened! Here is Katherine Tyler, my sister Margaret's girl, come all the way from Barbados!"

Three people stared up at her from the plain board table. Then, from his place at the head, a man unfolded his tall angular body and came toward her.

"You are welcome, Katherine," he said gravely, and took her hand in his bony fingers. She could not read the faintest sign of welcome in his thin stern lips or in the dark eyes that glowered fiercely at her from under heavy grizzled eyebrows.

Behind him a girl sprang up from the table and came forward. "This is your cousin Judith," her aunt said, and Kit gasped with pleasure. Judith's face fulfilled in every exquisite detail the picture she had treasured of her imagined aunt. The clear white skin, the blue eyes under a dark fringe of lashes, the black hair that curled against her shoulders, and the haughty lift of her perfect small chin—this girl could have been the toast of a regiment!

"And your other cousin, Mercy." The second girl had risen more slowly, and at first Kit was only aware of the most extraordinary eyes she had ever seen, gray as rain at sea, wide and clear and filled with light. Then, as Mercy stepped forward, one shoulder dipped and jerked back grotesquely, and Kit realized that she leaned on crutches.

"How lovely," breathed Mercy, her voice as arresting as her eyes, "to see you after all these years, Katherine!"

"Will you call me Kit?" The question sounded abrupt. Kit had been her grandfather's name for her, and something in Mercy's smile had reached straight across the gulf so that suddenly she wanted to hear the name spoken again.

"Have you had breakfast?"

"I guess not. I hadn't even thought of it."

"Then 'tis lucky we are eating late this morning," said her aunt. "Take her cloak, Judith. Come close to the fire, my dear, your skirt is soaking."

As Kit threw back the woolen cloak, Judith's reaching hand fell back. "My goodness!" she exclaimed. "You wore a dress like that to *travel* in?"

In her eagerness to make a good impression Kit had selected this dress with care, but here in this plain room it seemed overelegant. The three other women were all wearing some nondescript sort of coarse gray stuff. Judith laid the cloak thoughtfully on a bench and reached to touch Kit's glove.

"What beautiful embroidery," she said admiringly.

"Do you like them? I'll give you some just like them if you like. I have several pairs in my trunk."

Judith's eyes narrowed. Rachel Wood was setting out a pewter mug and spoon and a crude wooden plate.

"Sit here, Katherine, where the fire will warm your back. Tell us how you happened to come so far. Did your grandfather come with you?"

"My grandfather died four months ago," Kit explained.

"Why, you poor child! All alone there on that island! Who did come with you, then?"

"I came alone."

"Praise be!" her aunt marveled. "Well, you're here safe and sound. Have some corn bread, my dear. 'Twas baked fresh yesterday, and there is new butter."

Surprisingly, the bread tasted delicious, though of a coarse texture like nothing she had ever tasted before. Kit lifted the pewter mug thirstily, and abruptly set it down. "Is that *water?*" she asked politely.

"Of course, drawn fresh from the spring this morning."

Water! For *breakfast!* But the corn bread was

35

good, and she managed a second piece in spite of her dry tongue.

Rachel Wood could not seem to look away from the young face across the table, and every few moments her eyes brimmed over with tears.

"I declare, you look so like her it takes my breath away. But all the same, there is a hint of your father there, too. I can see it if I look closely."

"You remember my father?" Kit asked eagerly.

"I remember him well. A fine upstanding lad he was, and I never could blame Margaret. But it broke my heart to have her go so far."

But Rachel had come even farther. What could she have seen in that fierce silent man to draw her away from England? Could he have been handsome? Perhaps, with that strong regal nose and high forehead. But so terrifying!

Matthew Wood had not sat down at the table with the others. Though he had said nothing, Kit had been aware that not a motion had escaped his intent scowl. Now he pulled down a leather jacket from a peg on the wall and thrust his long arms into the sleeves.

"I will be working in the south meadow," he told his wife. "You had best not expect me till sundown."

At the open door, however, he stopped and looked back at them. "What is all this?" he inquired coldly.

"Oh," said Kit, scrambling to her feet. "I forgot. Those are my trunks."

"Yours? Seven trunks? What can be in them?"

"Why—my clothes, and a few things of Grand-father's."

"Seven trunks of clothes, all the way from Barbados just for a visit?"

The cold measured words fell like so many stones into the quiet room. Kit's throat was so dry she longed now to swallow the water. She lifted her chin and looked directly into those searching eyes.

"I have not come for a visit, sir," she answered. "I have come to stay with you."

There was a little gasp from Rachel. Matthew Wood closed the door deliberately and came back toward the table. "Why did you not write to us first?"

All her life, whenever her grandfather had asked her a question he had expected a direct answer. Now, in this stern man facing her, so totally different from her grandfather, Kit sensed the same quality of directness, and out of an instinctive respect she gave the only honest answer she could.

"I did not dare to write," she said. "I was afraid that you might not tell me to come, and I had to come."

Rachel leaned forward to put a hand on Kit's arm.

"We would not have refused you if you were in need," said her uncle. "But a step like this should not be taken without due pondering."

"Matthew," protested Rachel timidly, "what is there to ponder? We are the only family she has. Let us talk about it later. Now Katherine is tired, and your work has been delayed already."

Matthew Wood drew up a chair and sat down heavily. "The work will have to wait," he said. "It is best that we understand this matter at once. How did you come to set sail all alone?"

"There was a ship in the harbor and they said it was from Connecticut. I should have sent a letter, I know, but it might have been months before another ship came. So instead of writing I decided to come myself."

"You mean that, just on an impulse, you left your

rightful home and sailed halfway across the world?"

"No, it was not an impulse exactly. You see, I really had no home to leave."

"What of your grandfather's estate? I always understood he was a wealthy man."

"I suppose he was wealthy, once. But he had not been well for a long time. I think for years he was not able to manage the plantation, but no one realized it. He left everything more and more to the overseer, a man named Bryant. Last winter Bryant sold off the whole crop and then disappeared. Probably he sailed back to England on the trading ship. Grandfather couldn't believe it. After that he was never really well. The other plantation owners were his friends. Nobody ever pressed him, but after he died there just seemed to be debts everywhere, wherever I turned."

"Did you pay them?"

"Yes, every one of them. All the land had to be sold, and the house and the slaves, and all the furniture from England. There wasn't anything left, not even enough for my passage. To pay my way on the ship I had to sell my own Negro girl."

"Humph!" With one syllable Matthew disposed of the sacrifice, only a little less sharp than Grandfather's loss, of the little African slave who had been her shadow for twelve years. There was an awkward silence. Kit found Mercy's eyes and was steadied by the quiet sympathy she saw there. Then her aunt came to put an arm across her shoulder.

"Poor Katherine! It must have been terrible for you! You were perfectly right to come to us. You do believe she was right, don't you Matthew?"

"Yes," her husband conceded harshly. "She was right, I suppose, since we are her only kin. I will bring in the baggage." At the door he turned again. "Your grandfather was a King's man, I reckon?"

"He was a Royalist, sir. Here in America are you not also subjects of King James?"

Without answering, Matthew Wood left the room. Seven times he returned, bending his tall frame to enter the doorway, and with wordless disapproval set down one after the other the seven small trunks. They filled one entire end of the room.

"Where on earth can we put them?" quavered her aunt.

"I will find a place for them later in the attic," said her husband. "Seven trunks! The whole town will be talking about it before nightfall."

CHAPTER FOUR

As THE heavy door shut behind him the cloud gradually lifted from the room. Rachel moved nervously to the table and began to wrap the leftover corn bread in a clean linen napkin.

"Before I do another thing," she said, "I must take this to Widow Brown. She's still far too weak to fend for herself. Forgive me for leaving you, Katherine, but I'll be back in no time at all."

"In no time," echoed Judith bitterly, as her mother hurried out into the foggy morning. "Just as soon as she's built up the fire and made gruel and tidied the whole cabin. With more than a day's work waiting here at home."

"Why, Judith," Mercy rebuked her gently. "What would you have her do? You know what the Scriptures tell us about caring for the poor and the widows."

"There's no Scriptures saying Mother has to be the one to do all the caring," Judith retorted. "She wears herself out over people like Widow Brown, and honestly, Mercy, if Mother were ill how many of them to you think would lift a finger to help?"

"I'm sure they would," said Mercy promptly. "Besides, that's not the point. You'll give Kit a fine impression of us, Judith, and anyway, we'd better start on the work that's waiting right here."

Judith did not move. Her attention had turned again to the row of trunks. "Do you mean to say that every one of those trunks is full of dresses like the one you have on?"

"Well, dresses and petticoats, and slippers, and such. You have the same things yourselves, don't you?"

Mercy's laugh was a ripple of silver. "But we don't! We can't even imagine!"

"I can," said Judith. "I've seen the ladies in Hartford. Kit, how soon are you going to open them?"

"Right now, if you like," said Kit willingly.

Mercy was shocked. "Judith—what will our cousin think of us? Besides, there is all the work to be done."

"Oh, Mercy! There's always work!"

"I don't know—" said Mercy doubtfully. "Father says the Lord loveth not idleness. But then, the Lord doesn't send us a new cousin every day. Perhaps He would forgive us for a little rejoicing—"

"Oh, come, Kit, show us now!" urged Judith,

taking advantage of her sister's uncertainty. Kit was only too willing. As the first lid opened, all constraint was gone. Kit had never known many girls her own age. Her own eagerness rose at the sight of the two eager faces so close to hers. How amazing that a few clothes could cause such excitement. Kit felt a surge of generosity that was new and exhilarating.

"Imagine!" cried Judith, pulling out a handsome gown of filmy silk. "Five slits in the sleeves! Our minister preached against slit sleeves and Father won't let us make even one. And so many ribbons and bows! And, oh, Kit—a red satin petticoat—how gorgeous!"

"Here are the gloves." Kit opened a box. "There's a pair just like mine, Judith, and a pair for you, Mercy. *Please,* you must take them."

Judith had the gloves on before the sentence was finished, and stood stretching out her slender arms admiringly. Mercy stroked hers with a timid finger and laid them gently aside. Then Judith pounced on the dresses.

"Try it on," suggested Kit, seeing that Judith could scarcely take her eyes from a bright peacock blue paduasoy. Judith needed no urging. Dropping her own homespun skirt unashamedly on the floor, she drew the shining folds over her head.

"Why, 'tis perfect," exclaimed Kit. "It makes your eyes look almost green!"

Judith tiptoed across the floor, straining to see herself in the one small dim mirror that hung over a chest. Truly, in the vivid dress Judith was breathtaking, and she did not need the mirror to tell her so.

"Oh, if William could see me in this!" she breathed, ignoring Mercy's worried protests.

Kit laughed delightedly. "Well, 'tis yours, Judith. 'Twas made just for you. And there's a little cap with

41

ribbons to match—now where did I put it? There! Now which one will be best for Mercy?"

"Goodness, what use would I have for such things?" Mercy laughed. "I scarcely ever get to Meeting." Kit hesitated, chagrined. But Judith's eye had fallen on a light blue wool and she lifted it impulsively.

"This would be perfect for Mercy," she exclaimed. Kit unfolded the delicate English shawl and dropped it across Mercy's shoulders.

"Oh, Kit, how beautiful! I never felt anything so soft! Like a kitten's fur." Delight and protest struggled in Mercy's face. "I can't take anything so lovely."

Judith was back at the mirror. "Just wait till I walk into Meeting in this on Sunday morning," she squealed. "A few people I know won't hear a word of the sermon!"

"Why, girls! What on earth—?" Rachel Wood had come back unnoticed, and she stood now staring at her daughter in the peacock blue gown with something, half fear and half hunger in her eyes.

"Oh, Mother—look what Kit has given me!" cried Judith.

"I am looking," stammered her mother. "Judith—you look—I scarcely know you!"

"You should, Aunt Rachel," Kit spoke up boldly. "Because you must have looked just exactly like that yourself. I know because Grandfather has told me how beautiful you were."

The two girls stared at their mother in astonishment. Rachel looked dazed. "I had a dress just that color once," she said slowly.

Kit dived impulsively into the trunk. "Put this on, Aunt Rachel," she coaxed. "See? It ties under your chin like this. Oh, 'tis just perfect! Go and look at yourself."

Rachel shied away from the mirror, her cheeks pink with embarrassment. Under the little beribboned bonnet the years had dropped away from her face. At her brilliant eyes and tremulous smile her two daughters stared in unbelief.

"Oh, Mother! Wear that on Sunday! Promise you will!"

But the color had suddenly drained from Rachel's face. A chill swept across the room from the abruptly opened door. On the threshold stood Matthew Wood, staring from his awful height at the littered room, the gowns tumbled over chairs and benches, and the guilty faces of his womenfolk.

"What is the meaning of this?" he demanded.

"The girls were watching Katherine unpack," Rachel explained helplessly. "How are you back so soon, Matthew?"

"Can a man not come back for an axe helve without finding his house a shambles?"

"I guess we forgot ourselves." Rachel's fingers jerked at the bonnet strings.

Judith was not so easily intimidated. "Look, Father!" she attempted, "Kit has given me this dress. Did you ever see anything so handsome?"

"Give it back to her at once!"

"Father—no! I never had—"

"Do as I say!" he thundered.

"Uncle Matthew," broke in Kit. "You don't understand. I want her to have the dress."

Her uncle regarded her with scorn. "No one in my family has any use for such frippery," he said coldly. "Nor are we beholden on anyone's charity for our clothing."

"But they are gifts," cried Kit, tears of hurt and anger springing to her eyes. "Everyone brings—"

"Be quiet, girl! It is time you understood one thing at the start. This will be your home, since you have no other, but you will fit yourself to our ways and do no more to interrupt the work of the household or to turn the heads of my daughters with your vanity. Now you will close your trunks and allow them to get about the work they have neglected. Rachel, take off that ridiculous thing!"

"Even the gloves, Father?" Judith was still rebellious. "Everyone wears gloves to Meeting."

"Everything. No member of my household will appear in public in such unseemly apparel."

Mercy had said no word, but now as she folded the blue shawl and laid it quietly on top of the trunk, Rachel found courage for her only protest. "Will you allow Mercy to keep the shawl?" she pleaded. " 'Tis not gaudy, and 'twill keep off the draft there by the chimney."

Matthew's glance moved from the shawl to his daughter's quiet eyes, and barely perceptibly the grim line of his jaw relaxed. So there was one weakness in this hard man!

"Very well, Mercy may keep the shawl. I thank you for it." The bitter word was forced out just in time. Had it not been for this hint of grace, Kit's anger might have erupted in a scene that would have spoiled all her chances on this first morning. As it was she felt an unwilling respect that made her hold her tongue and set to work folding and replacing the piles of clothing.

Judith's tears were packed away in the folds of the blue dress. There was silence after the door had shut once more.

"Well," sighed Rachel, " 'tis all my fault. I can't blame you girls, but at my age—and the board not even cleared from breakfast."

Kit looked back at the table curiously. "Don't the servants do that?" she inquired.

"We have no servants," said her aunt quietly.

Surprise and chagrin left Kit speechless. "I can help with the work," she offered finally, realizing that she sounded like an overeager child.

"In that dress!" Judith protested.

"I'll find something else. Here, this calico will do, won't it?"

"To *work* in?" Disappointment had put an edge to Judith's tongue.

" 'Tis all I have," retorted Kit. "Give me something of yours then."

Judith's cheeks went scarlet. "Oh, wear that one. You can help Mercy with the carding. You won't dirty yourself at that."

Kit shortly repented her offer. For four mortal hours she sat on a wooden bench and struggled to grasp the tricky process of carding wool. Mercy demonstrated on two pieces of thin board to which were fastened strips of leather set with hooked wire teeth. From a great pile of heavy blue wool she pulled a small tuft, caught it in the wire teeth of one board, and drew across it the second board till the fibers were brushed flat.

"Isn't the color pretty?" she inquired. "Mother promised Judith that if she helped with the shearing this year we could buy some indigo from the West Indies. Judith hates handling the greasy wool and washing it, but she will be happy with the blue cloth." In one deft motion she plucked the wool from the teeth and rolled it into a fluffy ball.

It looked so easy, but the moment Kit took the wool cards into her hands she appreciated Mercy's skill. They were such awkward things. The wool fluffed and stuck to her fingers and snarled in clumps. She suspected that Judith had chosen this task on purpose.

"You're getting the knack," approved Mercy when a few misshapen little balls finally lay in the basket.

Kit eyed the great heap of wool. "You have to do all that by yourself?"

"Oh, the others help between times. But of course, there are so many things I can't do. You don't know how nice it is to have you to help. 'Tis a marvel how much faster the work goes when there's someone to talk to."

Fast! All this time and that great pile hardly touched! But Mercy had sounded sincere. How dreary it must be for her, working here day after day. Kit was ashamed of her own impatience. Suddenly, under Mercy's friendly smile, the question that had been troubling her all the morning burst out.

"Do you think I did wrong, Mercy, to come here?"

"You did exactly right," smiled Mercy.

"But your father—"

"Father doesn't mean to be unkind. It has been very hard for him here in Connecticut."

In the months since her grandfather died there had been no one whom Kit could trust. Now she found herself saying the words she had never dared to speak.

"I had to come, Mercy. There was another reason. I couldn't say it this morning, but there was a man on the island, a friend of grandfather's. He used to come often, and afterwards I found he had lent

46

Grandfather money, hundreds of pounds. He didn't want the money back—he wanted me to marry him. He tried to make me think that Grandfather had wanted it, but I'm sure that was not so. He wanted to pay everything. He would even have kept the house for us to live in. Everyone expected me to marry him. The women kept telling me what a wonderful match it was."

"Kit! How could they? Was he dreadful?"

"No, he wasn't really. He was very kind. But Mercy, he was fifty years old, and he had pudgy red fingers with too many rings on them. You see, Mercy, why I couldn't wait to write? You do see why I can't go back, don't you?"

"Of course you can't go back," said Mercy firmly. Her hand reached for Kit's and pressed it warmly. "Father has no intention of sending you back. You will just have to prove to him that you can be useful here."

By the end of that first day the word useful had taken on an alarming meaning. Work in that household never ceased, and it called for skill and patience, qualities Kit did not seem to possess. There was meat to be chopped, and vegetables to prepare for the midday meal. The pewter mugs had to be scoured with reeds and fine sand. There was a great kettle of soap boiling over a fire just behind the house, and all day long Judith and her mother took turns stirring it with a long stick. Judith set Kit to tend the stirring while she readied the soap barrel. Kit tried to keep a gingerly distance from the kettle. The strong fumes of lye stung her eyelids and stirring the heavy mass tired her arms and shoulders. Her stirring became more and more halfhearted till Judith snatched the stick in exasperation. "It will lump on you," she

47

scolded, "and you can just blame yourself if we have to use lumpy soap all summer."

Toward evening they set her at the easiest task they could devise—the making of corn pudding. The corn meal had to be added to the boiling kettle a pinch at a time. Before half of it was consumed, Kit's patience ran out. The smoke made her eyes water, and there was a smarting blister on one thumb. She suspected that Judith had invented the irksome procedure just to keep her busy, and in a burst of resentment she poured in the remaining cupful all at once. She learned her mistake when the lumpy indigestible mass was ladled onto her wooden trencher. There was nothing else for supper. After one shocked stare, the family downed the mess in a silence that made Kit writhe.

After the candles were lit, Rachel and the two girls picked up skeins of yarn and began to knit as Matthew drew the great Bible toward him across the table. Matthew's voice was harsh and monotonous. Kit could not keep her mind on the words. Every muscle in her body ached with weariness. As the reading went on her head grew heavier, and twice she jerked herself painfully back from the brink of sleep. The others, intent on their knitting, did not notice. Only when her uncle closed the Book and bent his head for the long evening prayer, did the clicking needles cease.

Kit, in her eagerness, went up ahead with a candle into the chilly bedchamber. But once there she remembered that in the morning she would need a fresh gown from the trunks to replace the soot-stained calico. Going back down the stairs she overheard some words not intended for her ears.

"Why does she have to sleep with me?" Judith demanded in a sulky tone.

"Why, daughter," her mother rebuked her, "are you not willing that your cousin should share with you?"

"If I have to share my bed will she share my work? Or will she expect us all to wait on her hand and foot like her black slaves?"

"Shame, Judith. The child tried her best, you know that."

"A five-year-old could do better. As if things weren't bad enough here in this house. If we had to have a cousin at all why couldn't it have been a boy?"

"A boy!" Rachel's answer was a long sigh. "Yes, a boy would have been different, that's true. Poor Matthew!"

Turning, Kit fled up the stairs. When Judith came to bed she was already under the covers, huddled far over to one side of the wide bed, her face hidden against a damp pillow. For a long time after Judith blew out the candle Kit lay rigid, fearful that a single sniff might give her away. But the feather mattress was deliciously soft, and her weary nerves gradually relaxed.

Suddenly, however, she sat straight up.

"What was that?" she quavered, forgetting her pride.

"What was what?" yawned Judith crossly. The long eerie noise sounded again. Indians?

"Oh, that! That's only a wolf!" scoffed Judith. "Goodness, you're not making all that fuss about one old wolf? Wait till you hear a pack of them."

CHAPTER FIVE

"THESE ARE the only clothes I have," protested Kit. "If they are not suitable, I shall stay here with Mercy."

Through the crystal Sabbath morning the Meeting House bell tolled steadily. Matthew Wood stood on the threshold of his home, his bushy eyebrows massed close together as he surveyed the three women who waited to accompany him. Beside the plain blue homespun and white linen which modestly clothed Aunt Rachel and Judith, Kit's flowered silk gave her the look of some vivid tropical bird lighted by mistake on a strange shore. The modish bonnet with curling white feathers seemed to her uncle a crowning affront.

"You will mock the Lord's assembly with such frippery," he roared.

This was the second time this morning that her uncle's wrath had descended on her head. An hour ago she had declined to go to Meeting, saying airily that she and her grandfather had seldom attended divine service, except for the Christmas Mass. What an uproar she had caused! There was no Church of England in Wethersfield, her uncle had informed her, and furthermore, since she was now a member of his household she would forget her popish ideas and attend Meeting like a God-fearing woman. This time, however, he was baffled; he knew as well as she that there were no garments to spare in that house.

Rachel laid a placating hand on her husband's sleeve. "Matthew," she pleaded, "everyone knows that the child has not had time to get new clothes. Besides, it would be wasteful to throw these aside. Katherine looks very pretty, and I'm proud to have her go with us."

Judith was certainly not proud of her. Judith was as outraged as her father, though for a different reason. Her pretty mouth had a sulky droop, and the long fringe of lashes barely hid the envy and rebellion in her blue eyes. This first venture outside her new home was not starting out auspiciously for Kit, but as they set out along the road she could not repress her curiosity and bouncing spirits. If they were going to church then there must be a town somewhere beyond this narrow road. Under a brilliant blue sky Wethersfield held far more welcome than on that first foggy dawn. There was a delicious crispness in the air.

The family walked along High Street, past a row of substantial frame houses, and came out on a small square clearing. Kit looked about eagerly. "Is it far to the town?" she whispered to Judith.

There was a silence. "This is the town," said Judith stiffly.

The town! Kit stared, too aghast to realize her own tactlessness. There was not a single stone building or shop in sight. The Meeting House stood in the center of the clearing, a square unpainted wooden structure, topped by a small turret. As they crossed the clearing Kit recoiled at the objects that stood between her and the Meeting House; a pillory, a whipping post and stocks.

Inside the small building, on rows of benches, sat the good folk of Wethersfield, men on one side and women on the other. At the door Matthew Wood left his family and moved with dignity to the deacon's bench directly in front of the pulpit. Rachel preceded the two girls down the aisle to the family bench. As Kit moved behind her the astonishment of the assembled townspeople met her with the impact of a gathering wave. It was not so much a sound as a stillness so intent that it made her ears ring. She knew that her cheeks were flaming, but she held her head high under the feathered bonnet.

The Puritan service seemed to her as plain and unlovely as the bare board walls of the Meeting House. She felt a moment's surprise when her uncle stepped forward to line the psalm. His firm nasal voice set the tune and pace, one line at a time, and the congregation repeated it after him. By the time the long psalm was over Kit was glad to sit down, but presently she longed to stand again. The hard edge of the narrow pew bit into her thigh, in spite of every gingerly effort to shift her weight. Kit's gaze flicked over the other churchfolk. A varied lot they were. Not all of them shared her uncle's opinions of seemly garb; some were as fashionably dressed as Kit herself. But the majority were soberly and poorly clad, and here and there, in the farthermost pews, Kit glimpsed the familiar black faces that must be slaves. All of them however were alike in their reverent silence. How could they sit there without twitching a muscle, even with the black flies buzzing under their bonnet brims? It was impossible that they could be listening to the sermon. She could not keep her mind on it for an instant.

A steady rustling sound told her that a few muscles were as unruly as her own. On the stairs leading to the gallery nearly twenty small boys were clustered, shoulder to shoulder, and the solid ranks undulated with the constant jerking of restless elbows straining under tight woolen jackets. A rosy-cheeked boy on the second step, with one fleeting motion, captured a fly and held it imprisoned against his knees. Four boys nearest him were convulsed. Snickers spilled out past the hands they clapped over their mouths. A man stepped menacingly from the corner brandishing a long pole, and Kit winced as two sharp raps descended on each luckless head. The cause of all the commotion sat serenely, his rapt, innocent gaze never straying from the minister's face, his hand still cupped over the imprisoned fly. Kit felt a giggle rising in her own throat, and looking frantically for distraction, caught John Holbrook's eye. He looked away without a sign of recognition.

Bother these people! Look at Judith, sitting there with her hands folded in her lap. Didn't her feet ever go to sleep? Nevertheless, if this were a test of endurance, then she could see it through as well as these New Englanders. She tilted her chin so that one plume swept gracefully against her cheek, discreetly curled and uncurled her numb toes inside the kid slippers, and set herself to endure.

The sun slanted directly downward through the chinks in the roof when the sermon ended. It must have been a good two hours, and would, Kit suspected, have been much longer had not the minister's voice grown increasingly hoarse till it threatened to fail altogether. Kit rose thankfully for the final prayer, and stood respectfully with the rest of the congregation till the minister had passed down the aisle to the door.

Outside the Meeting House the Reverend Gershom Bulkeley took Kit's hand in his. "So this is the orphan from Barbados?" he rasped. "How grateful you must be, young lady, for the kindness of your aunt and uncle in your time of need."

Two deacons also took her hand and stressed the word grateful. Had Uncle Matthew informed the whole town that he had taken her in out of charity? If so, then she was obviously a surprise to them, by the suspicion and downright hostility with which the deacons' wives were surveying her from feathered hat to slippered toe. She did not look like a pauper. Let them make what they liked of that!

Most of the churchgoers did not come near her. A little distance away she glimpsed Goodwife Cruff, surrounded by a close huddle of whispering women, all darting venomous glances in Kit's direction. Kit turned a defiant back on them, but first she sent a friendly wave to Prudence, whose peaked little face turned pink with delight.

With a flash of pleasure she saw John Holbrook approaching, but her impulsive greeting froze as she saw that Reverend Bulkeley had the young man firmly by the elbow. In the shadow of his teacher an extra staidness had fallen over the young divinity student, and his smile was lukewarm with dignity. Not till John had courteously acknowledged the minister's introductions did he turn to Kit.

"I was glad to see you in Meeting," he said gravely, "you must have found the sermon uplifting."

Kit was nonplussed.

"How very fortunate we were to hear Dr. Bulkeley," John continued, taking her silence for agreement. "He rarely preaches now, since his retirement. 'Twas a truly remarkable sermon. Every word seemed to me inspired."

Kit stared at him. Yes, actually, he was serious. Dr. Bulkeley had moved out of earshot, and there was no hint of flattery in John's earnest words. She was floundering for an answer when Judith spoke.

"Dr. Bulkeley's sermons are always inspired," she said demurely, "especially when he preaches about the final judgment."

John marked Judith's presence with surprise and respect. Under the white bonnet her face was sweetly serious, her eyes dazzlingly blue.

"His learning is incredible," he told her. "He can recite entire chapters of Scripture, and he knows law and medicine as well."

John's blush as he found the learned doctor again at his elbow was all the more flattering. Dr. Bulkeley glowed indulgently.

"I do know a bit of Scripture," he admitted. "But this young man has made a good start, a very good start indeed."

"You must bring your new pupil with you when you come to dine with us on Thursday," smiled Rachel Wood, and with a gracious acceptance Dr. Bulkeley steered his charge away. "And now, Katherine dear, here is another neighbor you must meet. Mistress Ashby, my niece from Barbados."

Kit curtsied, noting with satisfaction that this was one woman who did not despise vain adornment. Mistress Ashby's dove-colored damask with its gilt-edged lace must have come straight from England.

"And her son, William," continued her aunt. Braced to meet the reserve and suspicion she had encountered at every introduction so far, Kit was startled to meet the unmistakably dazzled gaze of William Ashby, and unconsciously she rewarded him with the first genuine smile she had managed this morning. Kit had no idea of what happened to her thin plain features when she smiled. William was speechless. As she turned to follow her aunt and Judith, Kit knew for certain that he had not moved, and that if she looked back she would see his sturdy frame planted motionless in the path. She did not look back, but she knew.

Walking back along the road Judith signaled Kit to fall behind the others. "You never mentioned that there was a handsome man on that boat," she whispered accusingly.

"Handsome? You mean John Holbrook?"

"You certainly seemed to know each other well enough."

"Well, there was no one else to talk to. But most of the time he sat by himself and studied."

"Have you set your cap for him?" asked Judith bluntly.

Kit colored to the edge of her bonnet. She would never get used to Judith's outspokenness.

"Goodness, no!" she protested. "Whatever made you think of such a thing?"

"I just wondered," Judith responded, and as Matthew Wood turned a stern look back at them, both girls walked on in silence.

"You certainly made an impression on William Ashby," Judith ventured presently.

There was no point in denying it. "Perhaps because I was someone new," said Kit.

"Perhaps. You aren't exactly pretty, you know. But naturally William would be impressed by a dress like that."

Kit wanted to change the subject. Wisps of smoke were beginning to rise from the chimneys of several small log lean-tos along the roadway. They seemed to offer a safe topic.

"Do people live in those tiny houses?" she inquired.

"Of course not. Those are Sabbath houses." Then Judith emerged from her own musings long enough to explain. "Families that live too far to go home between services cook their meal there on Sunday, and in the winter they can warm themselves at a fire."

A chill trickle of doubt began to cool the glow of the noontime sun and the memory of William Ashby's admiration. Surely Judith could not mean—

"Did you say—between services?" Kit inquired fearfully.

"Didn't you know there's a second service in the afternoon?"

Kit was appalled. "Do you mean we have to go?"

"Of course we go," snapped Judith. "That is what the Sabbath is for."

Kit came to a halt, and suddenly she stamped her foot in the dusty road. "I won't do it!" she declared. "I absolutely won't endure that all over again!"

But one look ahead at her uncle's shoulders, rigid in their Sunday black, and she knew that she would. Almost choking with helpless rage she stumbled after Judith, who had moved ahead too absorbed to even notice. Oh, why had she ever come to this hateful place?

CHAPTER SIX

REVEREND GERSHOM BULKELEY laid down his linen napkin, pushed back his heavy chair from the table, and expanded his straining waistcoat in a satisfied sigh.

"A very excellent dinner, Mistress Wood. I warrant there's not a housewife in the colonies can duplicate your apple tarts."

He had just better compliment that dinner, thought Kit. The preparation of it had taken the better part of four days. Every inch of the great kitchen had been turned inside out. The floor had been fresh-sanded, the hearthstone polished, the pewter scoured. The brick oven had been heated for two nights in a row, and the whole family had gone without sugar since Sunday to make sure that the minister's notorious sweet tooth would be satisfied.

Well, Dr. Bulkeley had been pleased, but had anyone else? Matthew Wood had eaten little and spoken scarcely a word. He sat now with his lips pressed tight together. Rachel looked tired and flustered, and even Mercy seemed unusually quiet. Only Judith had blossomed. In the candlelight she looked bewitching, and Reverend Bulkeley smiled whenever he looked at her. But the greatest part of his condescension he had bestowed on Kit, once he had understood that her grandfather had been Sir Francis Tyler. He himself had visited Antigua in the West Indies, he had told her, and he was acquainted with some of the plantation owners there. He went back to the subject now for the third time.

"So, young lady, your grandfather was knighted for loyalty by King Charles, you say? A great honor, a very great honor indeed. And I take it he was a loyal subject of our good King James as well?"

"Why, of course, sir."

"And you yourself? You are a loyal subject also?"

"How could I be otherwise, sir?" Kit was puzzled.

"There are some who seem to find it possible," remarked the minister, staring meaningfully at a ceiling beam. "See that you keep your allegiance."

With an abrupt scrape of wood Matthew pushed back his chair. "Her allegiance is in no danger in this house," he announced angrily. "What are you implying, Gershom?"

"I meant nothing to offend you, Matthew," said the older man.

"Then watch your words. May I remind you I am a selectman in this town? I am no traitor!"

"I said no such thing, nor did I mean it. Mistaken, Matthew, I hold to that, but not a traitor—yet."

"I am mistaken," Matthew Wood challenged him, "because I do not favor knuckling under to this new King's governor?"

"Governor Andros was appointed by King James. Massachusetts has recognized that."

"Well, we here in Connecticut will never recognize it—never! Do you think we have labored and sacrificed all these years to build up a free government only to hand it over now without a murmur?"

"I say you are mistaken!" growled Gershom Bulkeley. "Mark my words, Matthew. If you do not live to see the evil results, your children or their children will suffer. Call it what you will, this stubbornness can lead only to revolution."

Matthew's eyes flashed. "There are worse things than revolution!"

"I know more about that than you. I was surgeon in the Fort fight with the Indians. War is an evil, Matthew. Believe me, there can no good thing come of bloodshed."

"Who is asking for bloodshed? We ask only to keep the rights that have already been granted to us in the charter."

The two men sat glaring at each other across the table. Tears sprang to Rachel's eyes. Then Mercy spoke from the shadows.

"I had looked forward to hearing Reverend Bulkeley read to us this evening," she said gently.

Dr. Bulkeley sent her a gracious smile and considered. "I have to coddle this throat of mine," he decided. "But my young pupil here is a very exceptional reader. I shall pass the honor on to him."

Grudgingly Matthew Wood lifted the heavy Bible and placed it in John Holbrook's hand, and Rachel moved a pewter candlestick nearer to his elbow. John had been respectfully silent all the evening. Indeed, he had had little opportunity to be anything else, and he now seemed pleased out of all proportion at this slight notice from his master. Kit felt suddenly provoked at him. One week in Wethersfield seemed to have changed the dignified young man she had known on shipboard. Tonight he appeared to be a shadow, hanging on every word from this pompous opinionated man. Even now he dared not assert himself but held the Bible uncertainly in his hands and asked, "What would you have me read, sir?"

"I would suggest Proverbs, 24th Chapter, 21st

60

verse," said the old minister, with a canny gleam in his eye which Kit understood as John began to read.

"My son, fear the Lord and the King, and meddle not with them that are given to change, For their calamity shall rise suddenly, and who knoweth the ruin of them both?"

There was a harsh sound from Matthew, checked in response to his wife's pleading eyes. John continued reading.

As he read on, Kit forgot the meaning of the words and felt a stir of pleasure at the sound. John's voice was low-pitched but very clear, and the words fell with a musical cadence that was a delight. Every evening since she had come here she had sat waiting with impatience for her uncle's monotonous voice to cease. Tonight, for the first time, she caught the beauty of the ancient Hebrew verses.

When the reading was finished, family and guests bowed their heads and Reverend Bulkeley began the evening prayer. A little sigh escaped Kit. Her uncle's terse petitions were hard enough to endure; this prayer, she knew, would be a lengthy masterpiece. As the husky voice scraped inexorably on, she ventured to raise her head a little, and was gratified to see that Judith too was peeking. But Judith's attention was not wandering. She was studying, with deliberate appraisal, John Holbrook's bent head and the delicate chiseled line of his profile against the firelight.

A phrase of Dr. Bulkeley's prayer caught Kit's attention again. "And bless our sister in her weakness and affliction." Whom did he mean? Heavens, was he talking about *Mercy?* Had the man no perception at all? How Mercy must be shriveling at the fulsome words. After a few days in this household Kit had ceased to be aware of Mercy's lameness. No one in the family ever referred to it. Mercy certainly did not consider herself afflicted. She did a full day's work and more. Moreover, Kit had soon discovered that Mercy was the pivot about whom the whole household moved. She coaxed her father out of his bitter moods, upheld her timorous and anxious mother, gently restrained her rebellious sister and had reached to draw an uncertain alien into the circle. Mercy weak! Why, the man could not even use his eyes!

When the prayer was ended, the thanks repeated and the goodnights said, Rachel saw her guests to the door. She held out her hand to John Holbrook.

"I hope you will come again," she said kindly. "We would like you to feel welcome in our house."

John looked back to where Judith stood behind Mercy's chair. "Thank you, ma'am," he answered. "If I may, I would be very happy to come again."

As the heavy door finally closed, Matthew Wood turned fiercely toward his wife. "That is the last time," he pronounced, "that I will have Gershom Bulkeley under my roof!"

"Very well, Matthew," sighed Rachel. "But do not be too hard on him. Gershom is a good man, just set in his ways."

"He is a hypocrite and a whited sepulcher!" Matthew's fist crashed down on the table. "And I'll have no more texts read at me in my own house!"

Wearily the women set to work to clear the table, while Matthew raked up the fire in the hearth. All at once he straightened up. "There is another matter I forgot," he said. "Young William Ashby asked permission today to pay his respects to my niece."

A spoon clattered from Judith's fingers. There was utter silence in the room as Rachel and both her daughters turned to stare at Kit.

62

"You mean call on Katherine?" Aunt Rachel's voice was incredulous.

"That is what I said."

"But he has hardly seen her—only for a moment after Meeting."

"She was conspicuous enough."

Kit felt her cheeks growing hot. Judith opened her mouth to say something, glanced at her father and closed it again.

"I suppose we can hardly refuse," ventured Rachel. "He is a member of the Society in good standing, and he has gone about it quite properly."

"His father is another King's man," said her husband. "He proposed in council that we join with Massachusetts. But what can we expect, now that we harbor a Royalist under our own roof? Bring a candle, Rachel. We have wasted enough time for one night."

A constrained trio lingered after Rachel had climbed the stairs behind her husband. Mercy began quietly to make ready her own bed in the corner. A small wrinkle of concern marred her usually placid forehead.

"Well, I told you so!" Judith finally burst out. "I knew by the way he was staring at you after Meeting."

There was no use to pretend she didn't remember. Kit felt a small pleasurable stir of curiosity. "Do you know him, Mercy?"

"I know about him, of course," admitted Mercy.

"Who doesn't know about him?" added Judith. "Who hasn't heard that his father has three acres of the best land set aside, and the trees all marked to build the house the moment Master William makes up his mind? And he was just about to make it up, too, when you came along."

"We never really knew that, Judith," her sister reminded her gently. "We only thought so."

All at once Kit remembered. That first morning, when she was trying on the dress, Judith had said—

"Oh, dear," she exclaimed in dismay, "I don't want this William to come calling on me. Why, I've only seen him once, and I couldn't think of a word to say to him if he came. I'll tell Uncle Matthew so in the morning."

"Don't you dare say anything to Father!" Judith whirled on her.

"But if he—if you—"

"William never asked to call on me. I just said he was getting around to it."

"'Tis not quite fair, really," Mercy considered soberly, "to hold it against Kit, just because we thought—"

"Oh, I'm not holding it against Kit," Judith said airily. Suddenly she tossed her head. "As a matter of fact, Kit can have William with my blessing. I've changed my mind. I'm going to marry John Holbrook."

CHAPTER SEVEN

WHAT ON EARTH could she think of to say next? Kit wondered in desperation. She sat looking down at her folded hands, reluctant to lift her eyes to the young

64

man who sat on the bench across the wide hearth. She knew that when she looked up she would find William Ashby's gaze fixed steadily upon her. For the last half hour they had sat so. When a young man came to call what did one talk about? Was it all up to the girl? She had tried her best, but William seemed content just to sit, his back stiffly straight, his large capable hands resting squarely on his sturdy wool-clad knees. He looked impressive, in his cinnamon broadcloth coat and the fine linen shirt. His glossy beaver hat and white gloves were laid carefully on a chair near the door. William seemed to feel that merely by coming he had done his share. Apparently it was up to her to provide the conversation.

Aunt Rachel had laid a special fire in the company room and set lighted candles on the table. From the kitchen across the hall Kit could hear the voices of the family as they sat cozily about the fire that was still welcome on these cool May evenings. Tonight she longed to be with them. She would welcome even the Bible reading at this moment. She took a deep breath and tried again.

"Is it always so chilly in New England, even in May?"

William considered this. "I think this spring is a bit warmer than usual," he decided.

As though in answer to her urgent prayer for relief, a knock sounded on the outside door, and as Aunt Rachel went to answer, Kit heard John Holbrook's voice. Her aunt welcomed him cordially, and in a few moments put her head in at the parlor door, her understanding glance taking in the two silent young people.

"Why don't you both come and join us?" she suggested. "John Holbrook has come to call, and we can pop some corn for a treat." Bless Aunt Rachel!

Over a handful of fluffy white kernels William relaxed a trifle. There was something irresistible about popcorn. John, his pale cheeks flushed with the heat, managed the long shaker with a practiced hand. Judith blossomed suddenly in the firelight, and her laughter was infectious. Mercy's eyes were shining with pleasure. Rachel, with a ghost of the charm she must once have possessed, succeeded in drawing William, if not actually into the circle, at least to its warm circumference. Even Matthew unbent enough to ask courteously, "Does your father have all his field sown?"

"Yes, sir," replied William.

"Notice he's cutting some trees up Vexation way."

"Yes, I'm planning to build my house come autumn. We have marked some good white oak for the clapboards."

Kit stared at him. William had not spoken so many words all the evening. Aunt Rachel encouraged him.

"My husband tells me you have been appointed a Viewer of Fences," she smiled. "That is a fine honor for so young a man."

"Thank you, ma'am."

"With all the new land grants I've been hearing of, that will be an important duty," added Mercy helpfully.

"Yes," agreed William. "The Assembly has voted that there should be no unclaimed land left in all Hartford County."

"A wise move," put in Matthew. "Why should we leave land for the King's governor to grant to his favorites?"

William turned to the older man respectfully. "Are

66

you not afraid, sir," he asked, "that we are likely to anger the King the more by such hasty actions?"

"Are you so afraid to anger the King?" scoffed Matthew.

"No, sir, but we cannot hope to hold out against him. If we submit to his governor now, without a struggle, are we not more likely to retain for ourselves some rights and privileges? By provoking his anger we may lose them all."

Kit could scarcely believe her ears. William Ashby was neither speechless nor dim-witted. He even dared to stand up to her uncle! With new respect she moved to pass him the wooden bowl of popcorn, and to it she added a smile that caused him to lapse again into scarlet-faced silence. Matthew Wood did not notice the interruption.

"Surrender our charter and we lose all," he thundered. "That charter was given to Connecticut by King Charles twenty-five years ago. It guarantees every right and privilege we have earned, the very ground we stand on and the laws we have made for ourselves. King James has no right to go back on his brother's pledge. What do you say, Master Holbrook? Or has your teacher poisoned your mind as well?"

"I believe we should keep the charter, sir," John's eyes were on the fire, and his voice sounded troubled. "But Dr. Bulkeley says that Connecticut has misinterpreted the charter. His knowledge of the law is so wide. He says that justice is not always served by our courts and—"

"Bah!" Matthew Wood pushed back his chair and rose to his feet. "Justice! What do you young men know about rights and justice? A soft life is all you have ever known. Have you felled the trees in a wilderness and built a home with your bare hands? Have you fought off the wolves and the Indians? Have you frozen and starved through a single winter? The men who made this town understood justice. They knew better than to look for it in the King's favor. The only rights worth all that toil and sacrifice are the rights of free men, free and equal under God to decide their own justice. You'll learn. Mark my words, some day you'll learn to your sorrow!" He stumped off up the stairs without a goodnight.

Oh, dear! Could there never be a pleasant moment without this senseless argument? After Matthew's departure the conversation never really righted itself. Kit jumped as the square clock in the corner twanged eight o'clock. Only one hour! It seemed like the longest evening she had ever lived through. William rose deliberately to his feet.

"Thank you for your hospitality, Mistress Wood," he said politely.

John looked up, startled that the time had passed so quickly, and followed William's example. As the door shut behind their backs, a long sigh escaped Kit.

"Well, that's over with," she exclaimed. "At least we won't have to go through it again."

"Not till next Saturday night at least," laughed Mercy.

Kit shook her head positively. "He'll never come again," she said. Was she altogether relieved at the thought?

"Why, whatever makes you say that, child?" asked Rachel, busily raking up the fire.

"Couldn't you see? He hardly spoke a word to me. And then Uncle Matthew—"

"Oh, they all know about Father." Judith dismissed the quarrel airily. "William said he was starting to build his house, didn't he? What more could you want him to say?"

"He just happened to mention that."

"William Ashby never just happened to mention anything in his life," said Judith. "He knew exactly what he was saying."

"I can't see why just building a house—"

"Don't you know *anything*, Kit?" scoffed Judith. "William's father gave him that land three years ago, on his sixteenth birthday, and William said that he would never start to build his house until his mind was made up."

"That's ridiculous, Judith. He couldn't mean any such thing—so soon—could he, Mercy?"

"I'm afraid he could." Mercy smiled at her cousin's confusion. "I agree that William was telling all of us—you most of all—that his mind is made up. Whether you like it or not, Kit, William is going to come courting."

"But I don't want him to!" Kit was close to panic. "I don't want him to come at all. We—we can't even talk to each other!"

"Seems to me you're pretty choosy," snapped Judith. "Don't you know William is able to build the finest house in Wethersfield if he wants to? Does he have to keep you amused as well?"

Rachel put a reassuring hand on Kit's shoulder. "The girls are only teasing you, Katherine," she said gently.

"Then you don't think—"

"Yes, I do think William is serious. But you don't need to be worried, dear. No one is going to hurry you, least of all William himself. He is a very fine young man. Of course you feel like strangers now.

69

But I think you'll find sufficient to talk about before long."

But would they? Kit wondered, climbing the stairs to bed. Her doubts persisted through the week. A second Saturday passed, a third and a fourth, and William's calls fell into a pattern. I shall ask Mercy to teach me to knit, Kit decided after the second Saturday, and thereafter she armed herself with wool and needles. At least they kept her hands occupied and gave her an excuse for not meeting that implacable gaze.

William seemed to find nothing lacking in those evenings. For him it was enough simply to sit across the room and look at her. It was flattering, she had to admit. The most eligible bachelor in Wethersfield and handsome, actually, in his substantial way. Sometimes, as she sat knitting, aware that William's eyes were on her face, she felt her breath tightening in a way that was strange and not unpleasant. Then, just as suddenly, rebellion would rise in her. He was so sure! Without even asking, he was reckoning on her as deliberately as he calculated his growing pile of lumber.

Perhaps she would not have thought about William so much had there been anything else to break the long monotonous stretch from Saturday to Saturday. It was incredible that every day should be the same, varied only in the work that filled every hour from sunrise to dark. Surely, it seemed, there must come a moment when all the tasks would be done and some brief leisure earned, yet always a new chore loomed ahead. A shearing had brought a veritable mountain of gray wool to be washed and bleached and dyed, enough to keep Mercy carding and spinning and weaving for the next twelve months. There was water to draw and linen to scrub and, everlastingly, the endless rows of vegetables to weed and hoe. Kit had not found a single one of these tasks to her liking. Her hands were unskillful not so much from inability as from the rebellion that stiffened her fingers. She was Katherine Tyler. She had not been reared to do the work of slaves. And William Ashby was the only person in Wethersfield who did not expect her to be useful, who demanded nothing, and offered his steady admiration as proof that she was still of some worth. No wonder that she found herself looking forward to Saturday evening.

CHAPTER EIGHT

"THE ONION FIELD in the south meadow needs weeding," announced Matthew one morning in early June. "If Judith and Katherine can be spared, they can spend the morning at it."

The two girls who set out soon after breakfast did not provide such a contrast as on Meeting Day. Scandalized to see Kit wearing out her finery with scrubbing and cooking, Rachel and Mercy had made her a calico dress exactly the same as Judith's. It was coarsewoven and simply made, without so much as a single bow for trimming, but it was certainly far more suited to the menial work she had to do in it. Beyond a doubt, too, it had made for an easier relationship with her cousin. This morning Judith seemed almost friendly.

"What a wonderful day!" she exclaimed. "Aren't you glad we don't have to stay inside, Kit?"

Kit felt quite cheerful. It really was a wonderful day, with a bright blue sky, and the fields and woods all a soft green. The roadway was bordered with daisies and buttercups, pale and thin, of course, compared to the brilliant masses of color in Barbados, but pretty all the same. And for the first time since she had come to Wethersfield she did not feel chilly.

The girls passed the Meeting House, turned down Short Street and went on down the pathway that was known as the South Road. The Great Meadow, Judith explained, was the grassy land that lay within the wide loop of the river.

"No one lives there," Judith told her, "because in the spring the river floods over and sometimes the fields are completely covered. After the water goes down we can use the land. 'Tis good rich soil and every landowner has a lot for pasture or gardens. Father is entitled to a bigger lot, but he has no one to help him."

As they came out from the shelter of the trees and the Great Meadows stretched before them, Kit caught her breath. She had not expected anything like this. From that first moment, in a way she could never explain, the Meadows claimed her and made her their own. As far as she could see they stretched on either side, a great level sea of green, broken here and there by a solitary graceful elm. Was it the fields of sugar cane they brought to mind, or the endless reach of the ocean to meet the sky? Or was it simply the sense of freedom and space and light that spoke to her of home?

If only I could be here alone, without Judith or anyone, she thought with longing. Someday I am going to come back to this place, when there is time just to stand still and look at it. How often she would come back she had no way of foreseeing, nor could she know that never, in the months to come, would the Meadows break the promise they held for her at this moment, a promise of peace and quietness and of comfort for a troubled heart.

"What are you looking at?" demanded Judith, turning back impatiently. "Father's field is farther on."

"I was wondering about that little house," said Kit, by way of excuse. "I thought you said no one lived down here." Far over to the right, at the edge of a marshy pond, a wisp of smoke curled gently from a lopsided chimney. Beyond the little shack something moved. Was it a shadow, or a slight stooped figure?

"Oh—that's the Widow Tupper." Judith's voice was edged with contempt. "Nobody but Hannah Tupper would live there by Blackbird Pond, right at the edge of the swamp, but she likes it. They can't persuade her to leave."

"What if the river floods?"

"It did, four years ago, and her house was covered right over. No one knows where she hid, but when the water went down, there she was again. She cleaned out the mud and went right on as though nothing had happened. She's been there as long as I can remember."

"All alone?"

"With her cats. There's always a cat or so around. People say she's a witch."

"Do you believe in witches, Judith?"

"Maybe not," said Judith doubtfully. "All the same,

73

it gives me a creepy feeling to look at her. She's queer, that's certain, and she never comes to Meeting. I'd just rather not get any closer."

Kit looked back at the gray figure bent over a kettle, stirring something with a long stick. Her spine prickled. It might be only soap, of course. She'd stirred a kettle herself just yesterday; goodness knows her arms still ached from it. But that lonely figure in the ragged flapping shawl—it was easy enough to imagine any sort of mysterious brew in the pot! She quickened her step to catch up with Judith.

The long rows of onions looked endless, their sharp green shoots already half hidden by encroaching weeds. Judith plumped matter-of-factly to her knees and began to pull vigorously. Kit could never get over her amazement at her cousin. Judith, so proud and uppity, so vain of the curls that fell just so on her shoulder, so finicky about the snowy linen collar that was the only vanity allowed her, kneeling in the dirt doing work that a high-class slave in Barbados would rebel at. What a strange country this was!

"Well, what are you standing there for?" Judith demanded. "Father says we have to do three rows before we can go home for dinner." Kit lowered herself gingerly and gathered a halfhearted handful. At the second tug an onion shoot came too, and glancing to see if Judith had noticed, she guiltily thrust the tiny root back into the earth and patted it firm. Bother the things, she would have to keep her mind on them! All at once tears of self-pity brimmed her eyes. What was she doing here anyway, Sir Francis Tyler's granddaughter, squatting in an onion patch?

She jerked at the weeds. If she should marry William Ashby, would he expect her to weed his vegetables for him? Her hands stopped moving at all while she considered this. No, she was quite certain he never would. Did it seem likely that his mother, who sat so elegantly in meeting, had ever touched a chokeweed? There were no blisters under those soft gloves, Kit wagered. She knew by now that the humble folk who sat in the very back of the Meeting House were servants of the fine families of Wethersfield. William would own servants himself, beyond a doubt. She wiped a grimy hand across her eyes. Perhaps she could endure this work for a time if the future offered an escape.

A more immediate escape offered itself that very noontime. The two girls returned home to find Mercy brimming with excitement, her gray eyes sparkling.

"The most wonderful thing, Kit! Dr. Bulkeley has recommended to the selectmen that you help me with the school this summer."

"A school?" echoed Kit. "Do you teach a school, Mercy?"

"Just the dame school. For the younger children, in the summer months. With you to help me I can take more pupils."

"What do you teach them?"

"Their letters, and to read and write their names. They can't go to the grammer school, you know, till they can read, and many of their parents can't teach them."

"Where is this school?"

"Right here in the kitchen."

"I don't know much about children," said Kit dubiously.

"You know how to read, don't you? John Holbrook told Dr. Bulkeley you can read as well as he can."

Kit started. Had John repeated to Dr. Bulkeley that conversation on the *Dolphin*? Likely not, or he would never have recommended her. She had never dared to mention books in this household, where there was no book at all except the Holy Bible.

"Yes, of course I can read," she admitted cautiously.

"Well, they are going to send Mr. Eleazer Kimberley, the schoolmaster, to test you. Then the school will begin next week. Father is pleased too, Kit. We'll both be earning wages."

"Real wages?"

"Every child pays fourpence a week. Sometimes they pay with eggs or wool or such things instead. It will help, Kit, a great deal."

The more she thought about it, the more pleasant the dame school sounded to Kit. Surely, if she were earning wages they would no longer expect her to scrub floors and weed the onions. Even more, a feeling of satisfaction, even of triumph began to grow in her mind. Later that day, as she sat alone with Mercy over their wool combs, she spoke her thoughts aloud.

"If I am earning wages," she said suddenly, "then perhaps you will all think I am of some use, even if I'm not a boy." She could not keep out of her voice the bitterness that had rankled all these weeks.

Mercy laid down her carding and stared at her cousin.

"What do you mean, Kit?"

"That first night I was here," confessed Kit, "Judith said if only I had been a boy—"

"Oh, Kit!" Tears suddenly flooded Mercy's eyes. "You heard that? Why didn't you tell me before?"

Kit looked down in embarrassment. She wished now that she had held her tongue.

"She didn't mean what you think, Kit. It's just that

father needs a boy so much to help." Mercy hesitated.

"Mother has never told you much about our family, has she?" she went on. "You see, there was a boy, their first child, two years older than I. I barely remember him. We both caught some kind of fever. I got well, except for this leg, but he died."

"I didn't know," whispered Kit, stricken. "Poor Aunt Rachel!"

"There was another boy, after Judith," Mercy continued. "He lived only a week. Mother said it was the will of God, but sometimes I have wondered. He was very tiny, born early, but on the third day he had to be baptized. It was January and terribly cold. They said the bread froze on the plates at communion that Sunday. Father bundled him up and carried him to the Meeting House. He was so proud! Well, of course that was a long time ago, but after that Father changed. And it has been a struggle, trying to manage without a son to help. That's all we meant, Kit."

Kit sat silent, her own bitterness forgotten. I will try harder to understand him, she vowed. But oh, poor Aunt Rachel, who had been always laughing!

CHAPTER NINE

"Good children must,
Fear God all day,
Parents obey,

No false thing say,
By no sin stray."

Six voices chanted the words in unison. Two small heads bent earnestly over each of the three dog-eared primers which were all the dame school could boast.

"That's fine," praised Kit. "Now go on."

"Love Christ alway,
In secret pray,
Mind little play,
Make no delay,
In doing good."

At the opposite end of the kitchen Mercy, having generously alloted to Kit the primer readers, was laboring with the beginners. They sat hunched on the bench, each holding in hand a hornbook, a small stout-handled wooden slab on which was fastened a tiny sheet of paper, protected by a thin strip of transparent horn held in place by a narrow leather strip and tiny brass nails. At the top of the single page was printed the alphabet, and at the bottom the Lord's Prayer. The children wore their horns strung on cords around their necks. Now they squinted at the blurred letters and painfully repeated out loud:

"A, f, af
f, a, fa
a, l, al
l, a, la."

What patience Mercy had! If only patience were contagious like mumps. Kit sighed and turned back to the primer. Of all the dreary montonous sermons!

Grandfather would never have allowed her to learn from such a book. She wished she could remember how her grandfather had taught her the syllables and words. She suspected that he had made up his own lessons, and now, as her small pupils spelled out the gloomy text, she could not resist following his example. She seized a quill pen and printed two lines on a scrap of the curly birch bark which the children collected to use in place of costly paper. She passed the little scroll to young Timothy Cook.

"Timothy Cook
Jumped over the brook,"

he read with astonishment.

The other children giggled. "Write one about me," begged a dark-eyed little girl. Kit thought a moment and then printed out:

"Charity Hughes
Has new red shoes."

The six children followed every motion of her quill with breathless eagerness. Kit had no idea that her methods were novel and surprising. She only knew that the past ten days since the dame school had begun had been the pleasantest she had known in Connecticut. She and the children had taken to each other at first sight. Kit felt at ease with them as she had never managed to do with their elders. The children admired her pretty clothes, they brought her strawberries and daisies, they argued over who would sit next to her, and every day they waited with delighted expectation to see what she would do and say next.

There were eleven of them in all, eight small boys and three girls, ranging from four to seven years in age. Sober little adults they had appeared on that first day, dressed in fashions much like their parents'. One of them, to Kit's amusement, had given his name as Jonathan Ashby, a serious, stocky small edition of his brother William. But as their shyness wore off, so did their solemnness. They sat crowded together on the two long benches that Matthew had provided by the simple method of laying planks on rough wooden crosspieces. There was a daily scrambling for favored positions on the bench. If two or three of the heavier boys could band together at one end, they could make precarious sitting for the unlucky female at the other end. Altogether, it took alertness and patience to keep those restless little bodies still for four long hours at a stretch. While Kit resorted to ingenious tricks, Mercy possessed the patience. Kit marveled at the ease and gentleness with which Mercy controlled her charges, her warm sweet voice never raised, her lovely composure never ruffled. Now, as the chanting syllables came to an end, Mercy met Kit's eyes across the room and smiled.

"You have all done very well this morning," she said. "Now we will repeat the first part of the Catechism, and then Mistress Tyler will tell you a story."

Mercy worried about this indulgence, which had begun by accident on the second day, and proved such a success that she had weakly allowed it to continue. Was it right, she questioned Kit, to bribe children into good behavior by these stories? That was not the way the schoolmaster enforced discipline. But Kit could see nothing wrong in a reward at the end of the day's work. Truth to tell, she looked forward to the story as eagerly as the children. If only she had more to read to them! Last week she had told them the story of *Pilgrim's Progress,* drawing on every detail she could remember. What would she have given for that much-loved volume that had lain on Grandfather's table! But in a week's time she had stretched her memory to the utmost, and Pilgrim had traveled all the way from the Slough of Despond to the Celestial City. Now she had only the Bible to read to them, but there was far more between those black covers than the verses Uncle Matthew favored. Kit chose the stories she herself enjoyed most, and her reading had a zest and liveliness that enthralled the children. Even Mercy was surprised, and frequently a little disturbed at the drama that Kit seemed to discover in these long-familiar narratives.

Today she chose the parable of the Good Samaritan. "Now a certain man," she began, "went down from Jerusalem to Jericho and fell among thieves—" Suddenly she had an inspiration. Years ago, her grandfather had taken her to see a masque in Bridgetown, in which a troupe of players from England had acted out the ancient Christmas story.

"I have an idea!" she cried, laying down the Book. Eleven small faces turned toward her eagerly. It had not taken them long to discover that Kit's ideas usually meant something new and exciting.

"You all know this story, don't you?" The heads nodded earnestly. "Then, instead of my reading it to you, let's pretend that it is happening, right now, to us. Let's pretend that this room is the road to Jericho. One of you—you, Peter—will be the certain man traveling along the road. You can walk down between these benches, like this. And three of you can be the robbers, that set on him and strip him of his raiment and wound him. Martha and Eliza, you can be the

81

priest and the Levite, who pass by on the other side and just look at him and turn up your noses. And Jonathan can be the Good Samaritan who finds him and binds up his wounds. Charity, you can be the innkeeper, over here by the fireplace, and the Samaritan will bring the traveler to you to take care of."

"Kit—" broke in Mercy anxiously. "I never heard of anything like that before. Are you sure—?"

"Oh, Mercy! It's from the Bible! Now, each of you, try to imagine just how you'd feel if you really were those people. Just make believe this isn't a room at all—it's a hot dusty road, and Peter, you are getting very tired from walking so far."

The children were entranced. A game of pretending in school! They took their places, jabbering with excitement. Charity picked up the broom by the hearth and began to sweep. "An innkeeper is busy all the time," she said importantly. Jonathan Ashby stood stolidly beside Mercy, waiting for his chance to be the rescuer. Peter began his long journey between the benches.

But Kit had made one mistake. She had picked her characters too hastily. By chance she had chosen the three most obstreperous pupils in the school to be her thieves and robbers. And the hapless boy who represented the traveler was the priggish little scholar they most cordially disliked.

The unsuspecting traveler fell into his part as conscientiously as he read his primer. He walked primly between the benches from Jerusalem to Jericho. Out from behind the settle popped the robbers, and set upon him with a vengeance.

"Wait a minute!" warned Kit. "Tom—Stephen— we're only pretending!" But her warning was lost in the uproar. Such an opportunity, sanctioned by authority, had never been known before. Peter's raiment actually was in danger. His shrieks were genuine. Jonathan, forgetting his role entirely, rushed in with both fists flying. The innkeeper hurried to the wayfarer's defense with her broom. Both Kit and Mercy moved quickly, but not quickly enough.

From the corner of her eye Kit glimpsed the two tall figures in the kitchen doorway. Then, before she could reach the tussling children, a cane swung from nowhere and landed on an unwary back. A smart crackle of blows, a few agonized howls, and silence and order descended suddenly on the room. Across the subdued children's heads Kit and Mercy faced their two visitors, Mr. Eleazer Kimberley, the schoolmaster, and the Reverend John Woodbridge.

"What is the meaning of this disturbance?" demanded Mr. Kimberley. "We come to inspect your school, Mistress Wood, and we find bedlam."

Mercy opened her mouth to explain, but Kit broke in first. "It is all my fault, sir. I was just trying out a new idea."

"What sort of idea?"

"Well, sir, I was reading a story out loud to them from the Bible, and I thought instead it might be— more instructive maybe—to sort of—well, to act it out, and—"

"To *act it!*"

"Like a play, you know," Kit floundered, confused by the increasing horror on both their faces. Mr. Kimberley seemed to be strangling.

"Play-acting! And with the Bible!"

Reverend Woodbridge stared incredulously at Mercy. "What could you have been thinking of, Mercy, to allow such a thing?"

Mercy clasped her hands tight together. "I—I

didn't realize what we were doing, sir," she faltered. "I never thought that it was play-acting."

"I am shocked and disappointed," he said sternly. "I had heard such excellent reports of your school."

Mr. Kimberley flourished his cane at the silent children. "Go directly home, boys and girls. The school is dismissed. Do not come back tomorrow. We will send word if the school will continue."

"Oh, please, Mr. Kimberley," begged Kit, as the children, one by one, slipped through the door and escaped. "You can't not continue the school because of what I did. It wasn't Mercy's idea at all. Dismiss me, if you like."

Mr. Kimberley fastened upon her the look that was well known in his classroom. "Most assuredly you are dismissed, young lady," he said coldly. "We will have to consider seriously whether or not Mercy is responsible enough to continue such a position."

When the men had gone neither girl spoke a word. Mercy pulled herself about the room, righting an overturned chair, straightening out the scuffed primers. Two great tears ran slowly down her cheeks.

The sight of Mercy's tears was more than Kit could endure. If she looked at them for another instant she would fly into a thousand pieces. In a panic she fled, out the door and down the roadway, running, blind to reason or decorum, past the Meeting House, past the loiterers near the town pump, past the houses where her pupils lived. She scarcely knew where her feet were taking her, but something deep within her had chosen a destination. She did not stop until she reached the Great Meadow. There, without thinking, she left the pathway, plunged into a field, and fell face down in the grass, her whole body wrenched with sobs. The tall grass rustled over her head and hid her from sight, and the Meadows closed silently around her and took her in.

When Kit had sobbed herself out, she lay for a long time too exhausted to move or to think. Perhaps she slept a little, but presently she opened her eyes and became aware of the smell of the warm earth and the rough grass against her face. She rolled over and stretched, blinking up at the blue sky. The tips of the long grasses swished gently in the breeze. The hot sun pressed down on her so that her body felt light and empty. Slowly, the meadow began to fulfill its promise.

All at once, with an instinctive quickening of her senses, Kit knew that she was not alone, that someone was very close. She started up. Only a few feet away a woman was sitting watching her, a very old woman with short-cropped white hair and faded, almost colorless eyes set deep in an incredibly wrinkled face. As Kit stared at her she spoke in a rusty murmuring voice.

"Thee did well, child, to come to the Meadow. There is always a cure here when the heart is troubled."

For a moment Kit was too dumbfounded to move.

"I know," the murmuring voice went on. "Many's the time I've found it here myself. That is why I live here."

Kit stiffened with a cold prickle against her spine. Those thin stooped shoulders, that tattered gray shawl —this was the queer woman from Blackbird Pond— Hannah Tupper, the witch! The girl stared, horror-struck, at the odd-shaped scar on the woman's fore-head. Was it the devil's mark?

"Folks wonder why I want to live here so close to the swamp," the soft husky voice continued. "But I think thee knows why. I could see it in thy face a moment back. The Meadow has spoken to thee, too, hasn't it?"

The cold feeling began to pass away. In some unexplainable way this strange little creature seemed to belong here, so much a part of this quiet lonely place that her voice might have been the voice of the Meadow itself.

"I didn't really intend to come here," Kit found herself explaining. "I always meant to come back, but this morning I just seemed to get here by accident."

Hannah Tupper shook her head, as though she knew better. "Thee must be hungry," she said, more briskly. "Come, and I'll give thee a bite to eat." She hitched herself awkwardly to her feet. Reminded of the time, Kit leaped up and shook out her skirts.

"I must go back," she said hastily. "I must have been gone for hours."

The woman peered up at her. Her eyes, almost lost in the folds of leathery wrinkles, had a humorous gleam. A toothless smile crinkled her cheeks.

"Thee better not go back looking so," she advised. "Whatever it is, thee can stand up to it better with a bit of food inside. Come along, 'tis no distance at all."

Kit wavered. She was suddenly ravenous, but more than that, she was curious. Whatever this queer little woman might be, she was certainly harmless, and unexpectedly appealing. Like the school children, she had accepted Kit without a question or suspicion, and like a child she scuttled ahead now, confident that Kit would accept her in the same way. Giving way to her own impulse, Kit hurried after her. Late as it was, she was far from eager to return to her Uncle Matthew's.

The little hut with its sparsely thatched roof sagged

at one corner. It looked as though it could never survive a stiff wind, let alone a flood. Two goats munched at the edges of a small vegetable patch.

"There's a well behind the house," said Hannah. "Draw some water and wash thy face, child."

Kit let the bucket down, leaning over to watch it meet the far-off circle of reflected sky. The water was deliciously cold on her hot face, and she gulped it thirstily straight from the bucket. Then she smoothed her hair and retied her apron, and went into the little house. The one small room the house contained was scoured as a seashell. There was a table, a chest, a bedstead with a faded quilt, a spinning wheel, and a small loom. A few ancient kettles hung about the clean-swept hearth. From a square of sunlight on the floor an enormous yellow cat opened one eye to look at them.

Hannah had set a wooden trencher on the table with a small corncake studded with blueberries, and beside it a gourd filled with yellow goat's milk. She sat watching as Kit ate, taking nothing herself. Probably, Kit thought too late, swallowing the last crumb, that was every bit of dinner she had!

The girl looked about her. " 'Tis a pretty room," she said without thinking, and then wondered how that could be, when it was so plain and bare. Perhaps it was only the sunlight on boards that were scrubbed smooth and white, or perhaps it was the feeling of peace that lay across the room as tangibly as the bar of sunshine.

Hannah nodded. "My Thomas built this house. He made it good and snug or it wouldn't have stood all these years."

"How long have you lived here?" Kit asked curiously.

The woman's eyes clouded. "I couldn't rightly tell," she said vaguely. "But I remember well the day we came here. We had walked from Dorchester in Massachusetts, you see. Days on end we'd been, without seeing another human being. Someone had told us there would be room for us in Connecticut. But in the town there was not an inch of land to spare, not after they'd seen the brand on our foreheads. So we walked toward the river, and then we came to the meadow. It put us in mind of the marshes near Hythe. My husband was raised in Kent and 'twas like coming home to him. Here is where he would stay, and nothing could change him."

There were a hundred questions Kit dared not ask. Instead she looked about the room, and noticed with surprise the one ornament it contained. Jumping to her feet, she seized from the shelf the small rough stone and held it in her hand. "Why, 'tis coral!" she exclaimed. "How did it get here?"

A small secret smile brightened the wrinkled face. "I have a seafaring friend," Hannah said importantly. "Whenever he comes back from a voyage, he brings me a present."

Kit almost laughed. Of all the unlikely things—a romance! She could imagine him, this seafaring friend, white-haired and weatherbeaten, coming shyly to the door with his small treasures from some distant shore.

"Perhaps this came from my home," she considered, turning the stone in her hand. "I come from Barbados, you know."

"Do tell—from Barbados!" marveled the woman. "Thee seemed different somehow. Is it like paradise, the way he says? Sometimes I mistrust he's just telling tales to an old woman."

"Oh, everything he has told you is true!" answered Kit fervently. " 'Tis so beautiful—flowers every day of the year. You can always smell them in the air, even out to sea."

"Thee has been homesick," said Hannah softly.

"Yes," admitted Kit, laying down the stone. "I guess I have. But most of all, I miss my grandfather so much."

"That is the hardest," nodded the woman. "What was thy grandfather like, child?"

Tears sprang into Kit's eyes. No one, since she had come to America, had ever really wanted to hear about grandfather, except Reverend Bulkeley who had only been impressed by his royal favors. She scarcely knew where to begin, but all at once she was finding eager, incoherent words for the happy days on the island, the plantation, the long walks together and the swimming, the dim cool library and the books. Then she came to the flight to Connecticut and all the bitterness and confusion of the past weeks.

"I hate it here," she confessed. "I don't belong. They don't want me. Aunt Rachel would, I know, but she has too many worries. Uncle Matthew hates me. Mercy is wonderful and Judith tries to be friendly, but I'm just a trouble to them all. Everything I do and say is wrong!"

"So thee came to the meadow," said Hannah, patting the girl's hand with her small gnarled claw. "What went so wrong this morning?" She listened, nodding her head like a wizened owl, as the tale of the morning's woes came pouring out. As Kit reached the part about the schoolmaster and his cane, to her amazement a rusty chuckle interrupted her. Hannah's face had crumpled into a thousand gleeful wrinkles.

89

Kit hesitated, and all at once the memory struck her funny, too. Her breath caught tremulously, and then she was laughing with Hannah. But instantly she sobered again. "What am I to do now?" she pleaded. "How can I ever go back and face them?"

Hannah said nothing for quite a long time. Her faded eyes studied the girl beside her, and now there was nothing childlike in that wise, kindly gaze.

"Come," she said. "I have something to show thee."

Outside the house, against a sheltered wall to the south, a single stalk of green thrust upwards, with slender rapierlike leaves and one huge scarlet blossom. Kit went down on her knees.

"It looks just like the flowers at home," she marveled. "I didn't know you had such flowers here."

"It came all the way from Africa, from the Cape of Good Hope," Hannah told her. "My friend brought the bulb to me, a little brown thing like an onion. I doubted it would grow here, but it just seemed determined to keep on trying and look what has happened."

Kit glanced up suspiciously. Was Hannah trying to preach to her? But the old woman merely poked gently at the earth around the alien plant. "I hope my friend will come while it is still blooming," she said. "He will be so pleased."

"I must go now," Kit said, getting to her feet. Then something prompted her to add honestly, "You've given me an answer, haven't you? I think I know what you mean."

The woman shook her head. "The answer is in thy heart," she said softly. "Thee can always hear it if thee listens for it."

Back along South Road Kit walked with a lightness and freedom she had never known since the day she sailed into Saybrook Harbor. Hannah Tupper was far from being a witch, but certainly she had worked a magic charm. In one short hour she had conjured away the rebellion that had been seething in the girl's mind for weeks. Only one thing must be done before Kit could truly be at peace, and without speaking a word Hannah had given her the strength to do it. Straight up Broad Street she walked, up the path to a square frame house, and knocked boldly on the door of Mr. Eleazer Kimberley.

CHAPTER TEN

"YOU DIDN'T!" Mercy gasped. "Mr. Kimberley himself! How did you ever dare, Kit?"

"I don't know," admitted Kit. Now that it was over her knees were shaking. "But he was very fair. He listened to me, and he finally agreed I could have one more chance. I won't let you down again, Mercy, I promise."

"I never thought you had let me down," Mercy said loyally. "It's just that you do have a way of surprising people. You certainly must have surprised Mr. Kimberley. He isn't known for changing his mind."

"I surprised myself," Kit laughed. "I really can't take any credit for it, Mercy. I think I was bewitched."

"Bewitched?"

"I met the witch who lives down in the meadow. It was she who gave me the courage."

Mercy and her mother exchanged startled glances.

"You mean you talked with her?" An anxious frown wrinkled Mercy's forehead.

"I went into her house and ate her food. But I was joking about being bewitched. She's the gentlest little person you ever saw. You'd love her, Mercy."

"Kit." Aunt Rachel set down her heavy flatiron and regarded her niece seriously. "I think you had better not say anything to the others about meeting this woman."

"Why, Aunt Rachel, you of all people! You can't believe she's a witch?"

"No, of course not. That is just malicious gossip. But no one in Wethersfield has anything to do with Hannah Tupper."

"Why on earth not?"

"She is a Quaker."

"Why is that so dreadful?"

Rachel hesitated. "I can't tell you exactly. The Quakers are queer stubborn people. They don't believe in the Sacraments."

"What difference does that make? She is as kind and good as—as you are, Aunt Rachel. I could swear to it."

Rachel looked genuinely distressed. "How can you be sure? Quakers cause trouble wherever they go. They speak out against our faith. Of course, we don't torment them here in Connecticut. In Boston I've heard they even hanged some Quakers. This Hannah Tupper and her husband were branded and driven out of Massachusetts. They were thankful enough just to be let alone here in Wethersfield."

"Has she ever done any harm?"

"No—perhaps not, though there's been talk. Kit, I know your uncle would be very angry about this. Promise me you won't go there again."

Kit looked down at the floor. All her fine resolves about trying to understand and to be patient, and already she could feel the defiance rising again.

"You won't, will you, Kit?"

"I can't promise that, Aunt Rachel," said Kit unhappily. "I'm sorry, but I just can't. Hannah was good to me, and she's very lonely."

"I know you mean to be kind," insisted Rachel. "But you are very young, child. You don't understand how sometimes evil can seem innocent and harmless. 'Tis dangerous for you to see that woman. You must believe me."

Kit picked up her wool cards and set to work. She knew she looked stubborn and ungrateful, and she felt so. The hard little knot had kinked up inside her tighter than ever. Coming home through the meadow everything had seemed so simple, and here it was all tangled again. Only one thing was sure. She had found a secret place, a place of freedom and clear sunlight and peace. Nothing, nothing that anyone could say would prevent her from going back to that place again.

Should she tell William Ashby about Hannah? she wondered that evening as they sat talking in the summer twilight. No, he would doubtless be horrified. William still seemed a stranger, even though he came faithfully every Saturday evening and often now appeared unexpectedly on fine evenings between. She could never be sure what thoughts were hidden behind that impassive face, but she had learned to recognize the sudden stiffening of his jaw muscles that meant she had said something shocking. That happened often enough in spite of her best intentions. Better not to provoke it now by mentioning a harmless Quaker.

She would like to tell John Holbrook, she thought, but there was never a moment when she could speak to him alone. Frequently now, on these mild evenings of early summer, John joined the family as they sat outside. The women would carry their knitting to the doorstep, and they would all talk quietly there till the mosquitoes and the coming darkness drove them indoors. John had never asked formal permission to call; he had merely taken literally Rachel's invitation to come again. There had never been the slightest hint that he was courting Judith. He never seemed to single her out, but sometimes he consented when she suggested that they walk along the green in the twilight. That was all the encouragement Judith needed. Indeed, it was more than enough to satisfy the whole family of John's intentions.

Not even her father could have failed to guess that Judith was in love. She had never spoken another word, even to Mercy or Kit, after that first surprising disclosure. But there was a brilliance in her eyes, a warm color in her cheeks, and a new sweetness in her manner. Less and less often, as the summer set in, did her tart tongue discomfort her cousin. She did not even chatter as readily, and often she seemed to be withdrawn into some secret world. Kit watched her, half envious and half puzzled. The sober young divinity student seemed an odd match for Judith's high spirits. Truth to tell, Kit herself was a little disappointed in John. Beside William, who was so set in his ways, John seemed scarcely able to make up his mind at all. When the talk turned to politics, as it invariably did, William made a far better showing than John. Nothing the revered Dr. Bulkeley could say or do could be wrong in his pupil's eyes, even the fervent defense of the King's policies which went against all John's upbringing. Matthew Wood, after baiting John with fierce questions that threw the young student into confusion, had scornfully labeled him a "young toady with no mind of his own." For once Kit was inclined to agree with her uncle. Probably, she concluded now, it would do no good to ask John about Hannah Tupper. Whatever Dr. Bulkeley thought about Quakers, John would think so too.

She had to bide her time for two weeks before she could find another opportunity to visit the Meadows. Kit kept her word to Mr. Kimberley and threw herself so diligently into the school work that the children were bewildered. There were no more stories, no games, even no small unorthodox poems. After school hours there were the gardens to weed, and the first crop of flax to harvest in the hilly slopes above the town. Finally, on one hot afternoon, Kit and Judith finished their stint of onion rows a little early, and as they trudged back along the dusty path, Kit looked across the fields to the roof of the lopsided house by Blackbird Pond and knew that she could not pass by one more time.

"I am going over there to see Hannah Tupper," she announced, trying to sound matter-of-fact.

"The witch? Have you lost your senses, Kit?" Judith was scandalized.

"She's not a witch, and you know it. She's a lonely old woman, and Judith, you couldn't help liking her if you knew her."

"How do you know?" demanded Judith.

Kit gave her cousin a short and careful version of the meeting in the meadow.

"I don't see how you dared," Judith exclaimed. "Really, Kit, you do the oddest things."

"Come with me now, Judith, and see for yourself."

Judith couldn't be budged. "I wouldn't step inside that house for anything, and I don't think you should either. Father would be furious."

"Then you go on without me. I won't be long."

"What shall I tell them at home?"

"Tell them the truth if you like," responded Kit airily, knowing quite well that Judith, for all her disapproval, would never give her away. The common bond of just being young together in that household was strong enough for that. She set off through the long grass, leaving her cousin standing doubtfully in the path.

There was a pleasant humming sound in the small cabin. Hannah sat before her small flax wheel, her foot moving briskly on the treadle.

"Sit down, child, while I finish this spindleful." She smiled as though Kit had merely stepped outside the door a moment before. Kit perched on a bench and watched the whirring wheel.

"I came to tell you that I made my peace with the schoolmaster," she said at last. "I couldn't come before because I've been teaching in the school again."

Hannah nodded without surprise. "I thought thee would," she commented. "Does it go better with thee now?"

"Yes, I suppose so. At least Mr. Kimberley should be satisfied. He says that children are evil by nature and that they have to be held with a firm hand.

But it's not much fun trying to keep my hand firm and being so solemn all day long. I feel sorry for those little boys."

Hannah glanced over at Kit briefly. "So do I," she said dryly. "Did the schoolmaster make thee promise never to smile?"

Kit looked back at the faded eyes, sunk deep in wrinkles, and caught the twinkle there. Suddenly she laughed. "You're right," she admitted. "I haven't even dared to smile. I'm afraid if I let myself go an inch I'll do something disgraceful again. But Mercy smiles all day long, and still keeps order."

She reached down and scooped up the sleeping cat from the floor, settling its limp weight in her lap and tickling the soft chin until a contented purr almost matched the hum of the spinning wheel. The late afternoon sun slanted through the open door and fell across Hannah's gnarled hands as they moved swiftly and surely. Peace flowed into Kit. She felt warm and happy.

"How fast you go," she said, watching the thread fattening on the bobbin. "Did you grow the flax yourself?"

Hannah dipped her fingers into a gourd shell without slackening the wheel. "Some of the families in town always bring me their flax to spin," she explained. "I make a nice neat thread, if I do say so, but every year it seems to get harder to see it. I have to tell by the feel. Is it smooth enough, does thee think?"

Kit admired the fine perfect thread that slipped evenly through Hannah's fingers. "It's beautiful," she said, "Even Mercy can't spin it like that."

Hannah looked pleased as a child. "Fourpence a

skein," she said. "Enough to pay the taxes and buy what I need."

"Taxes? On the swamp land?" Kit was indignant.

"Of course," Hannah said matter-of-factly, "and the fines for not going to Meeting."

"They make you pay fines for that? Wouldn't it be better to go to Meeting instead?" Kit looked around at the much mended clothing and the sparse furnishings of the little room.

"I doubt they would welcome me," Hannah said, again dryly, "even if I chose to go. In Massachusetts we Quakers had our own meetings."

"Can I become a Quaker?" asked Kit, only half joking. "I'd rather pay a fine any day than go to Meeting."

Hannah chuckled. "Thee doesn't become a Quaker just to escape the Meeting," she said, and Kit flushed at the gentle reproof in her tone.

"How does one become a Quaker?" she asked seriously. "I wish I knew something about it, Hannah."

The old woman was silent for a moment. Before she could answer, a shadow fell across the sunlight. A tall figure filled the doorway. Kit started. For an instant she thought that Hannah actually had conjured up a vision. There, unbelievably, was Nathaniel Eaton, the captain's son, leaning easily against the doorpost, with that well-remembered mocking smile in his blue eyes.

"I might have known," he said, "that you two would find each other."

Hannah's face crinkled up with pleasure. "I knew thee would come today," she triumphed. "I saw the *Dolphin* pass Wright's Island this morning. Kit, my dear, this is the seafaring friend I told thee about."

Nat made a bow. "Mistress Tyler and I are already acquainted," he acknowledged. He tried to set down, without anyone's noticing, the small barrel he carried under one arm, but Kit's glance was quick. A keg of fine Barbados molasses. So it was not just coral trinkets and flower bulbs that this seafaring friend of Hannah's brought from afar! Hannah caught the action, too.

"Bless thee, Nat," she said quietly. "Now sit down and tell us where thee has been this time."

"Charlestown," he answered, settling on an up-turned barrel. Instantly the cat slid from Kit's lap and with a loud "R-rr-iouw" leaped into Nat's and circled contentedly. Nat winced as her claws dug rapturously into his coarse homespun trousers.

Hannah made fast the thread and sat with idle hands, her eyes never leaving the young sailor's face. "And thy father?"

"He is well and sends you his greetings."

"I've been listening for a breeze every morning, just thinking thee might be coming up the river. I said to Thomas just yesterday, 'Tom,' I said, 'I'm going to save the last of these berries, just in case the *Dolphin* comes soon.' He'll be pleased when I tell him you've been here."

Kit's breath caught suddenly in her throat. Hannah had spoken as though her husband, so many years dead, were still here in the little house. A cloud had passed across the old woman's eyes, a vagueness that Kit had noticed there before. Kit turned a troubled look to Nat. He seemed not to have noticed anything amiss, but very casually he reached out his hand and covered Hannah's worn fingers with his own.

"Has the old she-goat had her kids yet?" he asked

easily. "Don't tell me you've sold them before I could see them."

The vagueness was gone as suddenly as it had come. "I had to, Nat," Hannah said regretfully. "They were getting into the cornfield. They brought a good price—two hanks of wool for a new cape."

Nat leaned back now and surveyed Kit with frank interest. She had forgotten the intense blue of his eyes, like the sea itself.

"Tell me," he asked her, "how did they ever let you find your way to Hannah?"

Kit hesitated, and Hannah chuckled. "How did thee find a way here?" she demanded of him. "'Tis a strange thing, that the only friends I have I found in the same way, lying flat in the meadows, crying as though their hearts would break."

The two young people stared at each other. "You?" breathed Kit incredulously.

Nat laughed. "I'll have you know that *I* was only eight years old," he explained.

"Were you running away?"

"I certainly was. We were on the way down river, and my father had just told me he was leaving me at Saybrook to spend the winter with my grandmother and go to school. It seemed like the end of the world. I had never lived anywhere but the *Dolphin,* and it had never occurred to me that anyone but my father would teach me. I'd never in my life seen anything like the meadows. They went on and on, and all at once I was hungry and thoroughly lost and scared. Hannah found me and brought me here and washed the scratches on my legs. She even gave me a kitten to take back with me."

"A little gray tiger," Hannah remembered.

"That cat was our lucky piece for six years. Not

100

one of the men would have weighed anchor without her."

Kit was entranced. "I can just see you," she laughed. "Did Hannah give you blueberry cake, too?"

"Right here at the table," nodded Hannah. "I'd forgotten how a little boy could eat."

Nat reached again to cover her hand with his own. "Hannah's magic cure for every ill," he teased. "Blueberry cake and a kitten."

"Did you go back to school?" questioned Kit.

"Yes. Hannah walked back to the ship with me, and somehow I felt bold as a lion. I didn't even mind the thrashing that was waiting for me."

"I know," said Kit, remembering the walk up to Mr. Kimberley's door.

"And now thee can both have supper with me again," said Hannah, delighted as a child at the prospect of a party. But Kit jumped to her feet with a guilty glance at the sun.

"Oh, dear," she exclaimed. "I didn't realize it was time for supper."

Hannah smiled up at her. "God go with thee, child," she said softly. She did not need to say more. They both knew that Kit would come back.

Nat followed her to the door. "You didn't say what you were running away from," he reminded her "Has it gone so badly here in Wethersfield?"

She might have told him, but looking up she caught a hint of "I told you so" in those blue eyes that silenced her. Was Nat laughing at her for behaving like an eight-year-old? Her head went up.

"Certainly not," she said with dignity. "My aunt and uncle have been very kind."

"And you've managed to stay out of the water?"

That superior tone of his! "As a matter of fact,"

she told him haughtily, "I am a teacher in the dame school."

Nat swept her a bow. "Fancy that!" he said. "A schoolmistress!" Instantly she wished she had not said it.

But as Nat followed her into the road, his mocking tone changed. "Whatever it was," he said seriously, "I'm glad you ran to Hannah. She needs you. Keep an eye on her, won't you?"

What a contradictory person he was, she thought, hurrying along South Road. Always putting her at a disadvantage somehow, and yet, now and then, surprising her, letting her peek through a door that always seemed to slam shut again before she could actually see inside. She would never know what to expect next from him.

CHAPTER ELEVEN

MIDSUMMER HEAT lay heavily upon the Connecticut Valley. The bare feet of the children were covered with fine dry dust from the road. Inside the kitchen the small bodies squirmed on the hard benches, and eyes strayed from the primers to gaze through the door at the forbidden sunshine. Kit felt as restless as her pupils.

If only I could be like Mercy, Kit thought. When her own voice rose in exasperation she was ashamed, remembering Mercy's unfailing patience. Watching Mercy this morning, she thought again, soberly, of the words that Mercy had spoken earlier in the summer. There had been a rare afternoon when Judith had invited Kit to go with some other girls of the town to pick flowers and picnic along the shore of the river. At the last moment Kit had turned back to Mercy and cried impulsively, "Oh, if only you could go, too, Mercy! How can you bear it, always staying behind?"

And Mercy had answered serenely, "Oh, I settled that a long time ago. I remember it very well. Father had carried me to the doorstep, and I sat there watching the children playing a game in the road. I thought of all the things I would never be able to do. And then I thought about the things that I could do. Since then I've just never thought much about it."

Teaching the children was certainly something that Mercy could do, with love and skill. And yet, Kit often wondered, what was it worth, all this work to master their letters? She herself had been eager to learn, scarcely able to wait to open the wonderful volumes in Grandfather's library. But most of these children would never even imagine the adventure that words could mean. Here in New England books contained only a dreary collection of sermons, or at most some pious religious poetry.

Sighing, Kit glanced over the docilely bent heads of her charges toward the open doorway, and as she did so a sudden motion caught her attention. She moved quickly.

I'm sure someone is out there again, she thought. Today I'm going to find out.

Yes, for the third time a little bunch of flowers, buttercups and wild geraniums, lay on the doorstep.

As she bent to pick them up she was certain that a shadowy figure slipped behind a tree. Curiosity made her forget her pupils, and stepping into the road she saw the small figure plainly and recognized Prudence Cruff.

"Prudence," she called. "Don't run away. Is it you who left the flowers?"

The child came slowly from behind the tree. She was thinner than ever, clad in a shapeless sacklike affair tied about her middle. Her eyes, much too big for her pinched little face, gazed at Kit with longing. She reminded Kit of a young fawn that had wandered near the house one morning. It had drawn nearer just like this, quivering with eagerness at the food Mercy set out, yet tensed to spring at the slightest warning.

"Who are the flowers for, Prudence?"

"You." The child's voice was nothing but a hoarse whisper.

"Thank you. They're lovely. But why don't you come into the school with the others?"

"I'm too big," stammered Prudence.

"You mean you know how to read already?"

"Naw. Pa wanted me to go to school, but Ma says I'm too stupid."

"You don't really believe that, do you Prudence?"

A bare toe dug into the dirt of the roadway. "I dunno. I can hear you when the door is open. I bet I could learn as good as them."

"Of course you could, and you ought to. Why don't you come in with me right now, and see how easy it is?"

Prudence shook her head violently. "Somebody'd tell on me."

"What if they did?"

"Ma'd cane me. I'm not s'posed to speak to you."

Remembering Goodwife Cruff's hard thin mouth, Kit did not urge. "Prudence," she suggested instead, "you could learn to read by yourself if you really wanted to."

"I haven't any horn."

Kit remembered something. "Is there a place where you could meet me where no one would tell on you?" she asked. "Can you get to the Meadows?"

Prudence nodded. "Nobody cares where I go, just so's I get the work done," she said.

"Then if you'll try to meet me there this afternoon, I'll bring you a hornbook and I'll teach you to read some of it. Will you come?"

"If I get finished—" Prudence breathed.

"You know the path that leads from South Road over to Blackbird Pond?"

Prudence gulped. "The witch lives down there!"

"Don't be silly! She's a gentle old woman who wouldn't harm a field mouse. Anyway, you don't need to go that far. There's a big willow tree just down the path. I'll wait for you there. Will you try?"

The struggle behind those round eyes hurt to watch. "Maybe," whispered Prudence, and then she turned and ran.

Kit walked slowly back into the schoolroom. What excuse could she make to get into her trunks today? At the bottom of one of them, she had remembered, was a little hornbook. It had been a present, brought from England by friends of her grandfather's. It was backed by silver filigree, underlaid with red satin, and it had a small silver handle. She had never really used it; she remembered how she had astonished the visitors by reading every letter straight off, but she had cherished the gift for its delicate craftsmanship.

What a pity every child couldn't learn to read under a willow tree, Kit thought a week later. She and Prudence sat on a cool grassy carpet. A pale green curtain of branches just brushed the grasses and threw a filigree of shadows, as delicate as the wrought silver, on the child's face. This was the third lesson. At first Prudence had been speechless. In all her short life the child had seldom seen, and certainly never held in her hands, anything so lovely as the exquisite little silver hornbook. For long moments she had been too dazed to realize that the tiny alphabet fastened to it was made up of the same a's and b's and ab's that she had overheard through the school doorway. But now, by this third meeting, she was drinking in the precious letters so speedily that Kit knew she must soon find a primer as well.

" 'Tis getting late, Prudence. I don't want you to get into trouble, and I must go back, too."

The child sighed and held out the hornbook obediently.

"That is yours, Prudence. I meant it for a present for you."

"She'd never let me have it," the little girl said regretfully. "You'll have to keep it for me."

Kit made a decision. She had been wanting an excuse to take Prudence to Hannah. She had a feeling that the child needed that comforting refuge even more than she did herself.

"I know what we'll do," she suggested. "We'll leave the book here with Hannah. Then any time you want to use it you can come and get it from her."

Terror blanched the child's face.

"Prudence, listen to me. You're afraid of Hannah

because you don't know her, and because you've heard things that just aren't true."

"She'll cut off my nose if I go near her!"

Kit laughed, then took the child's hands in her own and spoke as earnestly as she knew how. "You trust me, don't you?"

The small head nodded solemnly.

"Then come with me and see for yourself. I promise you, on my honor, nothing will hurt you."

The bony hand in hers was trembling as they walked down the grassy path, but Prudence stepped resolutely beside her. Kit's heart ached suddenly with pity and gratitude at such trust.

"I've brought another rebel to visit you," she announced, as Hannah came to the door. Hannah's pale eyes twinkled.

"What a wonderful day!" she exclaimed. "Four new kittens, and now visitors! Come and see."

Under a corner of the cabin, on a pile of soft grass, the great yellow cat curled protectively around four tiny balls of fluff. Her topaz eyes glowed up at them, and her purr was boastful. Completely disarmed, Prudence went down on her knees.

"Oh, the dear little things," she whispered, reaching one reverent finger. "Two black ones, and one striped and one yellow one." Over her head Kit and Hannah smiled.

"If thee is very, very careful, thee can pick one up and hold it," Hannah told her.

With a black kitten cradled in her hands, Prudence watched them find a safe corner for the hornbook.

"Thee is welcome any time, child. I'll keep it safe for thee. Now show me what thee has learned today. What letter is this?"

In the clean white sand on the floor Hannah traced

107

a careful B. Looking at Prudence, Kit held her breath. But there was no trace of fear in those fawn-like eyes as Hannah held out the stick. Boldly Prudence reached to take it in her own hand, and carefully and proudly she traced the lines herself.

"I believe there must be a morsel of blueberry cake for such a smart pupil," praised Hannah.

The morsel of cake vanished in a twinkling. "Hannah's magic cure for every ill," Nat had said. "Blueberry cake and a kitten." Kit smiled to see it working its charm on Prudence. But there was an invisible ingredient that made the cure unfailing. The Bible name for it was love.

"Why do they say she's a witch?" Prudence demanded, as the two walked slowly back along the path.

"Because they have never tried to get to know her. People are afraid of things they don't understand. You won't be afraid of her now, will you? You will go to see her when you can, even if I'm not there?"

The child considered. "Yes," she said finally. "I'm going back first chance I get. Not just because the horn is there. I think Hannah is lonesome. Of course, she has the cat to talk to, but don't you think sometime she must want somebody to answer back?"

Watching Prudence scurry off toward home, Kit had a moment's misgiving. As always, she had acted on impulse, never stopping to weigh the consequences. Now, too late, she began to wonder. Had it been fair to draw Prudence into her secret world? She felt completely justified in deceiving her aunt and uncle; they were narrow-minded and mistaken. But the thought of Goodwife Cruff made her shudder. Yet Prudence had looked so miserable. She needed a friend. For a few hours those wary anxious eyes had been filled with shining trust and happiness. Wasn't that worth a little risk? Kit shook off her qualms and set her own face towards home and another dull evening.

William could talk of nothing but his house these days. Every evening he must report exactly which trees had been cut, which boards fashioned. Today, he reported, as the family moved inside to escape the twilight mist that rose from the river, he had overseen the carpenter who was splitting the white oak for the clapboards.

"I don't think I made any mistake in deciding on riven oak," he told them. "Of course, two shilling a day is high for a carpenter, but——"

Sometimes Kit wanted to stop her ears. Would she have to hear the price of every nail that went into those boards, and every single nail the finest that money could buy? She was tired of the house already before the first board was in place.

Judith, however, took a lively interest in such details. She had a flair for line and form and a definite mind of her own, and it was plain, to Kit at least, that as William planned his house Judith was comparing it, timber for timber, with the house she dreamed for herself. Her purpose was only too apparent as she made adroit attempts to draw John Holbrook into the discussion.

"I think you should have one of those new roofs, William," she said now. "Gambrel, they call them. Like the new house on the road to Hartford. I think they look so distinguished, don't you, John?"

Mercy laughed at John's bewilderment. "I don't believe John even notices there's a roof over his head," she teased gently, "unless the rain happens to leak through onto his nose."

"And then he'd just pick up his book and move somewhere else," added Kit.

William did not smile. He was considering the matter gravely. "Perhaps you're right, Judith. When I ride down Hartford way tomorrow I'll take a good look at that house. Of course, you never know whether to risk a new style like that."

Oh, for heaven's sake! Kit gave her yarn an impatient jerk that sent the ball bouncing across the floor. Too tardily William bent to catch it and had to get heavily down on his knees to retrieve it from under the settle. Now some men, Kit reflected, could pick up a ball of yarn without looking ridiculous. She thanked him with little grace.

It was Mercy, as usual, who quietly steered them into untroubled water. "What did you bring to read to us tonight, John?" she inquired. "Judith, light a pine knot for him to see by."

In this one thing they were all united. John loved to read out loud, and they were equally happy to listen. For all of them the days were filled with hard labor, with little enough to satisfty the hunger of their minds and spirits. The books that John shared with them had opened a window on a larger world. Perhaps each of them, listening, glimpsed through that window a private world, unknown to the others. Matthew Wood sat scowling, his keen mind challenging and weighing each new thought. Rachel, Kit suspected, welcomed the peace and relaxation of those moments as much as the reading itself. What William thought, it was impossible to discern. Kit often wished that John would read something besides the religious tracts he so admired, but even for her impatient spirits the beauty of his voice wove a magic spell.

Tonight it was poetry. "These were written by a woman in Boston," he explained. "Anne Bradstreet, wife of a governor of Massachusetts. Dr. Bulkeley feels they are worthy to be compared with the finest poetry of England. This is what she writes about the sun:

"Art thou so full of glory, that no Eye
Hath strength, thy shining Rayes once to behold?
And is thy splendid Throne erect so high?
As to approach it, can no earthly mould.
How full of glory then must thy Creator be?
Who gave this bright light luster unto thee;
Admir'd ador'd for ever, be that Majesty."

Kit's needles moved more slowly. Her jangling nerves relaxed, and as the clear low voice went on a contentment wrapped her round like the sunshine in the meadow.

John is a part of the family already, she reflected. We have all come to love him. Yet I still feel in awe of him, a little. Uncle Matthew thinks he is weak, but I suspect that underneath they are both made of the same New England rock. For John everything in his life, even the girl he marries, will always be second to his work. Does Judith realize that, I wonder, or does she think she can change him?

Suddenly, perhaps because the poetry had opened her heart, Kit raised her eyes and made a discovery. Mercy sat, as usual, slightly in the shadow beside the hearth, her needles moving so automatically that she rarely glanced at her work. Now a brightly glowing bead of resin threw a brief light across her face. Those great listening eyes were fastened on the face of the young man bent over his book, and for one instant Mercy's whole heart was revealed. Mercy was in love with John Holbrook.

Faster than thought the shadows claimed Mercy again. Kit glanced hastily around the circle. No one else had noticed. Judith sat dreaming, a little secret smile on her lips. Rachel nodded drowsily, too tired to keep her mind on the reading. Matthew sat intent, ready to pounce on a hint of heresy.

I must have imagined it, thought Kit, yet her hands were shaking. Mercy and John Holbrook! How right —how incredibly, utterly right—and how impossible!

I wish I had not seen it, she thought in a burst of sadness. Yet she knew she would never forget as long as she lived. The flame that had burned in Mercy's eyes had such purity, such complete selflessness, that everything Kit had ever known seemed dim in its light. What must it be to care for someone like that?

CHAPTER TWELVE

DAME SCHOOL ended in mid-August, and a hundred new tasks waited to fill the hours. The onions must be harvested, packed into the rough sacks that Mercy had sewn, and stacked ready to be hauled into Hartford or bartered for goods when a sailing ship came up the river. Early apples waited to be peeled and sliced and dried in the sun for the winter's use. There was cider to be made from the wild pears. The first corn stood high in the meadow, row after endless row, waiting to be plucked. Often Kit and Judith and even Rachel worked side by side with Matthew in the fields until sunset, and there was not a moment to spare. It was hard now to find the time for stolen visits with Prudence and Hannah. Occasionally, by chance, Kit would find herself alone, and rushing through her task at double speed, she would steal down the path to Blackbird Pond, hoping that Prudence too had been able to escape.

One sunny day a whole empty afternoon stretched unexpectedly before her. She had been helping Judith and Rachel to make the winter supply of candles. It was hot sticky work. For two days they had been boiling the small gray bayberries that Kit and Judith had gathered in the fields, and Rachel had skimmed off the thick greenish tallow. It simmered now in the huge iron kettle, beneath which the fire must be kept glowing all through the long hot day. At the opposite end of the kitchen, at a good distance from the heat of the fire, the candle rods hung suspended between chairbacks. Back and forth the three women walked, carrying the candle rods, dipping the dangling wicks into the tallow, hanging them back to cool, and dipping them again, till the wax fattened slowly into the hard slow-burning candles that would fill the house with fragrance all through the coming months.

Finally Rachel wiped the damp gray strands back from her forehead and surveyed the rows of sleek green candles.

"That's plenty for today, more than I counted on. The rods won't be free to use again till tomorrow. I have to look in on Sally Fry's new baby that's ailing, and you girls deserve a rest—you've been working since sunup."

Kit left the work gratefully. She had no intention of resting, however, and presently she was tripping out the door when her aunt called her back.

"Where are you going, Kit?"

Kit looked down, not answering.

Her aunt studied her. "Wait," she said then. She went into the kitchen and came back after a moment with a small package which she held out to Kit shamefacedly.

It was a bit of leftover apple tart. So Aunt Rachel had known all the time! Kit suddenly threw her arms about her aunt.

"Oh, Aunt Rachel—you are so good!"

"I can't help it, Kit," her aunt said worriedly. "I don't approve at all. But I can't bear to think of anyone going hungry when we have such plenty."

This time, as Kit drew near Blackbird Pond, she was startled by the sharp ring of an axe. She had hoped to find Prudence there. Instead, as she came around the corner of the thatched cottage, she discovered Nat Eaton, his wiry tanned body bared to the waist, his axe spouting a fountain of chips as he swung at a rotting log.

"Oh," she exclaimed in confusion, "I didn't know the *Dolphin* was in again."

"She's not. We're becalmed off Rocky Hill and I rowed ahead. Would you have stayed away?"

Kit was in a mood to overlook his mockery. "Barbados molasses and firewood," she commented instead. "I'm beginning to understand how Hannah can shift for herself out here. What a pile of wood, Nat, on a hot day!"

"Come time to use it I'll be bound for Barbados," replied Nat briskly. "Helps keep my hand in."

Hannah peered from the doorway. "More company!" she rejoiced. "Come inside where it's shady. Nat, thee has piled up more wood than an old woman could burn in a year."

Nat set down his axe. "Today is strictly business," he announced. "The next job is some new thatch for that roof. Some spots there's not enough to make a decent mouse's nest."

"Can I help?" Kit was astonished to hear her own voice.

Nat's eyebrow lifted. His quizzical blue eyes dwelt on her brown arms so deliberately that she closed her fists to hide the calluses on her palms.

"Maybe you could at that," he replied, with an air of bestowing a great favor. "You can gather up the grass while I cut."

Kit followed him into the swamp and stooped to gather great armfuls of the long grasses that fell behind his scythe. The strong sweet smell of it tickled her nostrils. When he propped two logs against the cottage wall to make a crude ladder, she amused him by climbing nimbly up after him. Together they spread the bunches of thatch, and Kit held them flat in place while he fastened them with stout vines, his brown fingers moving with the strength and sureness of long years in the rigging. When the last tuft was in place they sat on the fragrant springy cushion and rested, looking out over the sunny meadow toward the gleaming band of the river. For a long time neither of them spoke. Nat sat munching on a straw. Kit leaned her bare elbows back on the prickly thatch. The sun pressed against her with an almost tangible weight. All about them was a lazy humming

115

of bees, broken by the sharp clatter of a locust. The queer rasping call of the blackbird rose from the grass, and now and then they caught the flash of scarlet on the glossy black wings.

This is the way I used to feel in Barbados, Kit thought with surprise. Light as air somehow. Here I've been working like a slave, much harder than I've ever worked in the onion fields, but I feel as though nothing mattered except just to be alive right at this moment.

"The river is so blue today," she said sleepily. "It could almost be the water in Carlisle Bay."

"Homesick?" asked Nat casually, his eyes on the blue strip of water.

"Not here," she answered. "Not when I'm in the meadow, or with Hannah."

He turned to look at her. "How has it been, Kit?" he asked seriously. "I mean really. Are you sorry you came?"

She hesitated. "Sometimes I am. They've been good to me, but it's very different here. I don't seem to fit in, Nat."

"You know," he said, looking carefully away at the river, "once when I was a kid we went ashore at Jamaica, and in the marketplace there was a man with some birds for sale. They were sort of yellow-green with bright scarlet patches. I was bent on taking one home to my grandmother in Saybrook. But father explained it wasn't meant to live up here, that the birds here would scold and peck at it. Funny thing, that morning when we left you here in Wethersfield—all the way back to the ship all I could think of was that bird."

Kit stared at him. That cocky young seaman, striding back through the woods without even a proper goodbye, thinking about a bird! Now having spoken too seriously, he turned back her solemn regard with a laugh.

"Who would guess," he teased, "that I'd ever see you perched on a rooftop with straw in your hair?"

Kit giggled. "Are you saying I've turned into a crow?"

"Not exactly." His eyes were intensely blue with merriment. "I can still see the green feathers if I look hard enough. But they've done their best to make you into a sparrow, haven't they?"

"It's these Puritans," Kit sighed. "I'll never understand them. Why do they want life to be so solemn? I believe they actually enjoy it more that way."

Nat stretched flat on his back on the thatch. "If you ask me, it's all that schooling. It takes the fun out of life, being cooped up like that day after day. And the Latin they cram down your throat! Do you realize, Kit, there are twenty-five different kinds of nouns alone in the *Accidence*? I couldn't stomach it.

"Mind you," he went on, "it's not that I don't favor an education. A boy has to learn his numbers, but the only proper use for them is to find your latitude with a cross-staff. Books, now, that's different. There's nothing like a book to keep you company on a long voyage."

"What sort of books?" Kit asked in some surprise.

"Oh, most any sort. We pick them up in odd places. I like the old logbooks best, and accounts of voyages, but once a man left us some plays from England that were good reading. There was one about a shipwreck on an island in the Indies."

Kit bounced up off the grass in excitement. "You mean *The Tempest?*"

"I can't remember. Have you read that one?"

"It was our favorite!" Kit hugged her knees in delight. "Grandfather was sure Shakespeare must have visited Barbados. I suspect he liked to think of himself as Prospero."

"And you were the daughter I suppose? What was her name?"

"Miranda. But I wasn't much like her."

Nat laughed. "That Shakespeare should have gone on with the story. He didn't tell what happened when that young prince took her back with him to England. I bet she gave the ladies plenty to talk about."

"It wasn't England. It was Naples. And that's another thing, Nat," she remembered. "All this talk against England and the King. I don't understand it."

"No, I suppose you couldn't, not being brought up here."

"Why are they so disloyal to King James?"

"There are two sides to loyalty, Kit," said Nat, looking suddenly almost as serious as John Holbrook or William. "If the King respects our rights and keeps his word to us, then he will retain our loyalty. But if he revokes the laws he has made and tacks and comes about till the ship is on her beam ends, then finally we will be forced to cut the hawser."

"But that is treason!"

"What is treason, Kit? A man is loyal to the place he loves. For me, the *Dolphin* there is my country. My father would give his life for the right to sail her when and where he pleases, and so would I. Anyway, 'twould do little good with a gale blowing to wait for orders from His Majesty in England. I suppose it's like that for these people in Wethersfield. How can a king on a throne in England know what

118

is best for them? A man's first loyalty is to the soil he stands on."

That would please Uncle Matthew anyway, Kit thought, bewildered and a little dismayed to glimpse under Nat's nonchalant surface a flash of the same passion that made life in the Wood household so uncomfortable. Nat was a New Englander, too, had she forgotten? She was almost relieved to hear Hannah's voice at the foot of the ladder.

"Has thee finished the thatching yet? 'Tis high time thee had a bite of supper."

"Supper?" Kit had not even noticed the slanting sun. "Is it as late as that?"

Nat's hand on her wrist detained her as she scrambled toward the ladder. "You will come often to see her, won't you?" he reminded her.

"Of course." Kit hesitated. "I worry about her, sometimes," she whispered. "She seems so smart and spry, and then, the next moment, she seems to forget —she talks as though her husband were still alive."

"Oh, that!" Nat dismissed her fears with a single word. "Hannah's in good trim right enough, but her mind wanders now and then. Don't let it bother you. I have an idea Hannah is a lot older than we think, and she's lived through a lot. She and her husband starved in jail for months in Massachusetts. Finally they were branded and tied to a cart's tail and flogged across the boundary. From what I hear, Thomas Tupper was a sort of hero. If he still seems close enough to Hannah so she can talk to him after all these years, you wouldn't take that away from her, would you?"

As usual, Hannah did not urge her to stay. "My company always has to hurry off," she chuckled.

"Nat always is in a hurry, and thee, and now Prudence."

"Who is Prudence?" Pulling on his blue cotton shirt, Nat fell into step beside her along the path to the South Meadow.

"You remember the little girl with the doll?" Hurrying along the path, Kit told him about the reading lessons. She expected that when they reached South Road Nat would turn back, but to her consternation he strode along beside her, and even when she hesitated at Broad Street he did not take the hint. The happy mood of the afternoon was rapidly dissolving in apprehension. Why on earth had Nat persisted in coming, too? There would be enough explanations without a strange seaman to account for. But Nat easily matched her nervous pace with his swinging stride, apparently quite unaware of her desire to be rid of him.

There they all were, sitting outside near the doorstep. Then supper must be over. As they drew near, William rose heavily to his feet and stood waiting.

"Kit, where in the world have you been?" Judith spoke up. "William has been waiting for ever so long."

Kit looked from one to the other, from her aunt's barely restrained tears to her uncle's waiting judgment. There is nothing I can possibly tell them, she thought, except the truth.

"I've been helping to thatch Hannah Tupper's roof," she said. "I'm sorry that I didn't realize how late it was. Aunt Rachel, this is Nathaniel Eaton, Captain Eaton's son, from the *Dolphin*. He was mending Hannah's roof, and I helped him."

The family allowed Nat scanty nods of acknowledgment, but William did not alter a muscle of his tight-clenched jaw. The two young men measured each other for a long moment.

Nat turned to Matthew Wood. "I was at fault, sir," he said, with a dignity Kit would never have given him credit for. "I shouldn't have accepted her help, but 'tis a tricky job, and when she came along I was greatly obliged to her. I trust that none of you have been inconvenienced." He looked back at William, one eyebrow tilted at the old familiar angle. Kit stood helpless as he took his leave and strode lightly away. He had done his best, but the reckoning was still to come.

"Why should you take it upon yourself to mend a roof for the Quaker woman?" demanded her uncle.

"She lives all alone——" began Kit.

"She is a heretic, and she refuses to attend Meeting. She has no claim on your charity."

"But someone ought to help her, Uncle Matthew."

"If she wants help, let her repent her sin. You are never to go to that place again, Katherine. I forbid it."

Morosely Kit followed the family into the house.

"Don't mind too much, Kit," Mercy whispered. "Hannah will be all right if she has that seaman to help her. I liked his looks."

CHAPTER THIRTEEN

"To THINK you've never been to a husking bee!" exclaimed Judith. "Why, they're more fun than all the holidays put together."

"Just husking corn all the evening?" It sounded to Kit like an odd sort of party. Her arms still ached from wresting the heavy ears from the stalks, row after row, hour after hour.

"Oh, it doesn't seem like work when everyone does it together. We all sing, and Jeb Whitney brings his fiddle, and there's cakes and apples and cider. Oh, I always think autumn is the very best time of the year!"

"They say the crop is not too plentiful this year," Mercy put in slyly. "Could be there won't be as many red ears as usual."

Judith tossed her head. "I'll find one, never you fear," she said blithely. "I have my own methods."

"Red ears? Are they better than the others?" At Kit's innocent question her two cousins burst into peals of merriment.

"You wait and see," advised Judith. "Come to think of it, I guess I'll make certain that William gets one, too. Then you'll find out!" At her own sudden suspicion, Kit blushed crimson.

In a rare mood of intimacy Judith linked arms with

Kit as they set out along High Street to gather the last of the corn in the meadow. It was more than the sparkling September air that accounted for her high spirits.

"I just feel it in my bones," she confided, "that something wonderful is going to happen tonight at the corn husking."

Judith's excitement was contagious. Kit began to feel a tingle of anticipation. Though she still couldn't see how anyone could make a festivity out of hard dusty work, it was the first party of any sort to which she had been invited in Wethersfield. The few young people she had come to know, the ones she had seen at Sabbath Meeting and Lecture Day, would all be there.

"I never knew you could predict the future," she laughed, "but I hope you're right."

"I know I am," said Judith, "because this time I'm going to see to it that something happens. I've made up my mind."

"You mean—John Holbrook?"

"Of course I mean John. You know how he is, Kit. So serious and shy. He'll never be able to find his tongue if I don't help him out."

"But John is still a student—"

"I know. He hasn't any property like William, or any way to support me yet. That's why he doesn't speak. But I know how John feels, and I know how I feel, and why should we wait forever without even making plans? And what could ever be a better time than a husking bee?"

"Judith—" Kit ventured doubtfully, "do you really think—?"

"You'd better be thinking about your own affairs," laughed Judith. "William isn't like John. He's like me.

When he's made up his mind he isn't going to wait forever."

Why did Judith have to remind her? Kit thought wryly. Ever since the day of William's house-raising, when the neighbors had gathered together and, working from dawn to sunset, had raised a fine imposing frame and nailed the sturdy new clapboards in place, Kit had known that William was only waiting a propitious time to speak. She had long since decided what her answer would be. As William's wife she could come and go as she pleased. There would be no more endless drudgery, and she could snap her fingers at a woman like Goodwife Cruff. Besides, William admired her. In spite of the fact that he was often bewildered and scandalized, he was still as infatuated as he had been that first Sabbath morning. Then why did Judith's teasing always raise this cold little lump of foreboding?

She glanced longingly toward the little house by Blackbird Pond and promised herself that she would steal a few moments on the way home. But work as fast as she could, when she and Judith finished their task there was time for only a flying visit. Prudence had been there, Hannah told her, but had not dared to wait for a lesson.

"If only these old eyes of mine could make out the letters," Hannah regretted. "But actually the child doesn't seem to need much help. She's just hungry for more to read. Poor little mite. I keep hoping the goat's milk will put a little fat on her bones."

Judith was out of sight when Kit started back along South Road. But to her surprise she glimpsed a familiar wide black hat in the distance and paused to wait as John Holbrook came loping along the road to catch up with her.

"Dr. Bulkeley sent me to find some skunk cabbage," he explained, waving a bunch of green. " 'Tis a rare cure for asthma, he says. How do you come to be walking alone?"

"Judith went on ahead," she explained. Had he hoped to meet Judith on the road? "I stopped to see Hannah Tupper."

She said the name deliberately and was rewarded by his startled eyes.

"The Widow Tupper? Does your family know about that, Kit?"

"Judith and Mercy know. Hannah is a good friend of mine."

"She is a Quaker."

"Does that matter?"

"Yes, I think it does," he said thoughtfully. "Not that I hold anything against the Quakers. But this woman has no proper reputation. She's been accused twice of practicing witchcraft."

"That's just cruel gossip."

"Probably, but I'd hate to see it turned against you too. You know, Kit, there are a few people here in town who still haven't forgotten that day you jumped into the river. If they find out that you're acquainted with a witch—"

"John, how can you pay attention to anything so silly?"

"Witchcraft isn't silly, Kit. Dr. Bulkeley says—"

"Oh, Dr. Bulkeley says!" retorted Kit. "I'm tired of hearing what Dr. Bulkeley says. Don't you ever think for yourself any more, John?"

At the hurt in his blue eyes she was instantly contrite. "I'm sorry," she said, impulsively laying a hand on his sleeve. "I didn't mean that really. But since you've been studying with that man you seem to have changed somehow."

At once he forgave her. "You don't know him as I do," he explained. "Every day I realize more how much I have to learn. But it's not just the studies. We do change, Kit, in spite of ourselves—at least some of us do," he added, with a flash of the humor she had missed in him lately. "I don't want to preach at you, Kit. It's just that the Quakers have a name for stirring up trouble, and it seems to me you manage to get into enough by yourself."

"I know," Kit agreed cheerfully, "but it's Hannah who's helping me to change. If you only knew her—"

John walked beside her, listening earnestly as she tried to make him understand the lonely woman in the meadow. Presently they reached the crossing at Broad Street where John would turn toward Dividend, and they stood for a moment, both unwilling to end this rare moment of comradeship. John took off his hat, leaned his elbows on the fencepost and stood gazing reflectively back at the Meadows, the wind stirring his fair hair. All at once he turned and smiled at Kit with the same unexpected sweetness that had warmed her heart that first day in Saybrook harbor.

"Five months," he said, "since we came here together on the *Dolphin*. Such high hopes we had, you and I. It has turned out well for you, hasn't it, Kit? A fine big house going up, and a good dependable fellow like William. I hope you will be very happy."

Kit colored and looked down at the browning grass. She did not want to talk about William. "And you, John?" she asked instead.

"Perhaps," he answered, and the smile lingered at the corners of his mouth. "We shall see."

Sooner than you think, maybe, thought Kit. "Are you going to the husking bee tonight?" she inquired mischievously.

"I don't know," he considered. "Will Mercy be there?"

"Mercy? Why no, I don't suppose she can be. It's more than a mile away."

"Then I think I shall spend the evening at your house instead. I seldom have a chance to talk to her."

"But they say a husking bee is such—" Slowly she began to realize what he had said.

"John! Why should you want to talk to Mercy?"

His eyes twinkled. "Why do you think I come so often?"

"But I thought—we all thought—I mean—"

"It has always been Mercy, from the very beginning. Didn't you guess that?"

"Oh *John!*" In a burst of incredulous joy Kit flung both arms rapturously about his neck. With a startled glance up the road, John tactfully freed himself. His very ears were pink, but his eyes were shining down at her.

"I'm glad you approve," he said. "Do you think I have a chance, Kit?"

"A chance! Just you try! Oh, John, I'm so happy I could dance a jig!"

"I can't try yet," he reminded her soberly. "I have nothing to offer her, nothing at all."

"You'll have a church of your own some day. Only—could Mercy—do you think she could manage a minister's household? There are so many things Mercy can't do, John."

"Then I will do them for her," he said quietly. "I don't want a wife to wait on me. For Mercy just to

127

be what she is—I could never do enough to make up for it."

"Then tell her, tonight, John," she urged, remembering the longing in Mercy's eyes.

"Perhaps," he answered again. "We shall see."

Walking home past Meeting House Square Kit could hardly keep from dancing. She wanted to shout and sing. Mercy and John Holbrook! How right! How exactly, unbelievably right! How could she keep from telling someone? They must see that she was bursting with excitement. Judith would surely—

Judith! Her jubilant feet came suddenly to a halt. How could she have forgotten? Ought she to have said something to John, warned him somehow? No, she could hardly have done that, in fairness to Judith. He was so completely unaware, so serious and shy, as Judith herself had said, so wrapped in his books and his dreams of Mercy that he had never even noticed that Judith had set her cap for him. What was this something that Judith was so sure was going to happen tonight? What sort of scheme did Judith have up her sleeve?

Well, if he doesn't go to the husking bee, nothing can happen, she thought practically. And who knows, if he's there with Mercy— Oh dear, Judith is going to mind terribly. But she is so proud. She'll put her nose in the air and pretend she never had such an idea in her head. And she'll get over it, I know, because John isn't really suitable for Judith. If only he will speak tonight!

Judith lingered exasperatingly in front of the little mirror that evening. She was wearing the new blue wool dress for the first time, with a snowy white collar and deep cuffs, and she had never looked lovelier. Her eyes were a deep blue in the candlelight, the clear white of her skin flushed with a secret excitement. Kit fidgeted impatiently. It didn't matter how she looked. William was waiting already, and they must all get away quickly before John arrived. If only Aunt Rachel and Uncle Matthew could find something to do, and Mercy could be sitting alone in the firelight!

They were too late, however. John Holbrook stepped inside the door just as the two girls rustled down the stairs, and his eyes were lively with admiration as he waited, with a courtly bow, to let them go ahead of him into the kitchen. Judith tipped back her head and smiled up at him provocatively. Rachel put aside her work, and even Matthew came to the door to see the young folks off.

"I'm so glad you've come," Judith dimpled. "Now we can all walk together."

"I'm not going to the husking," John told her, smiling. "I think I shall stay here and visit with Mercy instead."

"But they're all expecting you. Mercy doesn't mind, do you, Mercy?"

John shook his head, still smiling. There was a reflection of Judith's excitement in his own pale face.

"I think I shall stay here," he insisted. "There is something I want to speak to your father about."

His words had a breath-taking effect. Judith took a step backward, one hand at her throat, and a wave of scarlet spread from the white collar to her black curls.

"Tonight?" she whispered in unbelief. Then suddenly joy came flooding past every doubt and restraint.

"Oh, Father!" she cried impetuously. "He doesn't need to miss the husking, does he? You know what he wants to ask! Say yes, now, so we can go to the party together!"

Matthew Wood was bewildered. "Why, daughter," he rebuked her, "what sort of talk is this?"

"Shameless talk, and I don't care!" laughed Judith, tossing her black curls. "Oh Father, you must have guessed. John doesn't need to tell you."

Such radiance was irresistible. Matthew Wood's stern features softened, and when he turned to John he was actually smiling.

"If you will come courting such a headstrong, brazen girl," he said indulgently, "then I can only give you both my blessing. Perhaps you can teach her some meekness."

John stood dumbfounded, his pale face shocked completely colorless. He seemed totally unable to collect his wits.

Tell them! urged Kit, silently and desperately. You've got to say something, John, right away!

As if he had heard her, John opened his white lips and made a hoarse sound. "Sir—I—" he attempted. Then, still incredulous, he looked back at Judith. Every trace of pride and haughtiness was wiped from her face. Such utter happiness and trust shone from those blue eyes that John faltered, and in that moment of hesitation he was lost.

William's heavy hand descended on his shoulder. Aunt Rachel held out both hands to him, with tears in her eyes. Then Mercy came slowly from the hearth, her head up, her great eyes clear and lustrous. "I am so glad for you both," she said warmly. Only Kit could say nothing.

Perhaps I dreamed it, she thought, watching Mercy. But she knew she had not dreamed the love in Mercy's eyes that summer evening. Now no one but herself would ever know. She had counted on Judith's pride. But Mercy did not have Judith's pride; it was something much stronger than pride that upheld her.

Presently the four set out together into the still, frosty twilight. Judith took John's arm confidingly, still carried quite beyond constraint on her wave of happiness.

"You'll never know," she chattered. "You saved me from being the most outrageous hussy, John. I had a scheme. I'm not sure I would have dared, actually. But now—"

Now what? Kit asked, walking behind them. She ached with her own stifled protests. He can't do this! she told herself over and over. But she knew that he could. John understood Mercy. He knew that she had never in her life reached her hand for so much as a crust of bread that Judith might want. If he should hurt Judith now, Kit knew, Mercy would never forgive either him or herself.

Lost in her own thoughts, Kit barely noticed that William's dignified pace was even more deliberate than usual. They had dropped some distance behind the others when a purposeful hand grasped her own elbow.

"Wait a moment, Kit," said William. "Let them go ahead. I want to talk to you."

The quiet resolution in his voice penetrated her racing thoughts. Reluctantly she gave him a corner of her attention. The intent look in his eyes, even in the waning light, warned her of what was coming.

Oh, no! Not after all that had happened! She was tempted to run for the shelter of the fireside and Mercy.

"I didn't mean to speak tonight," William was saying. "But watching those two—don't you envy them their happiness, Kit?"

I can't bear it, she thought in panic. "Not tonight!" The last two words escaped into a half-whisper. William took them literally.

"Tomorrow then. Let me speak to your uncle. You won't need to help me out," he added with unwonted humor. "I am quite capable of speaking for myself."

Kit stood shivering in the damp twilight. This silk dress is not warm enough for New England, she thought irrelevantly. Then she made an effort to gather her forces. William's question was not unexpected after all. She had thought that her answer was all ready.

"Please, William," she whispered. "Don't speak to him yet."

William looked down at her, perplexed.

"Why not? Don't you want to marry me, Kit?"

She hesitated. "I had not thought of getting married so soon."

"Judith is just sixteen," he reminded her.

"I know. But I'm still a stranger, William. There are so many things I have to learn."

"That's true," he agreed. He was silent a moment. "I won't hurry you, Kit," he said reasonably. "The house can't be finished before spring, anyway. I'll wait for your answer."

What her answer would be he seemed to have not the slightest doubt. As they walked on, his hand remained on her elbow with a new possessiveness.

Laughter spilled from the open door. The great barn was glowing with lanterns swinging from the handhewn timbers. There was a fragrance of new hay and the warm reassuring smell of cattle. The gaily dressed young people sat in a circle around a vast mound of silk-tasseled corn, and already the husking had begun. Shouts of welcome greeted the newcomers, and the circle shifted to make room for them. To Kit's surprise the husking was fun, enlivened by singing and wagers and jokes that seemed uproariously funny. She was astonished. Wethersfield was not always a dull solemn place! Had her uncle ever been to a husking? she wondered.

All at once a new shout went up. Judith sat with a half-shucked ear of corn in her lap, and from the ruffled silk peeped bright orange-red kernels. Judith laughed and tossed back her head with all her old arrogance.

"I haven't any need for a thing like that!" she said triumphantly. "What am I offered for it?"

Without waiting for an answer, she tossed it straight across the circle into William's hands. There were a few quick giggles, a hush of curiosity. Kit sat helpless, her cheeks on fire, and then the laughter and the cheering left her giddy as William stepped resolutely forward to claim his forfeit.

CHAPTER FOURTEEN

AFTER THE KEEN still days of September, the October sun filled the world with mellow warmth. Before Kit's eyes a miracle took place, for which she was totally unprepared. She stood in the doorway of her uncle's house and held her breath with wonder. The maple tree in front of the doorstep burned like a gigantic red torch. The oaks along the roadway glowed yellow and bronze. The fields stretched like a carpet of jewels, emerald and topaz and garnet. Everywhere she walked the color shouted and sang around her. The dried brown leaves crackled beneath her feet and gave off a delicious smoky fragrance. No one had ever told her about autumn in New England. The excitement of it beat in her blood. Every morning she woke with a new confidence and buoyancy she could not explain. In October any wonderful unexpected thing might be possible.

As the days grew shorter and colder, this new sense of expectancy increased and her heightened awareness seemed to give new significance to every common thing around her. Otherwise she might have overlooked a small scene that, once noticed, she would never entirely forget. Going through the shed door one morning, with her arms full of linens to spread on the grass, Kit halted, wary as always, at the sight of her uncle. He was standing not far from the house, looking out toward the river, his face half turned from her. He did not notice her. He simply stood, idle for one rare moment, staring at the golden fields. The flaming color was dimmed now. Great masses of curled brown leaves lay tangled in the dried grass, and the branches that thrust against the graying sky were almost bare. As Kit watched, her uncle bent slowly and scooped up a handful of brown dirt from the garden patch at his feet, and stood holding it with a curious reverence, as though it were some priceless substance. As it crumbled through his fingers his hand convulsed in a sudden passionate gesture. Kit backed through the door and closed it softly. She felt as though she had eavesdropped. When she had hated and feared her uncle for so long, why did it suddenly hurt to think of that lonely defiant figure in the garden?

Judith's voice interrupted her groping thoughts. "Hurry up, Kit," she called. "That's the third group of people that've gone past the house. They say there's a trading ship coming up the river. If we finish the washing we can watch it come in."

Kit's heart leaped. "What ship?"

"What does that matter? It will bring mail, and perhaps some new bolts of cloth, and maybe the scissors we ordered from Boston. Anyway, it's fun to see a ship come in, and there won't be many more this fall."

An odd confusion, half eagerness and half reluctance, tossed Kit's spirits to and fro. She was minded to stay at home and help Mercy, even as her feet hurried her along the path beside Judith. But the moment they rounded the bend in the road she forgot her uncertainty. There was the *Dolphin* coming up the river with all her sails. The curving tail of the prow was chipped and dull, the hull was battered and knobby with barnacles, the canvas dark and weathered, yet how beautiful she was! In a surge of memories, Kit could almost feel the deck lifting beneath her feet, and a longing almost like homesickness caught at her throat. How she would love to sail on the *Dolphin* again! Forgotten was the smell of horses, the motionless waiting, the sudden terror of gale and lightning. She remembered only the endless shining reaches of water that stretched to the end of the world, the vast arc of the milky way, and the scouring rush of salt wind that blew back her hair. What would she give to stand on the deck of the

Dolphin, facing down the river, toward the open sea and Barbados!

The *Dolphin* rounded to, her top sails were furled, and with a great creaking of lines and shudder of canvas, she came to rest alongside the Wethersfield dock. The onlookers crowded forward as bales and barrels and knobby bundles were passed over the sides into their eager .hands. Kit and Judith stood a little aside, enjoying the bustling scene. The excitement of the crowd seemed to be contagious. When Judith spoke, Kit was surprised to find that her own lips were strangely unmanageable. A queer trembling made her clench her fists tight. She could not turn her eyes away from the deck of the ship.

At last she glimpsed a fair head emerging from the hatchway, almost hidden behind a vast load. It was some time before Nat Eaton, carelessly scanning the busy wharf, caught sight of her. Then he raised one hand in the briefest possible greeting. Kit knew how Nat could be when he was absorbed in the ship's business. She waited, pretending an interest in each bit of cargo that came over the rail. Gradually the citizens of Wethersfield claimed their orders, the merchants from Hartford counted off the barrels of nails and oil and salt, and only a handful of idlers still stood about.

"Come on, Kit," urged Judith. "There's nothing more to see."

No, Kit had to agree, there was not the slightest excuse for lingering further. With a little shrug she turned away, and immediately she heard his voice.

"Mistress Tyler! Wait a moment!" She whirled back to see Nat bounding over the rail. He came toward her with his light buoyant step, carrying under his arm a bulky package wrapped in a bit of sailcloth.

"Good day to you, Mistress Wood," he greeted Judith respectfully. Then he turned to Kit. "Would you be kind enough to deliver a bit of cargo for me?" The words were acceptable enough, it was the indifferent tone that was bewildering.

"'Tis a length of woolen cloth I picked up for Hannah," he explained, holding out the package.

Kit took it reluctantly. "She'll be waiting for you to come yourself."

"I know, but my father is anxious to be off. Lose this wind and we'll be delayed here for days. Hannah might need this. If you can spare the time from your fashionable friends."

Kit's mouth opened, but before she could speak he went on.

"An interesting cargo we had this trip. One item in particular. Sixteen diamond-paned windows ordered from England by one William Ashby. They say he's building a house for his bride. A hoity-toity young lady from Barbados, I hear, and the best is none too good for her. No oiled paper in her windows, no indeed!"

She was taken aback by the biting mockery in his voice.

"You might have mentioned it, Kit," he said, lowering his voice.

"There—there's nothing definite to tell."

"That order looks definite enough."

While she searched for something to say she knew that his eyes had not missed the hot surge she could feel sweeping up from the collar of her cloak to the hood at her forehead.

"May I congratulate you?" he said. "To think I

worried about that little bird. I might have known it would gobble up a nice fat partridge in no time." Then, with a quick bow to Judith, he was gone.

"What bird? What was he talking about," panted Judith, breathlessly keeping up with Kit's sudden haste. Her head turned away to hide her angry tears, Kit did not answer.

"Honestly, Kit, you do know the oddest people. How did you ever meet a common riverman like that?"

"I told you he was the captain's son."

"Well I certainly don't think much of his manners," observed Judith.

To Kit's relief a distraction awaited them at home. Rachel stood in the doorway peering anxiously up the road.

"I declare," she fretted. "There is no peace for the poor man. Someone came to fetch him just now. Said a rider came out from Hartford with news this morning, and there's a great crowd at the blacksmith's shop. Can you see anything up the road, Judith?"

"No," said Judith. "The square seems quiet."

"I think it is something to do with that Governor Andros of Massachusetts, the one who is determined to take the charter away. Oh dear, your father will be so upset."

"Then let's get him a good dinner," suggested Judith practically. "Don't worry, Mother. The men can take care of the government."

Following them into the house, Kit felt grateful to the unpopular Andros. Whatever he had done, he had saved her, for the moment at least, from any more of Judith's questions.

Matthew Wood did not come home for the good meal they had made ready. Late in the afternoon he came slowly into the kitchen. His shoulders sagged and he looked ill.

"What is it, Matthew?" Rachel hovered over his chair. "Has something terrible happened?"

"Only what we have expected," he answered wearily. "Governor Treat and the council have warded it off for nearly a year. Now Sir Edmond Andros has sent word, three days since, that he is setting out from Boston. He will arrive in Hartford on Monday to take over as royal governor in Connecticut."

"Lay a fire in the company room," he added. "There are some who will want to talk tonight."

One other chance bit of news reached them before nightfall. For all his haste, Captain Eaton had missed the wind after all, and the *Dolphin* lay becalmed just off Wright's Island. Kit took a revengeful pleasure in the thought. She hoped they had a good long wait ahead of them. It would serve Nat right if they sat there till the ice set in. He might perfectly well have delivered his own package. And she would make very sure of one thing. She would take care not to deliver it herself till the *Dolphin* was well on its way toward Saybrook.

CHAPTER FIFTEEN

"IT MEANS the death of our free commonwealth!"
" 'Twill be the end of all we've worked for!"

The angry voices came clearly through the closed door of the company room. It was impossible not to overhear. Mercy's spinning wheel faltered, and Rachel's hand, lighting a pine knot, trembled so that a spark fell on the table unheeded and left a small black scar. Frequently in the past month the same grim-faced men had called upon Matthew Wood, but tonight the voices had a frightening quality.

"They must think it a desperate matter to meet like this on the eve of the Sabbath," said Mercy.

"Your father never touched his supper," fretted Rachel. "Do you suppose it would do to offer them all a bite when they come out?"

Kit dropped a stitch for the third time. She had little concern for the colony of Connecticut, but she was seething with curiosity over one aspect of tonight's business. Some time ago William had arrived, offered his usual courteous greetings to the women, and then, instead of taking his place by the fireside, had astounded her by knocking boldly on the company room door. More surprising still, he had been admitted, and there he had stayed, behind that closed door, for the past half hour. Pride could not restrain her tongue another moment.

"What in the world is William doing in there?" she burst out. "Why would Uncle Matthew let him in?"

"Didn't you know?" Judith threw her a condescending glance.

"Know what?"

"William came over to father's way of thinking two months ago. Even before his house was raised, when he had to pay such high taxes on his land."

Now how did Judith know that? Kit stared at her. "I never heard him say a word about it."

140

"Maybe you just weren't listening." Judith's tone had more than a touch of smugness.

Chagrined, Kit jerked at another dropped stitch. It was true, sometimes when William and Judith were talking about the house it was all she could do to keep her mind from wandering. But she knew she would have remembered anything as important as this. Was William ashamed to admit to her that he had turned against the King? Or did he think she was too stupid to understand?

The voices broke out again. "This Governor Andros says right out that deeds signed by the Injuns are no better than scratches of a bear's paw! We are all to beg new grants for land we've bought and paid for. Why, the fees alone will leave us paupers!"

"They can come into our Meeting House and order us to kneel and whine tunes like their Church of England."

"My cousin in Boston actually had to put his hand on the Holy Book to swear in court. I'll shoot any man tries to make me do that!"

They could hear Matthew's voice, cold and steady, never raised or out of control. "Whatever happens," he was saying, "we do not want any shooting here in Connecticut."

"Why not?" broke in another voice. "Should we hand over our freedom without a murmur like Rhode Island?"

"I say defy him!" came a hoarse shout. "Nine train bands we have ready in Hartford county. Nigh unto a thousand men. Let him look into a row of muskets and he'll change his tune!"

"It would mean senseless bloodshed," Matthew said clearly.

For nearly an hour the voices went on, the angry

shouting gradually giving way to low tense words that could not be distinguished. Finally a silent, tight-mouthed group of men emerged, with no interest in the refreshment that Rachel timidly offered. When they had gone Matthew lowered himself heavily into a chair.

"It is no use," he said. "We must spend the Sabbath in prayer that God will grant us patience."

Rachel searched for some words of comfort. "I know it is a disappointment," she attempted. "But will it truly change our lives so very much? Here in Wethersfield, I mean? We will still all be together in this house, and surely we will not lose our rights as citizens of England."

Her husband brusquely waved away her comfort. "That is all a woman thinks about," he scoffed. "Her own house. What use are your so-called rights of England? Nothing but a mockery. Everything we have built here in Connecticut will be wiped out. Our council, our courts will be mere shadows with no real power in them. Oh, we will endure it of course. What else can we do? If only we could somehow hold back the charter itself. This man has no right to take it from us."

Not till later, when she and Judith undressed, shivering, in the chilly upstairs chamber, did Kit dare to venture a comment. "They don't seem to realize," she whispered, "how powerful the Royal Fleet is. Once when the Royalists were trying to hold Bridgetown, Barbados, Parliament sent a troopship and subdued them in no time."

"Oh, I don't think there'll be any fighting," said Judith confidently. "It's just that men like Father don't like to be dictated to. But Dr. Bulkeley says the charter was never intended to be as free as they have made it. He thinks the men of Connecticut have taken advantage of the King's generosity."

"So I suppose John thinks so too?" Kit couldn't resist adding.

Once Judith would have flared, but her new happiness was hard to shake. "Poor John," she laughed now. "He's so mixed up between Dr. Bulkeley and Father. Honestly Kit, I agree with Mother. I don't believe it will change our lives much. Men make an awful fuss about such things. I just wish it hadn't happened four days before Thanksgiving. It's going to spoil the holiday to have everyone so gloomy."

"I'd be curious to see this Governor Andros," said Kit. "You remember Dr. Bulkeley told us he used to be a captain of the dragoons in Barbados."

"Maybe we can see him," said Judith, blowing out the candle and hopping into bed. "If he comes up from New London he'll have to cross the river at Smith's ferry. I'm going to get a peek at him no matter what father says. You don't often get a chance to see all those soldiers in uniform!"

For a good many Wethersfield citizens curiosity got the better of loyalty on the next afternoon. Kit and Judith met a fair number of farmers and their wives traveling along South Road and ranging along the bank of the river. They had a good hour's wait ahead of them, lightened by the arrival of an escort from Hartford, led by Captain Samuel Talcott, one of the Wethersfield men, Kit noted with surprise, who had occasionally joined the meetings in her uncle's company room.

"I'd have no part in greeting that Andros," commented one farmer. "The crabs would pick my bones before I'd do it."

"Look at the fine horse all ready for His Highness!

143

They should have asked me. I'd have found the horse for him all right!"

Captain Talcott sensed the growing anger in the waiting crowd and raised his voice. "There is to be no demonstration," he reminded them. "The governor comes here under orders from His Majesty. He will be received with all due courtesy."

Presently a murmur arose as the first red-coated horsemen appeared on the opposite shore. "There he is!" excited voices cried. "The tall one just getting off his horse! He's getting into the first boat there!"

The ferryboats crossed the wide river without mishap, and the party from Boston stepped out onto the shore at Wethersfield. More than seventy men there were, with two trumpeters and a band of grenadiers. Kit thrilled at the sight of the familiar red coats. How tall and handsome and trim they looked, beside the homespun blue-coated soldiers.

And Andros! He was a true cavalier, with his fine embroidered coat, his commanding air, and the wealth of dark curls that flowed over his velvet collar. How elegantly he sat the saddle of his borrowed horse. Why, he was a gentleman, an officer of the King's Dragoons, a knight! Who were these common resentful farmers to dispute his royal right? He made their defiance seem childish.

Governor Andros had no cause to complain of his reception at Wethersfield. The people kept a respectful silence. The Hartford escort saluted and showed a praiseworthy discipline. As the band rode out of sight along the road a few fists were shaken, and some small boys hurled clumps of mud after the last horses' hoofs. For the most part it was a somber group that straggled back to their neglected chores. The magnificence of Andros and his procession had shaken their

144

confidence. They all knew that this haughty man was on his way to meet with their council, and that before night fell he would hold their very lives in his hand.

Resignation and despair settled over the household that evening, as though, Kit thought, it were the eve of that Doomsday that the minister warned of in Sabbath Meeting. There was no company to look forward to. William was a member of the militia in Hartford, and John had sent word that he must care for two of Dr. Bulkeley's patients while the doctor attended the session. In Matthew's scowling presence the others scarcely dared whisper. Kit was thankful when she and Judith could escape to the cold sanctuary of the upstairs chamber.

They had been fast asleep for some time when they were startled awake by the thudding of hoofs in the road below and the whinny of a horse suddenly reined in. There was an echoing rap of a musket against the door.

Matthew must have been awake and waiting, for before the rapping ceased they heard the bolt slide back. Instantly Judith was out of bed with Kit scrambling after her. Snatching heavy cloaks to pull over their nightclothes, the girls flung open the chamber door. From the opposite room came Rachel, still fully dressed. The three women crowded together on the narrow stairs. To Kit's astonishment the man who stepped through the door into the light of Matthew's candle was William.

"It's safe, sir!" he burst out, before the door was shut. "The charter's safe, where he can never lay a hand on it!"

"Thank God!" exclaimed Matthew reverently. "You were at the meeting, William?"

"Yes, sir. Since four o'clock. Sir Edmond got a

stomach full of talking this day. The speeches of welcome lasted near to three hours, before he could get in a word of business."

"And the charter?"

"It was there, all the time, in the middle of the table in plain sight. Sir Edmond made a long speech about how much better off we were all going to be. It got dark, and finally he asked for lights. Before long the room got hot and full of smoke and when someone opened a window, the draft blew out the candles. It took quite a few minutes to get them lighted. Nobody moved. Far as I could see everybody stayed right in their places. But when the candles were lit the charter had disappeared. They looked high and low for it, all over the room, and never found a trace."

"Was the governor angered?"

"You'd have admired him, sir. You couldn't help it. He sat there cool as an icicle. He knew the paper wasn't going to be found, and he wouldn't stoop to ask a question about it. As it was, he could afford to ignore it."

"Aye," said Matthew grimly. "He had the power in his hands without it."

"Yes. Governor Treat read a statement, and they all signed it. The Colony of Connecticut is annexed to Massachusetts. Governor Treat will be appointed Colonel of Militia."

"And Gershom Bulkeley?"

"They say he will be appointed a Justice of the Peace for his loyalty."

"Hmm," snorted Matthew. He thought the news over for a moment. "The charter," he insisted, "do you know what happened to it?"

William hesitated. For the first time he acknowledged the presence of the three women by one brief embarrassed glance up the stairs.

"No sir," he answered. "The room was dark."

"Then how do you know it is safe?"

"It is safe, sir," said William positively.

"Then we can hold up our heads," said Matthew, taking a long breath. "Thank you for coming, my boy."

When the door was shut behind William, Matthew turned to the women on the stairs. "We can praise God for this night," he said. "Now get to bed, all of you. And remember, if there is any talk about this, you have heard nothing—nothing at all, do you understand?"

"Can you sleep now, Matthew?" asked his wife anxiously.

"Aye," agreed Matthew, "I can sleep now. There are hard times ahead for Connecticut. But some day, when the hard times have passed, as they must pass, we will bring our charter out of hiding and begin again, and we will show the world what it means to be free men."

The two girls crept back into the cold chamber and climbed shivering into bed. As Kit lay wide awake in the blackness, some distant shouts, a snatch of raucous, unrestrained singing such as she had never heard before in Wethersfield, sent her mind back to the days of her childhood. She surprised Judith by a sudden giggle.

"I know where the charter went," she whispered. "The spirits took it."

"What are you talking about?" Judith was almost asleep.

"I just remembered it is All Hallows Eve. This is the night the witches are supposed to ride abroad on

147

broomsticks, and the spirits do all sorts of queer things."

"Nonsense," said Judith. "We don't hold with saints' days here in New England. Besides, William knows perfectly well where that charter is. I could tell he does."

Snubbed again, Kit fell silent and listened to that unaccustomed shouting in the distance. She felt curiously elated. She knew she had overheard an account of serious insubordination to the King, yet in her heart she was glad that her uncle had known this small victory. Now perhaps they would have some peace in the house. No, it was more than that. Tonight she had understood for the first time what her aunt had seen in that fierce man to make her cross an ocean at his side. There was a sort of magnificence about him, even without the fine uniform that made Governor Andros so splendid. Lying there in the dark, Kit had to admit it—she was proud of him.

CHAPTER SIXTEEN

"THERE WILL BE no Thanksgiving this week," announced Matthew when he came home at noontime the next day. "It seems we have no authority here in Connecticut to declare our own holidays. His Excellency, the new governor, will declare a Thanksgiving when it pleases him."

"Oh dear!" exclaimed Judith in disappointment. "We had planned such a lovely day. And Mercy has pies baked already."

"We can be thankful among ourselves that we have an abundance to eat and the good health to enjoy it."

"But there won't be any games, and the train band won't drill?"

"There is no occasion to celebrate," he reminded her. "Better for the young people to remember that idleness breeds mischief. A disgraceful thing happened last night. Never since we have lived in Wethersfield has there been such a disturbance on All Hallows Eve."

"I thought I heard some shouting," said Rachel. "It reminded me of home. In England the boys used to light bonfires and march through the streets—"

"Such things are best not mentioned," her husband silenced her. "All Saints' Day is a papist feast. But our own young people had no share in this, thank goodness. 'Twas a rowdy band of rivermen from a trading ship."

"Did they do any damage?"

"Little enough, since we have a constable who is quick to his duty. The three ringleaders are cooling their heels now in his shed, and on Lecture Day they will sit for all to see in the town stocks."

"What did they do, Father?" inquired Judith coolly. Across the table her eyes met Kit's deliberately.

"They came roistering into town just before midnight. I am sorry to tell you, Katherine, that your friend William Ashby seems to have been the only one singled out for their insulting prank."

Kit dared not ask the question, but her uncle went on.

"They illuminated his house," he told them gravely.

"You mean they burned it down?" gasped Rachel.

"No. They well might have. They put lanterns in the window frames that are waiting for the new panes. Lanterns made out of pumpkin heads, with candles inside, and unholy faces cut in the sides to show the light."

"Jack-o-lanterns!" exclaimed Judith. Kit choked suddenly on a giggle that rose unexpectedly from nowhere. Instantly she was horrified at herself, and in mortified confusion kept her eyes on the wooden trencher before her.

Her uncle shot a suspicious glare at the two girls. "Whatever they are called, they are the devil's invention. 'Twas an outrageous piece of blasphemy. I trust they will be dealt with severely."

Thursday Lecture day, the day of public punishment, was two days away. Somehow, Kit knew, she would have to endure the waiting. Though actually, she knew already what she would see. It did no good to remind herself that there were dozens of trading ships on the river, and that the *Dolphin* might well be out to sea by now. Kit had no doubt at all who one at least of the culprits in the stocks would be, and neither, by the smug set of her pretty lips, had Judith.

By Thursday noon Kit gave up trying to keep her mind on her work. No matter how she shrank from the ordeal before her, she knew she could not stay away. The one thing she could not face was the thought of taking that walk to the Meeting House in the presence of Judith. An hour before meeting time, when all the family seemed occupied, she slipped out of the house and set out along High Street with a hard little lump of dread crowding her ribs.

At first she could barely glimpse the stocks. They were surrounded by the usual crowd of idlers and passersby. It was no place for a girl alone, but she had to see. Clenching her fists tight she moved closer.

Yes, they were all three *Dolphin* men, and none of them showed the slightest sign of repentance. One of the three sat with his head down in sullen disgust. Nat and the redheaded seaman who had painted the *Dolphin*'s figurehead that morning on the river were cheerfully exchanging insults with a cluster of young bound boys who had stopped to enjoy the spectacle, the two culprits holding their own in an unchastened manner that delighted the onlookers. In spite of their ready answers, the sport had been one-sided, as Kit could see by the daubs of mud that stained the rough boards of the stocks. Even as she watched, an apple core sailed through the air and bounced off Nat's forehead. A cheer went up at such marksmanship, but Nat's comment drew an even louder roar of approval.

"Watch your tongue, you scoundrel!" shouted a farmer, catching sight of Kit's flustered face. "There's a lady present."

Nat twisted his head the inch or so that the boards allowed him and stared at her without the slightest recognition. Her presence had spoiled the sport. The servant boys drifted away, and presently the three prisoners sat for a moment neglected. Impelled by some urge, half pity and half annoyance, Kit came forward from the shelter of the trees.

Nat watched her come without a flicker in his blue eyes. Now that she stood directly in front of him she could see the bruise that the careless missile had left. Suddenly she felt the tears rising.

"Kit, for heaven's sake," Nat hissed in an exasperated whisper, "get away from this place! Quick!"

Deliberately Kit stepped closer. She marked the

way the tight boards were chafing the hard brown wrists. "This is horrible, Nat!" she burst out. "I can't bear to see you in this hateful thing!"

"I'm quite comfortable, thank you," he assured her. "Don't waste your pity on me. 'Tis as roomy as many a ship's berth I've slept in."

"Isn't there anything I can do? Are you hungry?"

"You can stop trying to be a lady of mercy. 'Twas well worth it. I'd gladly sit here another five hours for a sight of Sir William's face that evening."

He was impossible! With a flounce of petticoats she turned away. It did not help to note that her foolish concern had been witnessed by a whole group of early Lecturegoers. This would certainly give them something to wag their tongues over. Head held high, she forced herself to keep a ladylike pace. At the door of the Meeting House she stopped to read the posted notice.

That for stealing pumpkins from a field, and for kindling a fire in a dwelling they three shall be seated in the stocks from one hour before the Lecture till one hour after. That they shall pay a fine of forty shillings each, and that they be forbidden hereafter, on certainty of thirty lashes at the whipping post, to enter the boundaries of the township of Whethersfield.

Kit's courage failed her altogether. She simply could not go into that Meeting House. She could not bear to sit there and hear that sentence read aloud. She could not face the family, or the whispering and staring that would turn her own family pew into a pillory. Gathering her skirts about her she hurried across the green, skirted the square in a wide arc, and fled home to her uncle's house. It was the first time since she had come to Wethersfield in the spring that she had dared to miss a Thursday Lecture.

The family had already left for the Meeting House and Mercy, busy at her spinning, did not hear her return. Kit crept up the stairs, but the empty bedchamber was not the refuge she needed. She had to talk to someone. Mercy would listen with gentleness, of course. But how could she ever explain to Mercy about Nat? There was only one person who could understand.

It is a good chance to take Hannah the piece of cloth, anyway, Kit reasoned. At least this one afternoon I can be very sure of not meeting any seafaring friends there. She stole down the stairs again and took a winding path through the back meadows to Blackbird Pond.

"Don't fret, child," Hannah said philosophically, when Kit had poured out the story. "The stocks aren't so dreadful. I've been in them myself."

"But Nat is banished from Wethersfield. He won't be able to leave the ship or to come to see you any more."

"Well now, that is a shame," agreed Hannah, unperturbed. In spite of her woe, Kit had to smile. Why hadn't she remembered that ever since he was eight years old Nat had been finding his way to Blackbird Pond through devious meadow routes? Hannah knew that no threats could keep Nat from coming again. As always, here in this house, things seemed to look much less desperate.

"This William Ashby," Hannah said thoughtfully. "I never heard Nat mention him."

"He had come to call the night that Nat walked home with me. Nat met him there."

"Does thee mean he had come to call on thee?"

"Yes." Why hadn't she ever told Hannah about William?

"Is the young man courting thee, Kit?"

Kit looked down at her hands. "I guess you'd call it that, Hannah."

Hannah's shrewd little eyes studied the girl's downcast face. "Does thee plan to marry him?" she asked gently.

"I—I don't know. They all expect me to."

"Does thee love him?"

"How can I tell, Hannah? He is good, and he's fond of me. Besides," Kit's voice was pleading, "if I don't marry him, how shall I ever escape from my uncle's house?"

"Bless thee, child!" said Hannah softly. "Perhaps 'tis the answer. But remember, thee has never escaped at all if love is not there."

Presently Kit opened the door to Prudence's timid knock and was comforted by the pleasure that rushed into the child's face. Prudence had further news of the culprits.

"Nat won't be able to come to see you," she told Hannah. "They marched the three of them straight to the landing and put them on the *Dolphin*. But Nat waved to me as he went by."

"You know Nat?" Kit asked the child, surprised.

"Of course I know him. He comes to see Hannah. Last time he listened to me read."

Why should it disturb her to think of Nat's sharing the reading lessons? Kit wondered, trying to be reasonable. How many of his visits had she missed? She was a little jealous to think of them all here cozily together while she was hard at work in the cornfield. Annoyed at herself, she picked up the sail-wrapped

154

bundle. "He sent you a present, though," she told Hannah brightly.

Hannah ruefully surveyed the length of gray woolen. "Now isn't that kind of Nat?" she exclaimed. "So soft and tight-woven. Much too fine for the likes of me. But thee knows, the truth is these old eyes of mine can't even see to thread a needle."

"Then Prudence and I will make you a dress," promised Kit blithely.

"Can you sew, truly?" demanded Prudence, overwhelmed at still another accomplishment.

"Of course I can sew. I've never made a woolen dress, but I learned to embroider before I was your age. I'll borrow a pattern and scissors from Mercy and you'll see!"

While the reading lesson began, Kit spread the cloth on the floor, turning it this way and that, as she had seen Mercy do, trying to plan how to use the length to the best advantage. The idea of cutting and sewing a dress by herself was novel and exciting.

"Will you really let me sew some stitches?" asked Prudence, watching her with shining eyes.

"Really and truly," promised Kit, smiling back at her. What fun it would be to make something warm and pretty for Prudence, she thought with longing. Did they never give the child anything decent to wear? Those skimpy sleeves did not even cover her elbows, and the scratchy linsey-woolsey cloth kept her thin shoulders constantly twitching.

She knew she could never give Prudence even the smallest gift. The lessons were risky enough. Looking at the child, Kit felt again a fleeting uneasiness. What misery would be the child's lot if these meetings were discovered? The miracle that had been taking place before their eyes had made it all too easy to forget the danger.

For Prudence was an entirely different child from the woebegone shrinking creature who had stood in the roadway outside the school. The tight little bud that was the real Prudence had steadily opened its petals in the sunshine of Kit's friendship and Hannah's gentle affection. Her mind was quick and eager. She had memorized the hornbook in a few days' time and sped through the primer. After that she had plunged headlong into the only other reading matter available, Hannah's tattered Bible. Kit had chosen the Psalms to begin with, and slowly, syllable by syllable, Prudence was spelling out the lines, while Hannah sat listening, her own lips often moving with the child's in the lines she remembered and could no longer read.

There were days on end, of course, when Kit could not manage to keep the tryst. But Hannah and Prudence were fast friends now, and she knew that the reading went companionably on. There were more frequent days when Prudence could not escape her mother's sharp eye, and other days when her small face looked so pinched and exhausted that Kit wondered painfully if the child had been punished for tasks she had left unfinished. Always before she had been able to shake off her doubts. But today she had had too sharp a lesson in the retribution of this Puritan Colony. For the first time she felt a twinge of real fear.

"Hannah," she said softly over Prudence's head, "I am afraid to go on like this. What would happen if they found us out? Nat is strong enough to take it. But Prudence—"

"Yes," agreed Hannah quietly. "I know that soon thee would begin to consider that."

"What should I do, Hannah?"

"Has thee looked for an answer?"

Prudence looked up. "You won't say I can't come, Kit?" she pleaded. "I don't care what they do to me. I can stand anything, if only you'll let me come!"

"Of course you can come," said Kit, stooping to give the child a reassuring hug. "We'll find an answer, somehow. Look now, I've brought you a present, too." From her pocket she drew three precious objects that had required some ingenuity to gather, a partly used copybook from her trunk, a small bottle of ink, and a quill pen.

" 'Tis high time you learned to write," she said.

"Oh Kit! Now? This very minute?"

"This very minute. Watch me carefully." Opening to a clean page she carefully wrote the child's name on the first line. "P-R-U-D-E-N-C-E. Now see if you can copy that."

The small hand trembled so that the first eager stroke sent a great blot of ink sprawling across the page. Prudence raised stricken eyes.

"Oh Kit! I've spoiled your lovely book!"

" 'Tis no matter. You should see the great blots I used to make. Now—very carefully—"

Finally it was completely written, Prudence, in quite respectable letters, without a single blot. Prudence was awestruck at her own handiwork. Hannah came to peer closely and admire.

"Let me do it again," pleaded the child. "This time I won't make the R so wiggly." She grasped the quill in tense, careful fingers, and her lips silently formed each letter as she traced the lines. Over her bent head Kit and Hannah exchanged an affectionate smile. For a time they both sat listening to the small sounds in the house, the scratching of the pen, the rustling and snapping of the fire, and the slow purr of the yellow cat.

How peaceful it is, thought Kit, lazily stretching her toes nearer to the blaze. Why is it that even the fire in Hannah's hearth seems to have a special glow? Like the sunshine on the day that I sat on the new thatch with Nat. If only, right now, on that bench across the hearth— But what ridiculous daydream was this? Kit shook herself upright.

" 'Tis too dark to work any more," she said. Prudence laid down the quill with a long sigh, and plopping down on the hearth, dragged the limp drowsy cat into her arms.

"I wish I could live here with you and pussy," she said wistfully, laying her thin cheek against the soft golden fur.

"I wish thee could too, child," said Hannah gently.

"Remember Nat said it was like the psalm I was reading that day?" the child said dreamily. "Peace be within thy walls."

"Well," Kit interrupted too briskly, "there won't be any peace anywhere if we don't get home in a hurry." She flung open the cottage door, and a bit of milkweed whisked in on a rush of November wind, spilling shreds of spidery white down. Prudence ran back to fling her arms about Hannah.

Kit would remember many times the picture she carried with her along the darkening road. Was there some premonition, she would wonder, that made that moment so poignant, some foreknowledge that this was the last afternoon the three would ever spend together in the small cottage? She would remember, too, that all the way home she tried without success to find the answer that Hannah had promised could always be found in her own heart.

Rachel greeted her reproachfully. "You're very late, Kit. It was wrong of you to stay away from Lecture. Your uncle was very displeased. And John Holbrook walked back with us to say goodbye to you and Mercy."

"Goodbye? Where is John going?"

Rachel looked across the room at Judith, who was setting the table near the fire. But Judith, her eyes red from weeping, said nothing.

"What has happened, Aunt Rachel?" asked Kit, bewildered.

"John has enlisted in the militia. There's a detachment going out from Hartford to aid some of the towns north of Hadley in Massachusetts against the Indian attacks, and John volunteered to go with them."

"To fight?" Kit was too astonished to be tactful. "Why, John is the last person I'd think to be a soldier."

" 'Tis a doctor they needed, and John has learned a good deal of medicine this year."

"But why now, right in the middle of his studies?"

"I think it was his way of breaking with Dr. Bulkeley," explained Rachel. "He has tried so hard, poor boy, to reconcile Gershom's ideas with his own bringing up. Now it seems the doctor is going to publish a treatise in favor of Governor Andros and the new government, and John just couldn't stomach it any longer. We all think it is to his credit."

"I don't!" spoke up Judith. "I think it is nothing but stubbornness."

"That's not fair, Judith," Mercy spoke from the hearth. She looked a little more pale and tired than usual. "I think you should be proud of him."

"Well, I'm not," answered Judith. "What difference does it make what Dr. Bulkeley writes? Now John won't get a church of his own, and he can never get married or build a house!" Her tears broke out afresh.

"He'll come back," Rachel reminded her. "The trip was only to be for a few weeks."

"He'll be gone for Christmas. If he cared anything about me he wouldn't have gone at all."

"For shame, Judith!" said her mother. "You had better dry those tears before your father comes in."

Mercy spoke thoughtfully. "Try to understand, Judith," she said slowly. "Sometimes it isn't that a man doesn't care. Sometimes he has to prove something to himself. I don't think John wanted to go away. I think, somehow, he had to."

Judith had shut her mind to any consolation. "I don't know what you're talking about," she snapped. "All I know is we were perfectly happy, and now he has spoiled everything!"

CHAPTER SEVENTEEN

FIVE DAYS after John Holbrook's departure Judith fell ill. Her mother, inclined at first to attribute her complaints to moping, took a second look at her flushed cheeks and put her to bed. Within two more days alarm had spread to every corner of Wethersfield. Sixteen children and young people were stricken with the mysterious fever, and none of the familiar remedies seemed to be of any benefit. For days Judith tossed on the cot they had spread for her in front of the hearth, burning with fever, fretful with pain, and often too delirious to recognize the three women who hovered about her. A young surgeon was summoned from Hartford to bleed her, and a nauseous brew of ground roasted toads was forced between her cracked lips, to no avail. The fever simply had to run its course.

On the fourth day Kit felt chilly and lightheaded, and by twilight she was thankful to sink down on the mat they dragged to the fireside near her cousin. Her bout with the malady was short, however. Her wiry young body, nourished by Barbados fruits and sunshine, had an elastic vitality, and she was back on her feet while Judith was still barely sitting up to sip her gruel. Dressing rather shakily, Kit was compelled to ask Mercy's assistance with the buttons down her back, and was shocked when her older cousin suddenly bent double in a violent fit of coughing. Kit whirled round on her.

"How long have you been coughing like that?" she demanded. "Let me feel your hand! Aunt Rachel, for heaven's sakes, get Mercy to bed quick! Here she's trying to wait on us!"

Tears of weakness and protest ran down Mercy's cheeks as Rachel stooped to take off her oldest daughter's shoes. Kit heated the warming pan to take the chill off Mercy's bed in the corner, and Mercy buried her face in the pillows as though it were a shame past bearing that she should cause so much trouble.

Mercy was seriously ill. Twice the young doctor

rode out from Hartford to bleed her. The third time he stood looking soberly down at her. "I dare not bleed her further," he said helplessly.

Rachel raised timid eyes to her husband. "Matthew—do you think—that perhaps Gershom Bulkeley might know something to help her? He is so skilled."

Matthew's lips tightened. "I have said that man does not come into my house," he reminded her. "We will hear no more about it."

Rachel, already worn from the long vigil with Judith, was near the breaking point. Matthew, after working in the fields all day, forced his wife against her will to get some rest while he sat by his daughter's bedside at night. Judith watched helplessly, still too weak even to comb her own hair. The meals fell to Kit, and she did the best she could with them, measuring out the corn meal, stirring up the pudding, spooning it into a bag to boil, and cursing the clumsiness that she had never taken the pains to overcome. She built up the fire, heated kettles of water for the washing, so that Mercy might have fresh linen under her restless body. She fetched water, and strained a special gruel for Judith, and spread her uncle's wet clothes to dry before the fire. At night she dozed off, exhausted, and woke with a start sure that something was left undone.

Mercy lay on some remote borderland between sleeping and waking. Nothing could rouse her, and every breath was such a painful struggle that the slow rasp of it filled the whole house. Fear seeped in at the corners of the room. The family dared not speak above a whisper, though certainly Mercy was beyond hearing. On the fourth morning of Mercy's illness Matthew did not go to work at all, but sat heavily at the table, turning the pages of the Bible, searching in vain for some hope to cling to, or shut himself in the company room where they heard his heavy tread back and forth, back and forth, the length of the room. Toward noontime he took down his coat from the peg. "I am going out for a time," he said hoarsely.

He had one sleeve in the coat when a knock sounded at the door, and as he drew back the bolt a man's voice grated harshly through the silent room.

"Let me in, man. I've something to say."

Matthew Wood stepped back from door, and the Reverend Bulkeley loomed on the kitchen threshold.

"Matthew," he said, "you're a stubborn mule and a rebel. But this is no time for politics. Time was your Mercy was like my own daughter. Let me see her, Matthew. Let me do what I can, with God's help, to save her."

Matthew's voice was almost a sob. "Come in, Gershom," he choked. "God bless you! I was coming to fetch you."

Dr. Bulkeley's solid presence brought to them all new hope. "I have a theory," he told them. "I've read something like it, and 'twill do no harm to try. Cook me some onions in a kettle."

For four long hours Kit labored at Dr. Bulkeley's bidding. She sliced onions, blinking her eyes against the stinging tears. She kept the fire blazing under the iron kettle. When the onions were cooked to just the right softness, Dr. Bulkeley piled them in a mass on a linen napkin and applied the blistering poultice to Mercy's chest. As soon as the poultice cooled a new one must be ready.

Late in the afternoon the doctor rose to his feet. "There are others I must tend to," he muttered. "Keep her warm. I'll be back before midnight."

Kit busied herself to prepare a meal which none of them could eat. With fingers so heavy from fatigue and fear that she could scarcely force them to move, she cleared the table and put away the untouched food. She wondered if ever again she would escape from the sound of that dreadful breathing. Her own lungs ached with every sighing breath that Mercy drew.

Then without warning a new fear came rushing in upon her. From without the house there was an approaching sound of stamping feet and murmuring voices, gathering volume in the roadway outside. There was a crashing knock on the outer door. The three women's eyes met in consternation. Matthew Wood reached the door in one stride and flung it open.

"How dare you?" he demanded in low-voiced anger. "Know you not there is illness here?"

"Aye, we know right enough," a voice replied. "There's illness everywhere. We need your help to put a stop to it."

"What do you want?"

"We want you to come along with us. We're going for the witch."

"Get away from my house at once," ordered Matthew.

"You'll listen to us first," shouted another voice, "if you know what's good for your daughter."

"Keep your voices down, then, and be quick," warned Matthew. "I've no time to listen to foolishness."

"Is it foolishness that there's scarce a house in this town but has a sick child in it? You'd do well to heed what we say, Matthew Wood. John Wetherell's boy died today. That makes three dead, and it's the witch's doing!"

"Whose doing? What are you driving at, man?"

"The Quaker woman's. Down by Blackbird Pond. She's been a curse on this town for years with her witchcraft!"

The voices sounded hysterical. "We should have run her out long ago."

"Time and again she's been seen consorting with the devil down in that meadow!"

"Now she's put a curse on our children. God knows how many more will be dead before morning!"

"This is nonsense," scoffed Matthew Wood impatiently. "There's no old woman, and no witchcraft either could bring on a plague like this."

"What is it then?" shrilled a woman's voice.

Matthew passed a hand over his forehead. "The will of God—" he began helplessly.

"The curse of God, you mean!" another voice screamed. "His judgment on us for harboring an infidel and a Quaker."

"You'd better come with us, Matthew. Your own daughter's like to die. You can't deny it."

"I'll have naught to do with it," said Matthew firmly. "I'll hold with no witch hunt."

"You'd better hold with it!" the woman's voice shrilled suddenly. "You'd better look to the witch in your own household!"

"Ask that high and mighty niece of yours where she spends her time!" another woman shouted from the darkness. "Ask her what she knows about your Mercy's sickness!"

The weariness dropped suddenly from Matthew Wood. With his shoulders thrown back he seemed to tower in the doorway.

"Begone from my house!" he roared, his caution drowned in anger. "How dare you speak the name of a good, God-fearing girl? Any man who slanders one of my family has me to reckon with!"

There was a silence. "No harm meant," a man's voice said uneasily. " 'Tis only woman's talk."

"If you won't come there's plenty more in the town who will," said another. "What are we wasting our time for?"

The voices receded down the pathway, rising again in the darkness beyond. Matthew bolted the door and turned back to the dumbfounded women.

"Did they wake her?" he asked dully.

"No," sighed Rachel. "Even that could not disturb her, poor child."

For a moment there was no sound but that tortured breathing. Kit had risen to her feet and stood clinging to the table's edge. Now the new fear that was stifling her broke from her lips in an anguished whisper.

"What will they do to her?"

Her aunt looked up in alarm. Matthew's black brows drew together darkly. "What concern is that of yours?"

"I know her!" she cried. "She's just a poor helpless old woman! Oh, please tell me! Will they harm her?"

"This is Connecticut," answered Matthew sternly. "They will abide by the law. They will bring her to trial, I suppose. If she can prove herself innocent she is safe enough."

"But what will they do with her now—tonight—before the trial?"

"How do I know? Leave off your questions, girl. Is there not trouble enough in our own house tonight?" He lowered himself into a chair and sunk his head in his hands.

"Go and get some sleep, Kit," urged Rachel, dreading any more disturbance. "We may need you later on."

Kit stared from one to the other, half frantic with helplessness. They were not going to do anything. Unable to stop herself she burst into tears and ran from the room.

Upstairs, in her own room, she stood leaning against the door, trying to collect her wits. She would have to get to Hannah. No matter what happened, she could not stay here and leave Hannah to face that mob alone. If she could get there in time to warn her—that was as far as she could see just now.

She snatched her cloak from the peg and, carrying her leather boots in her hand, crept down the stairs. She dared not try to unbolt the great front door but instead tiptoed cautiously through the cold company room into the back chamber and let herself out the shed door into the garden. She could hear shouts in the distance, and slipping hurriedly into her boots she fled along the roadway.

In Meeting House Square she leaned against a tree for an instant to get her bearing. The crowd was gathering, a good twenty men and boys and a few women, carrying flaring pine torches. In the hoarse shouting and the heedless screaming of the women there was a mounting violence, and a terror she had never known before closed over Kit's mind like fog. For a moment her knees sagged and she caught at the tree for support. Then her mind cleared again, and skirting the square, darting from tree to tree like a savage, she made her way down Broad Street and out onto South Road.

She had never before seen the Meadows by moon light. They lay serene and still, wrapped in thin veils of drifting mist. She found the path easily, passed the dark clump of willows, and saw ahead the deep shining pool that was Blackbird Pond and a faint reddish glow that must be Hannah's window.

Hannah's door was not even bolted. Inside, by the still-flickering embers of the hearth, Hannah sat nodding in her chair, fast asleep. Kit touched the woman's shoulder gently.

"Hannah dear," she said, struggling to control her panting breath. "Wake up! 'Tis Kit. You've got to come with me, quickly."

"What is it?" Hannah jerked instantly awake. "Is it a flood?"

"Don't talk, Hannah. Just get into this cloak. Where are your shoes? Here, hold out your foot, quick! Now—"

There was not a moment to spare. As they stepped into the darkness the clamor of voices struck against them. The torches looked very near.

"Not that way! Down the path to the river!"

In the shelter of the dark bushes Hannah faltered, clutching at Kit's arms. She could not be budged. "Kit! Why are those people coming?"

"Hush! Hannah, dear, please—"

"I know that sound. I've heard it before. They're coming for the Quakers."

"No, Hannah, come—I"

"Shame on thee, Kit. Thee knows a Quaker does not run away. Thomas will take care of us."

Desperately Kit shook the old woman's shoulders. "Oh, Hannah! What shall I do with you?" Of all times for Hannah to turn vague!

But Hannah's brief resolution suddenly gave way,

and all at once she clung to Kit, sobbing like a child.

"Don't let them take me again," she pleaded. "Where is Thomas? I can't face it again without Thomas."

This time Kit succeeded in half dragging the sobbing woman through the underbrush. They made a terrible rustling and snapping of twigs as they went, but the noise behind them was still louder. The crowd had reached the cottage now. There was a crashing, as though the furniture were being hurled to splinters against the walls.

"She was here! The fire is still burning!"

"Look behind the woodpile. She can't have got far."

"There's the cat!" screeched a woman in terror. "Look out!"

There was a shot, then two more.

"It got away. Disappeared into thin air."

"There's no bullet could kill that cat."

"Here's the goats. Get rid of them too!"

"Hold on there! I'll take the goats. Witched or no, goats is worth twenty shillings apiece."

"Scotch the witch out!"

"Fire the house! Give us a light to search by!"

Desperately the two women pushed on, over a marshy bog that dragged at their feet, through a cornfield where the neglected shocks hid their scurrying figures, past a brambly tangle, to the shelter of the poplar trees and the broad moonlit stretch of the river. There they had to halt, crouching against a fallen log.

Behind them a flare of light, redder than the moonlight, lit up the meadows. There was a hissing and crackling.

"My house!" cried out Hannah, so heedlessly that

Kit clapped a hand over her mouth. "Our own house that Thomas built!" With the tears running down her own cheeks, Kit flung both arms around the trembling woman, and together they huddled against the log and watched till the red glow lessened and died away.

For a long time the thrashing in the woods continued. Once voices came very close, and the search party went thwacking through the cornfield. Two men came out on the beach, not twenty feet from where they hid.

"Could she swim the river, think you?"

"Not likely. No use going on like this all night, Jem. I've had enough. There's another day coming." The men climbed back up the river bank.

When the voices died away it was very still. Serenity flowed back over the meadows. The veil of mist was again unbroken. After a long time, Kit dared to stretch her aching muscles. It was bitterly cold and damp here by the river's edge. She drew Hannah's slight figure closer against her, like a child's, and presently the woman's shuddering ceased, and Hannah drifted into the shallow napping of the very old.

There was no such escape for Kit. Her first surge of relief soon died away, and her thoughts, numbed by the sheer terror of pursuit, began to stir again in hopeless circles. What chance did they have when morning came? Should she rouse Hannah now and push on down the river? But where could they go? Hannah was exhausted; all her strength seemed to have died with the dying flames of her house. She could take Hannah home with her, where at least there would be warm clothes and hot food. But her uncle was a selectman. It would be his bounden duty to turn Hannah over to the law. And once they had her locked up in jail, what then? What use would a trial be with no one to speak in her defence but a foolish girl who was suspected of being a witch herself? Hannah could not even be trusted to answer the questioning straight. Like as not her mind would wander and she would talk about her Thomas.

Yet as the long hours wore away Kit could find no better solution. Whatever might happen, Hannah needed immediate care. Even the jail would be better than this unprotected place. As the first gray light slanted along the river, Kit made up her mind. They would not risk the main roads. They would pick their way along the shore of the river and cut through the meadows back to her uncle's house.

Then, unbelievably, out of the mist came the miracle. First two points of mast, then sails, transparent and wraithlike in the fog, then, as Kit strained her eyes, the looming hull, the prow, and the curved tail of a fish. The *Dolphin!* Glory be to heaven! The most beautiful sight in the world! The *Dolphin,* moving down toward Wright's Island on a steady breeze.

Kit leaped to her feet. "Hannah! Wake up! Look —look there!" Her stiff lips could scarcely babble. She flung her arms into the air, waving wildly. She could hear a man's voice across the water, but the fog rolled tantalizingly between her and the ship. She tore off her petticoat and waved it hysterically. But she dared not shout, and if she could not attract their notice the *Dolphin* would sail past down the river and their chance would be gone.

Kicking off her shoes, Kit waded into the water, plunged in and struck out toward the ship. It was a very short swim, but she had overdrawn her strength for days past. She was panting when the black hull loomed over her head, and at first she could barely raise her voice above the wash of the ship. She drew a careful breath and tried again.

There was a cry above her and a sound of running feet. "Ahoy! All hands! Man overboard!"

" 'Tis a woman!"

"Hold on there, ma'am, we're coming!"

She heard shouted orders; a thumping and creaking of ropes. Then the lifeboat swung out over her head and lowered with a smack into the water. Nat and the redheaded sailor were inside, and she had never before been so happy to see anyone.

"I knew it," groaned the redheaded one, as she clung, gasping, to the side of the boat.

"Kit! What kind of a game is this?"

"Hannah—she's in terrible trouble, Nat. They burned her house. Please—can you take her on the *Dolphin?*"

They dragged her over the side of the boat. "Where is she?" Nat demanded. "Tell the captain to heave to!" he yelled up toward the deck. "We're going ashore."

"There," pointed Kit, "by that pile of logs. We've been there all night. I didn't know what to do, and when I saw the ship—" All at once she was sobbing and babbling like a three-year-old, about the witch hunt, and the chase through the cornfield, and the man who had come so close. Nat's hands closed over hers hard and steady.

" 'Tis all right, Kit," he said, over and over. "We'll take you both on and get you some dry clothes. Just hold on a few minutes more till we get Hannah." The boat scraped the shore.

Still dazed, Hannah accepted the miracle and the prospect of a journey like a docile child. Then after two shaky steps she turned obstinate. She would not set foot in the boat without her cat.

"I can't go off without her," she insisted. "I just can't, and thee ought to know that, Nat. She'd just grieve her heart out with no home to go to and me gone off on a ship."

"Then I'll get her," said Nat. "You wait here, and keep quiet, both of you."

Kit was outraged. If she had been Nat she would have picked Hannah up and carried her off in the boat with no more nonsense. As he strode up the bank, she scrambled after him through the wet underbrush. "You're crazy, Nat!" she protested, her teeth chattering with cold. "No cat is worth it. You've got to get her out of here. If you could have heard those people—"

"If she's set on that cat she's going to have it. They've taken everything else." Nat stood in the midst of the charred cinders that had been the little house. "Damn them!" he choked. "Curse all of them!" He kicked a smoldering log viciously.

They searched the trampled garden and presently they heard a cautious miaow. The yellow cat inched warily from beneath a pumpkin vine. She did not take to the idea of capture. They had to stalk her, one on each side of the garden, and Nat finally dived full length under a bush, dragged the cat out, and wrapped it tightly in his own shirt. Back at the shore Hannah received the writhing bundle with joy and climbed obediently into the rowboat.

"Where are we going, Nat?" she asked trustfully.

"I'm taking you to Saybrook for a visit with my grandmother. You'll be good company for her, Hannah. Come on, Kit. Father will go on without us."

"I'm not going, Nat. All I wanted was to see Hannah safe."

Nat straightened up. "I think you'd better, Kit," he said quietly. " 'Till this thing blows over, at least. This is our last trip before winter. We'll find a place for you in Saybrook and bring you back first trip next spring."

Kit shook her head.

"Or you can go on to the West Indies with us."

Barbados! The tears sprang to her eyes. "I can't, Nat. I have to stay here."

The concern in his eyes hardened to awareness. "Of course," he said courteously. "I forgot. You're going to be married."

" 'Tis Mercy," she stammered. "She's terribly ill. I couldn't go, I just couldn't, not knowing—"

Nat looked intently at her, and took one step nearer. The blue eyes were very close. "Kit—"

"Ahoy, there!" There was a bellow from the *Dolphin*. "What's keeping you?"

"Nat, quick! They'll hear the shouting!"

Nat jumped into the boat. "You'll be all right? You need to get warm—"

"I'll go home now. Only hurry—"

She stood watching as the boat pulled away from the sand. Halfway to the ship Nat turned to stare back at her. Then he raised an arm silently. Kit raised her own arm to wave back, and then she turned and started back along the shore. She dared not wait to see them reach the *Dolphin*. In another moment she would lose every shred of commonsense and pride and fling herself into the water after the rowboat and plead with them not to leave her behind.

Though it was long past daybreak now, her luck still held. She met no one in the north field. Once she dodged behind a brushpile as the town herder came by with some cows to pasture. She reached the house without further danger. The shed door was still unbolted, and she let herself in and crept noiselessly through the house. She heard a murmur of voices, and as she reached the hallway the door to the kitchen opened.

"Is that you, Kit?" Aunt Rachel peered at her. "We decided to let you sleep, poor child. Dr. Bulkeley has been here all night. Praise God—he says the fever is broken!"

In her joy and weariness, Aunt Rachel did not even notice the sodden dress and hair under Kit's woolen cloak.

CHAPTER EIGHTEEN

IN DRY CLOTHES, with some hot corn mush and molasses inside her, Kit leaned against the back of the settle and soaked in the warmth of the fire. Lightheaded with weariness and relief, she looked around the familiar room. How beautiful and safe it looked, with the sunshine slanting in the window! The regular breathing from Mercy's curtained bed sounded almost normal. Dr. Bulkeley had said that Judith might get up this morning. Rachel had consented to go up to her own bed for a short sleep, on their promise to waken her at once if Mercy should rouse, and Matthew was preparing to get back to his work.

Watching him draw on his heavy boots, Kit knew that she could not let him go without speaking. All night, just beyond the fringe of her thoughts, through the terror of the hunt and the long cold hours of waiting, she had cherished one small warming memory. There on the beach it had been the one thing that had held her back when Nat had offered her a chance to escape. She had to make sure that this memory was rightfully hers. She got up shakily, and went to stand before her uncle.

"Uncle Matthew," she said softly. "I heard what you said last night to those people, and I want to thank you for it."

" 'Tis no matter," he answered gruffly.

"But it is a matter," she insisted. "I've been nothing but a trouble to you from the beginning, and I don't deserve your standing up for me."

Her uncle studied her from under his bushy eyebrows. " 'Tis true I did not welcome you into my house," he said at last. "But this last week you have proved me wrong. You haven't spared yourself, Katherine. Our own daughter couldn't have done more."

Suddenly Kit wished, with all her heart, that she had never deceived this man. She would like to stand here before him with a clear conscience. She was ashamed of the many times—more times than she could count—when she had skipped off and left her work undone.

I shall tell him some day, she vowed to herself, when I am sure that Hannah is safe. And I will do my full share, beginning this very moment. I don't even feel tired any more.

She helped Judith into her clothes and drew a

chair for her near the sunny window. She drew a great kettle of water from the well and set it to boil for the wash. She swept up the scuffed sand and spread a fresh layer in a fine pattern. She stirred up a corncake for the midday meal. Hannah was safe, and Mercy was going to get well. That should be enough, and surely if she worked hard enough she could forget this strange feeling of emptiness, the haunting regret that a secret and lovely thing was gone forever.

Matthew came back presently for the noon meal. Kit thrust the iron peel into the oven and drew out the corncake, plump and golden and crisp about the edges, and Judith said the smell of it made her feel hungry for the first time. Mercy stirred and asked, in a quite natural voice, for a sip of water, and Rachel's haggard face lighted with a smile.

They were not alarmed this time by the knock on the door. Matthew went to answer it, and the others sat calmly at the table. They heard the scuff of boots in the hallway, and a man's voice.

"We have business with you, Matthew."

"There is illness here," he answered.

"This can't wait. Better summon your wife, too, and that girl from Barbados. We'll be brief as we can."

The men stood aside to let Rachel and Kit walk ahead into the company room. There were four callers, one a deacon from the church, the constable of the town, and Goodman Cruff and his wife. They were not excited this morning. They looked hard and purposeful, and Goodwife Cruff's eyes glittered toward Kit with contempt and something else she could not interpret.

"I know you don't hold with witchcraft," the constable began, "but we've summat to say as may change your mind."

"You arrested your witch?" asked Matthew with impatience.

"Not that. The town's rid of that one for good."

Matthew stared at him in alarm. "What have you done?"

"Not what you fear. We didn't lay hands on the old woman. She slipped through our trap somehow."

"And we know how!" hissed Goodwife Cruff. Kit felt a wave of fear that left her sick and dizzy.

The deacon glanced at Goodwife Cruff uneasily. "I don't quite go along with them," he said. "But I got to admit the thing looks mighty queer. We've combed the whole town this morning, ever since dawn. There's not a trace of her. Don't see how she could have got far."

"We know right enough. They'll never find her!" broke in Goodwife Cruff. "No use trying to shush me. Adam Cruff, you tell them what we saw!"

Her husband cleared his throat. "I didn't rightly see it myself," he apologized. "But there's some as saw that big yeller cat of hers come arunnin' out of the house. Couple of fellers took a shot at it. But the ones as got a good look claims it had a great fat mouse in its mouth, and it never let go, even when the bullets came after it."

His wife drew a hissing breath. *That mouse was Hannah Tupper!* 'Tis not the first time she's changed herself into a creature. They say when the moon is full—"

"Now hold on a minute, Matthew," cautioned the constable at Matthew's scornful gesture, "you can't gainsay it. There's things happen we better not look at too close. The woman's gone, and I say good riddance."

"She's gone straight back to Satan!" pronounced Goodwife Cruff, *"but she's left another to do her work!"*

Kit could have laughed out loud, but a look at Goodwife Cruff sobered her. The woman's eyes were fastened on her face with a cunning triumph.

"They found summat when they searched her place. Better take a look at this, Matthew." The constable drew something shining from his pocket. It was the little silver hornbook.

"What is it?" asked Matthew.

"Looks like a sort of hornbook."

"Who ever saw a hornbook like that?" demanded Goodman Cruff. " 'Tis the devil's own writing."

"Has the Lord's Prayer on it," the constable reminded him. "Look at the letters on the handle, Matthew."

Matthew took the thing in his hands reluctantly and turned it over.

"Ask *her* where it came from," jibed Goodwife Cruff, unable to keep silent.

There was a harsh gasp from Rachel. Matthew lifted his eyes from the hornbook to his niece's white face. "Can this be yours, Katherine?" he asked.

Kit's lips were stiff. "Yes sir," she answered faintly.

"Did you know you had lost it? Was it stolen from you?"

"No sir. I knew it was there. I—I took it there myself."

"Why?"

Kit looked from one grim waiting face to another. Did they know about Prudence? If not, she must be

179

very careful. "It—it was a sort of present," she said lamely.

"A present to the widow?"

"Not exactly—"

"You mean she had some sort of hold over you—some blackmail?"

"Oh no! Hannah was a friend of mine! I'm sorry, Uncle Matthew, I meant to tell you, truly I did, as soon as I could. I used to go to see her, on the way home from the meadow. Sometimes I took things to her—my own things, I mean." Poor Rachel, how that apple tart must be torturing her conscience!

"I don't understand this, Katherine. I forbade you —you understood it perfectly—to go to that woman's house."

"I know. But Hannah needed me, and I needed her. She wasn't a witch, Uncle Matthew. If you could only have known her—"

Matthew looked back at the constable. "I am chagrined," he said with dignity, "that I have not controlled my own household. But the girl is young and ignorant. I hold myself to blame for my laxness."

"Take no blame to yourself, Matthew." The constable rose to his feet. "I'm sorry, what with your daughter sick and all, but we've got to lock this girl up."

"Oh no!" burst out Rachel. "You can't let them, Matthew!"

"Since when," asked Matthew, his eyes flashing, "do you lock up a girl for disobedience? That is for me to settle."

"Not disobedience. This girl is charged with witchcraft."

"That is ridiculous!" thundered Matthew.

"Watch your words, man. The girl has admitted to

being a friend to the witch. And there is a complaint against her, made according to law and signed."

"Who dared to sign such a charge?"

"I signed it!" shouted Goodman Cruff. "The girl put a spell on half the children in this town, and I'll see her brought into court if it's the last thing I ever do!"

Matthew looked defeated. "Where do you aim to take her?" he asked.

"Shed back of my place will do. There's no proper jail short of Hartford, and I've lost near a day's work already."

"Wait a minute. How long do you intend to keep her?"

"Till the trial. When Sam Talcott gets back tomorrow he'll likely examine her with the ministers present. That's what they did to Goody Harrison and that Johnson woman. Been twenty years since we had a witch case hereabouts. Reckon there'll be a jury trial in Hartford."

"Suppose I give you my word that until Captain Talcott returns I'll keep her locked in her room upstairs?"

"What good is his word?" demanded Goodwife Cruff. "Has he known where she was these past months?" She wants to see me in jail, Kit thought. She felt numbed by the hatred in the woman's eyes.

"I'd trust you all right," the constable considered. "But they's some I don't trust. They was out of their minds down there last night. One more death in this town and I won't be responsible for what happens. The girl will be safe with me, that I warrant."

Rachel started forward, but Matthew motioned her back. "Get her coat," he ordered. They stood waiting silently in the hallway while Rachel climbed the stairs, weeping, and came back with her own woolen cloak.

"Yours feels damp," she quavered. "Keep this on you, Kit. It may be cold in that place."

The Cruffs walked behind them all the way along High Street, down Carpenter's Lane to the constable's house, and stood by till they saw Kit safely in the shed and heard with their own ears the heavy bolt drop in place outside the door.

The shed was entirely empty save for a pile of straw in one corner of the dirt floor. There was no window, but the rough boards let in chinks of daylight as well as drafts of cold November air. Kit leaned against the doorpost and let the tears run down her cheeks.

Toward late afternoon, when one side of the shed was already deep in shadows, she heard footsteps, the bolt drew back, and the constable's face peered through the door.

"Brought some supper," he growled. "And my wife sent this." He thrust toward her a heavy quilt, none too clean even in that dim light, but a gesture of kindness nonetheless.

"We never had a girl in here before," he explained uneasily. "Funny thing. I'd never a picked you for a witch. But you can't tell."

"Please," Kit ventured. "Those other women you spoke of—Goody Harrison and the other? What happened to them?"

"Goody Harrison was banished from the colony. They hanged Goody Johnson." Then seeing the horror that blanched her face he reconsidered.

"I hardly think they'd be so hard on you," he consoled her. "Being you're so young and the first offense.

More likely brand you, or cut off an ear." He slammed shut the door again.

Whatever might be in that wooden bowl, she had no heart even to taste it. She had begun to shake again, and the quilt did not warm her. She had never in all her life known the feeling of a locked door. It was all she could do to hold herself from pounding against it and screaming.

If she should scream, who would hear her? Who was there anywhere who could help her? John Holbrook perhaps. In his quiet way he had a sort of strength and conviction. They might have listened to John. But he was far away in the wilderness of Massachusetts. Nat Eaton? He was halfway down the river, and banished from town as well. William? Why of course! William could help her. Why hadn't she thought of him at once? Anything William said would carry weight in the town. His position, his character, were unquestioned. Could the magistrate for one moment hold the Cruffs' word against a man like William?

The thought steadied her. She thought of him coming to champion her, confident, unruffled, those wide dependable shoulders like a fortress between her and the angry face of Goodwife Cruff. Dear dependable William! Perhaps he would come tonight. Kit drew a deep breath, and sitting on the floor, her knees drawn tight against her chest, she waited for William.

It was Rachel who finally came instead. Long after dark Kit heard her whisper outside the shed wall, so timid and faint that at first she thought she must have imagined it.

"Kit? Can you hear me? Are you all to rights?"

"Yes! Oh, Aunt Rachel, you shouldn't have left them!"

"I had to know how you are. I knew you'd want to know, Kit. Dr. Bulkeley says Mercy's fever is nearly gone."

"I'm so glad. I wanted to help, and now I've left it all for you to do. Oh, Aunt Rachel—can you ever forgive me?"

"Shush, child. 'Tis myself I can't forgive. To think I knew all along you were going to that place and I never spoke up."

"I'd have kept going anyway. But I never knew I'd shame you all like this. Aunt Rachel—what do they do to witches?"

There was a small sound outside the boards. "Nothing, child," whispered Rachel. "They won't do anything to you. We'll think of something." But she had not spoken fast enough—that little sobbing catch of breath had answered first. "The inquiry will be in the morning. Have courage, dear! But you've got to help us, Kit. If there's something you haven't told, something you're holding back, you must tell everything." How much courage must it have taken for Rachel to brave her husband's anger, and the dark and the strange terror of a prison shed!

"I wish I could get some food in to you. Are you very frightened, Kit dear?"

"Not now," lied Kit. "Not now that you've come. Thank you, Aunt Rachel."

Sustained by her aunt's visit, Kit was able to face the morrow with less panic. She sat down and forced herself to take stock of her chances. She couldn't imagine that they could have much evidence against her. But it didn't seem to take much evidence to rouse these people's suspicions. What had poor Hannah ever done to harm them? Goodwife Cruff had hated her ever since that first day on the *Dolphin*, and she would never rest now till she had her vengeance. Nobody in the town would have much sympathy for a disobedient girl. If only she could have obeyed her impulse this morning and told her uncle the whole story. Though perhaps he too was helpless. She saw now that she had undermined his authority in all eyes by flouting his orders.

Suppose they discovered that Prudence too had disobeyed? It did not bear thinking. And she was entirely responsible for Prudence's actions, Kit admitted with a sick heart. Who had inveigled the child with promises, and thought of the hiding place under the willow tree, and persuaded her—no dragged her against her will—to meet Hannah? Oh, why hadn't she seen what she was doing? How could she have been so wicked? What difference did it make whether Prudence could read or not, when she was half starved and beaten and overworked?

If I wanted to neglect my own work, Kit groaned in remorse, I might at least have been out in the Cruffs' field helping the poor child!

And yet, how lovely it had been, that last afternoon in the cabin. Leaning her forehead on her knees, Kit could almost feel herself there again. She could hear the crackling of the flames, the bubbling of the stew in the kettle, the scratching of the pen in Prudence's fingers, the creak creak of Hannah's chair and the drowsy purring of the yellow cat. She could see the glow of the fire, but she could not feel its warmth. It was like gazing in at a window, from the cold outside, at a forbidden room she could never enter again.

She had not slept all the night before on the beach.

Now, huddled inside the ragged quilt, she was sucked down, in spite of herself, into a black whirlpool of slumber, where nightmare phantoms whirled with her, nearer and nearer, toward some unknown horror.

CHAPTER NINETEEN

THE SUN had been slanting through the chinks in the shed wall for hours when Kit heard the heavy bolt withdrawn and the shed door opened. This time it was the constable's wife, with a wooden trencher of mush. In spite of its dubious appearance it sent a faint curl of steam into the frosty air, and Kit forced herself to take a few spoonfuls while the woman stood watching, hands on her hips.

"I reckoned you'd be half froze," the woman observed. "To tell the truth I couldn't sleep half the night thinking of you out here. 'Tis good enough for thieves and drunkards, I says to my man, but 'tis no place for a female, witch or no. I've seen the girl in Meeting, I says, sitting there decent as you please, and it goes against reason she could be a witch. There's some folks in this town always bent on stirring up trouble."

Kit looked up at her gratefully. " 'Twas good of you to send the quilt," she said. "How long will they keep me here, do you think?"

"My man has orders to take you to the Town House in an hour."

So soon! Kit put down the spoon, her stomach curling. "What will happen there?"

"The magistrate and the ministers will examine you. If they think you be guilty they'll send you on to Hartford to wait trial. At any rate, you'll be off our hands. My man and I, we don't relish this work much. We'll be glad when his term is up."

Kit laid down the trencher in dismay. "But I can't go like this! I've been sitting in the dirt all night!" The face she lifted to the woman was even sorrier than she realized, streaked with mud and tears.

"You're no treat to look at, that's sure," the woman admitted. "If they took you for a witch right now I'd scarce blame them. Wait a minute."

She went away, taking the precaution of bolting the door securely, and returned presently with a basin of water and a rough wooden comb. Gratefully, Kit did what she could to make herself respectable. The dress, dirty and crumpled, could not be helped.

It required the constable and two sturdy members of the Watch to conduct a timid witch up Carpenter's Lane, along Broad Street, up Hungry Hill to the Town House. The small building seemed full of people as she entered. Benches and chairs along the two walls were crowded with men from the town, with here and there a sharp-faced woman, cronies of Goodwife Cruff. At a table at the end of the room sat Captain Samuel Talcott, Magistrate from Wethersfield to the General Court of Connecticut, and a group of men whom Kit knew as the town selectmen. Her uncle sat in his place among them, his lips tight, his eyebrows drawn fiercely together. What anguish it must cost him, Kit thought with shame, to have to sit here and pass judgment on a member of his own household. At the opposite end of the table sat the two ministers, Reverend John Woodbridge and Dr. Gershom Bulkeley, both famed for their relentless sermons against witchcraft. Kit's heart sank. There was no one, no one in the whole room, save her uncle, who would speak a word in her defense. William had not come.

Captain Talcott rapped on the table and a hush fell over the room. "Good folk, we will proceed at once to the business at hand. We have come here in order to inquire and search into the matter of Mistress Katherine Tyler, lately of Barbados, who is accused by sundry witnesses of the practice of witchcraft. Mistress Tyler will come forward."

Prompted by the constable's elbow, Kit got to her feet and moved haltingly across the room to stand facing the magistrate across the table.

"You will listen to the charge against you."

A clerk read from a parchment, giving full weight and due to every awful word.

"Katherine Tyler, thou art here accused that not having the fear of God before thine eyes thou hast had familiarity with Satan the grand enemy of God and man, and that by his instigation and help thou hast in a preternatural way afflicted and done harm to the bodies and estates of sundry of His Majesty's subjects, in the third year of His Majesty's reign, for which by the law of God and the law of the Colony thou deservest to die."

There was a murmur along the benches. Kit's hands felt icy, but she kept her eyes steadily on the magistrate.

"Mistress Tyler, you are accused by Adam Cruff

with the following actions. Firstly that you were the familiar friend and companion of the Widow Hannah Tupper of Blackbird Pond, an alleged witch who has within the past week disappeared in a suspicious manner. Such friendship is a lawful test of guilt, inasmuch as it is well known that witchcraft is an art that may be learned and conveyed from one person to another, and that it has often fallen out that a witch, upon dying, leaveth some heir to her witchcraft.

"Secondly, that you are guilty of actions and works which infer a court with the devil, which have caused illness and death to fall upon many innocent children in this town."

The clerk sat down. Captain Talcott eyed the girl before him. Quite plainly he had a distaste for the duty at hand, but his stern soldierly countenance did not soften.

"Mistress Tyler," he said, "you have heard the complaints against you. We will proceed with the first accusation. Is it true that you were a friend and companion of the Widow Tupper?"

For a moment Kit feared that her voice would not come. "Yes, sir," she managed shakily.

"Is it true that on sundry occasions during the summer you have entered her house and visited with her?"

"Yes, sir."

"Is it true that you were also acquainted with a certain cat which the widow entertained as a familiar spirit?"

"It—it was just an ordinary cat, sir, like any cat."

"You will answer yes or no. Is it true that you have engaged with the Widow Tupper in various enchantments with the direct intent of causing mischief to certain people?"

"Oh no, sir! I don't know what you mean by enchantments."

"Do you deny that on a certain day in August last, on passing the pasture of Goodman Whittlesley you cast a spell upon his cattle so that they were rooted to the ground where they stood and refused to answer his call or to give any milk on that evening?"

"I—I don't understand, sir. How could I do such a thing?"

"Goodman Whittlesley, will you repeat your complaint for this assembly?"

Her head reeling, Kit stood helpless as, one after the other, they rose and made their complaints, these men and women whom she scarcely recognized. The evidence rolled against her like a dark wave.

One man's child had cried aloud all night that someone was sticking pins into him. Another child had seen a dark creature with horns at the foot of her bed. A woman who lived along South Road testified that one morning Kit had stopped and spoken to her child and that within ten minutes the child had fallen into a fit and lain ill for five days. Another woman testified that one afternoon last September she had been sitting in the window, sewing a jacket for her husband, when she had looked up and seen Kit walking past her house, staring up at the window in a strange manner. Whereupon, try as she would, the sleeve would never set right in the jacket. A man swore he had seen Kit and Goody Tupper dance round a fire in the meadow one moonlit night, and that a great black man, taller than an Indian, had suddenly appeared from nowhere and joined in the dance.

Matthew Wood leaped suddenly to his feet. "I protest this mockery!" he roared, in a voice that silenced every whisper. "Not one word of this nonsense could be proved in the Court of Assistants. There is not one shred of lawful evidence in the lot! I beg you, Sam Talcott, make an end of it!"

"Do I infer that you are willing to vouch for your niece's good character, Matthew Wood?"

"Certainly. I will vouch for it."

"We are to understand then that these visits to the Widow Tupper were taken with your approval?"

Taken aback, Matthew glared at the magistrate. "No, I had no knowledge of them," he admitted.

"Did you ever, at any time, indicate to your niece that she was not to associate with this woman?"

"Yes, I forbade her to go."

"Then the girl has been disobedient and deceitful."

Matthew clenched his fists in frustration. "The girl has been thoughtless and headstrong at times. But her upbringing has been such as to encourage that."

"You admit then that her education has been irregular?"

"You can twist what I say as you will, Sam Talcott," said Matthew in steely anger. "But I swear before all present, on my word as a freeman of the colony, that the girl is no witch."

"We are obliged to listen to the testimony, Matthew," said Captain Talcott reasonably. "I will thank you to keep silent. What is your opinion of the case, Dr. Bulkeley?"

Dr. Bulkeley cleared his throat. "In my opinion," he said deliberately, "it is necessary to use the greatest caution in the matter of testimony. Since the unnatural events so far recounted appear to rest in each case upon the word of but one witness, the legality of any one of them is open to question."

"It is ridiculous to talk of legality," interrupted Matthew. "There has not one word been spoken that makes sense!"

For the last few moments Goodwife Cruff had been vehemently prodding her husband. He rose now obediently. "Sir, I've summat to say as makes sense," he announced, assuming a bold tone, "and there's more than one witness to prove it. I've got summat here as was found in the widow's house that night."

With a sinking heart Kit watched as he drew an object from his pocket. It was not the hornbook, as she expected. It was the little copybook. At sight of it Goodwife Cruff's anger burst through all restraints.

"Look at that!" she demanded. "What do you say about that? My Prudence's name, written over and over. 'Tis a spell, that's what it is! A mercy the child is alive today. Another hour and she'd have been dying like the others!"

The magistrate accepted the copybook reluctantly, as though it were tainted.

"Do you recognize this book, Mistress Tyler?"

Kit could barely stand upright. She tried to answer, but only a hoarse whisper came out.

"Speak up, girl!" he ordered sharply. "Does this book belong to you?"

"Yes sir," she managed.

"Did you write this name?"

Kit could barely swallow. She had vowed she would never deceive her uncle again! Then, remembering, she looked back at the copybook. Yes, the name on the first line was in her own hand, large and clear for Prudence to copy. "Yes sir," she said, her voice loud with relief. "I wrote the name."

Matthew Wood passed a hand over his eyes. He

looked old, old and ill as he had looked that day beside Mercy's bed.

"Why should you write a child's name over and over like that?"

"I—I can't tell you sir."

Captain Talcott looked perplexed. "There are no other children's names here," he said. "Why did you choose to write the name of Prudence Cruff?"

Kit was silent.

"Mistress Tyler." The magistrate spoke to her directly. "I had considered this morning's inquiry merely a formality. I did not expect to find any evidence worthy of carrying to the court. But this is a serious matter. You must explain to us how this child's name came to be written."

As Kit looked back at him mutely, the restraints that held the tensely waiting crowd gave way. Men and women leaped to their feet, screaming.

"She won't answer! That proves she's guilty!"

"She's a witch! She's as good as admitted it!"

"We don't need a jury trial. Put her to the water test!"

"Hanging's too good for her!"

In the midst of the pandemonium Gershom Bulkeley quietly reached for the copybook, studied it carefully, and turned a shrewd, deliberative eye upon Kit. Then he whispered something to the magistrate. Captain Talcott nodded.

"Silence!" he barked. "This is the Colony of Connecticut! Every man and woman is entitled to a trial before a jury. This case will be turned over to the General Session in Hartford. The inquiry is dismissed."

"Hold a minute, Captain!" called a voice. A commotion near the door had been scarcely noticed.

'There's a fellow here says he has an important witness for the case."

Every voice was suddenly stilled. Almost paralyzed with dread, Kit turned slowly to face a new accuser. On the threshold of the room stood Nat Eaton, slim, straight-shouldered, without a trace of mockery in his level blue eyes.

Nat! The wave of joy and relief was so unexpected that she almost lost her balance, but almost instantly it drained away and left a new fear. For she saw that beside him, clinging tightly to his hand, was Prudence Cruff.

Goodwife Cruff let out a piercing scream. "Take her out of here! The witch will put an evil eye on her!" She and her husband both started forward.

"Stand back!" ordered the magistrate. "The child is protected here. Where is the witness?"

Nat put his hands on the child's shoulders and gently urged her forward. With one trusting look up at his face, Prudence walked steadily toward the magistrate's table.

Suddenly Kit found her voice. "Oh please sir!" she cried, the tears rushing down her face, "let them take her away! It is all my fault! I would do anything to undo it if I could! I never meant any harm, but I'm responsible for all of it. Please—take me to Hartford. Do what you want with me. But—oh, I beg you—send Prudence away from this horrible place!"

The magistrate waited till this outburst was over. " 'Tis a trifle late to think about the child," he said coldly. "Come here, child."

Kit sank on her knees and buried her face in her hands. The buzz in the room roared like a swarm of bees around her head. Then there was a waiting hush. She could scarcely bear to look at Prudence, but she forced herself to raise her head. The child was barefoot and her snarled hair was uncovered. Her thin arms, under the skimpy jumper, were blue with cold. Then Kit stared again. There was something strange about Prudence.

"Will you stand there, child, in front of the table?" Captain Talcott spoke reassuringly.

Watching Prudence, Kit suddenly felt a queer prickling along her spine. There *was* something different about her. The child's head was up. Her eyes were fastened levelly on the magistrate. Prudence was not afraid!

"We will ask you some questions, Prudence," said the magistrate quietly. "You will answer them as truthfully as you possibly can. Do you understand?"

"Yes sir," whispered Prudence.

"Do you know this young woman?"

"Oh yes, sir. She is my teacher. She taught me to read."

"You mean at the dame school?"

"No, I never went to the dame school."

"Then where did she teach you?"

"At Hannah's house in the meadow."

A loud scream from Goodwife Cruff tore across the room.

"You mean Mistress Tyler took you to Hannah Tupper's house?"

"The first time she took me there. After that I went by myself."

"The little weasel!" cried Goodwife Cruff. "That's where she was all those days. I'll see that girl hung!"

It is all over, thought Kit, with a wave of faintness.

Gershom Bulkeley still held the little copybook. He spoke now, under his breath, and passed the book to Captain Talcott.

"Have you ever seen this book before?" the magistrate questioned.

"Oh yes, sir. Kit gave it to me. I wrote my name in it."

"That's a lie!" cried Goodwife Cruff. "The child is bewitched!"

Captain Talcott turned to Kit. "Is it true," he asked her, "that the child wrote her own name in this book?"

Kit dragged herself to her feet. " 'Tis true," she answered dully. "I wrote it for her once and then she copied it."

"You can't take her word for anything, sir," protested Goodman Cruff timidly. "The child don't know what she's saying. I might as well tell it, Prudence has never been what you'd call bright. She never could learn much."

The magistrate paid no attention. "Could you write your name again, do you think?"

"I—I think so, sir."

He dipped the quill pen carefully in the ink and handed it to the child. Leaning over the table, Prudence set the pen on the copybook. For a moment there was not a single sound in the room but the hesitant scratching.

Goodman Cruff was on his feet. Propelled by a curiosity greater than any awe for the magistrate, he came slowly across the room and peered over his child's shoulder.

"Is that proper writing?" he demanded in unbelief. "Prudence Cruff, does it say, right out as it should?"

The magistrate glanced at the writing and handed the copybook to Gershom Bulkeley.

"Very proper writing, I should say," Dr. Bulkeley commented, "for a child with no learning."

The magistrate leaned to take the pen out of the small fingers. Goodman Cruff tiptoed back to the bench. The bluster was gone from him. He looked dazed.

"Now Prudence," the magistrate continued. "You say that Mistress Tyler taught you to read?"

"What sort of reading?" Goodwife Cruff rose in a frenzy. "Magic signs and spells I tell you! The child would never know the difference."

Gershom Bulkeley also rose to his feet. "That at least will be easy to prove," he suggested reasonably. "What can you read, child?"

"I can read the Bible."

Dr. Bulkeley picked up the Great Bible from the table and turned the pages thoughtfully. Then, moving to hand the Book to Prudence, he realized that it was too heavy for her to hold and laid it carefully on the table beside her. "Read that for us, child, beginning right there."

Kit held her breath. Was it the tick of the great clock that sounded so frightening, or her own heart? Then across the silence came a whisper.

"Buy the truth, and sell it not;
also wis-wisdom, and in-in-instruction, and
understanding."

The childish voice slowly gained strength and clarity till it reached every corner of the room.

"The father of the right-righteous shall greatly rejoice; and he that begetteth a wish child shall have joy of him. Thy father and thy mother shall be glad, and she that bare thee shall rejoice."

197

In the warm rush of pride that welled up in her, Kit forgot her fear. For the first time she dared to look back at Nat Eaton where he stood near the door. Across the room their eyes met, and suddenly it was as though he had thrown a line straight into her reaching hands. She could feel the pull of it, and over its taut span strength flowed into her, warm and sustaining.

When finally she looked away she realized that everyone in the room was staring at the two parents. They had both leaned forward, their mouths open in shock and unbelief. As she listened, Goodwife Cruff's face darkened and her eyes narrowed. She saw now that she had been tricked. The fresh anger that was gathering would be vented on her child.

On the father's face a new emotion seemed to be struggling. As the thin voice ended, Goodwife Cruff drew in her breath through her teeth in a venomous hiss. But before she could release it her husband sprang forward.

"Did you hear that?" he demanded widely, of everyone present. All at once his shoulders straightened. "That was real good reading. I'd like to see any boy in this town do better!"

"It's a trick!" denied his wife. "That child could never read a word in her life! She's bewitched, I tell you!"

"Hold your tongue, woman," shouted her husband unexpectedly. "I'm sick and tired of hearing about Prudence being bewitched. All these years you been telling me our child was half-witted. Why, she's smart as a whip. I bet it warn't much of a trick to teach her to read."

Goodwife Cruff's jaw dropped. For one moment she was struck utterly dumb, and in that moment her husband stepped into his rightful place. There was a new authority in his voice.

"All my life I've wished I could read. If I'd had a son, I'd of seen to it he learned his letters. Well, this is a new country over here, and who says it may not be just as needful for a woman to read as a man? Might give her summat to think about besides witches and foolishness. Any rate, I got someone now to read the Good Book to me of an evening, and if that's the work of the devil, then I say 'tis a mighty queer thing for the devil to go working against himself!"

The magistrate had not interrupted this speech. There was a glint of amusement in his eye as he asked, "I take it then, Goodman Cruff, that you withdraw your charges against this young woman?"

"Yes," he answered loudly. "Yes. I'll withdraw the charges."

"Adam Cruff!" His wife had found her voice. "Have ye lost your senses? The girl has bewitched you too!"

In the back of the room someone tittered. A man's laugh rang out—was it Nat's? All at once, like a clap of thunder, the tension of the room broke into laughter that shook the timbers and rattled the windows. Every man in the room was secretly applauding Adam Cruff's declaration of independence. Even the magistrate's stern lips twisted slightly.

"There seems to be no evidence of witchcraft," he announced, when order had been restored. "The girl has admitted her wrong in encouraging a child to willful disobedience. Beyond that I cannot see that there is any reasonable charge against her. I pronounce that Mistress Katherine Tyler is free and innocent."

But suddenly Goodwife Cruff's anger found a new outlet. "That man!" she shrilled. "Isn't he the seaman? The one who was banished for setting fire to houses? Thirty lashes they promised him if he showed his face here again!"

There was renewed uproar. The constable looked to the magistrate for orders. Captain Talcott hesitated, then shrugged his shoulders. "Arrest him," he snapped. "The sentence still stands."

"Oh no!" Kit pleaded in alarm. "You can't arrest him, when he only came back to help me."

With a shrewd look at his niece, Matthew Wood interceded for her. " 'Tiz the truth, Sam," he observed. "The lad risked the penalty to see justice done. I suggest you remit the sentence."

"A good suggestion," agreed the magistrate, relieved to have an end to the matter. But Nat had slipped out of the room and his halfhearted pursuers reported not a single trace of him.

"They won't find him," a voice whispered in Kit's ear. A small hand crept into hers. "He's got a fast little pinnace hidden on the riverbank. He told me to say goodbye to you if he had to hurry away."

"Prudence!" Kit's knees had suddenly turned to water. "How—how did it all happen?"

"He came and found me this morning. He said he got worrying about you and came back and sort of spied around till he heard about the meeting. He said I was the only one could save you, and he promised he would stay right here and help as long as we needed him."

"Oh I'm so grateful to both of you!" Kit's tears started again. "And I'm so proud of you, Prudence! Will you be all right, do you think?"

"She'll be all right." Goodman Cruff, coming to claim his daughter, had overheard. "Time somebody looked after her so's she won't need to run off any more. Next summer she'll go to your school, like I always wanted."

"Goodwife Cruff," the magistrate called back the departing woman. "I remind you that the penalty for slander is heavy. A fine of thirty pounds or three hours in the stocks. Mistress Tyler would be within her rights to press her own charges."

"Oh no!" gasped Kit.

Matthew Wood stood beside her. "Let us make an end of this," he said. "We have no desire to press charges. With your permission, Captain, I shall take Katherine home."

CHAPTER TWENTY

THE DAY of the first snowfall Mercy got out of bed. Judith, venturing outside as far as the well, came back, her cheeks glowing, with bits of feathery white clinging to her cloak and to her dark curls.

" 'Tis snowing!" she announced.

"Snowing!" Mercy struggled up on one elbow, her voice eager. "Come, let me touch it, Judith!" Judith drew near the bed, and held out her sleeve. The flecks of white vanished under Mercy's reverent fingertip.

"I must see it!" Mercy insisted. "Just for a moment, Mother. I can't miss the first snowfall."

It took much preparation, as though for a long

journey. Two pairs of knitted wool stockings between her feet and the cold boards, the blue shawl wrapped securely about her ears, and a heavy quilt swaddled around her from head to foot. They formed a little procession, Rachel and Judith supporting the invalid at each elbow, and Kit following behind to hold up the trailing ends of the quilt from the sanded floor. Very slowly they crossed the room to the front window, and Mercy sank weakly into a chair and rested her chin against the window frame.

Outside, the gray afternoon was speckled with drifting white. Already a thin powdery dusting had gathered in the wagon ruts of the road. The flakes fell softly, vanishing in the heaps of brown leaves, swirling in little smoky coils.

"I love the first snowfall better than anything in the world," sighed Mercy, her eyes worshipful.

"I can't imagine why," said Judith practically. "It means you can scarcely step foot out the door again till spring."

"I know. But 'tis so beautiful. And it makes the house seem so warm and safe. To think that Kit has never seen snow before! Go to the door, Kit, and feel it for me."

Kit went obediently to the door and stepped outside. The white flakes made a queer sort of confusion before her eyes; they brushed her cheeks like tiny flower petals and caught on her eyelashes. For a moment her heart lifted with a trace of Mercy's excitement. Then the cold dampness soaked through her thin slippers and she shivered.

I'm not sure I like it, she thought. It's curious and lovely in a way, but it makes everything so dark, and somehow it makes me feel shut off. Somewhere, far beyond this endless curtain of white, green leaves and flowers were growing under a bright warm sun. Would she ever see them again?

Next morning her dark fears were swept away in a rush of wonder. Under a cloudless blue sky stretched a breath-taking glittering universe, carved of dazzling white coral, unreal and silent. Every familiar sign was altered. There was no trace of life or motion. It was as though no eye but hers had ever looked out upon this purity and perfection.

Then as she looked, a living thing dared to intrude upon this untouched wilderness. Through the white carven carpet that had been High Street pushed four oxen, buried up to their middles, dragging behind them a heavy plow. Snow fell away from the great blade in a gigantic wave. "They are breaking out the road," explained Judith. "Now we will be able to get to the Lecture."

That evening, for the first time since Kit's arrest, William came to call. He had stayed away, he explained, out of consideration for the illness in the house. He inquired courteously after Mercy's health, and she smiled at him from the bed where she sat propped against the feather pillows. Rachel fluttered to draw a chair for him. On the opposite side of the hearth Kit was intent on her spinning. She had taken over Mercy's flax wheel and was slowly mastering the art of winding a fine uniform thread. It took concentration and a steady hand. Now the humming of the wheel barely slackened as she raised her eyes for one grave cool look. William's eyes flickered away toward the leaping flames. It was Judith who kept the conversation going. She had fiercely resented her enforced absence from church and lectures. Now she demanded to know everything that had happened, which of her friends were up and about, when there might be a sleighing party.

"I hope John gets back soon," she sighed. "Thankful Peabody's wedding is to be in December, and I can't bear it if he isn't here for that."

"They say in the town that there's been no word from the detachment since they stopped at Hadley. There's been new Indian raids up Deerfield way."

Judith dropped her knitting and stared at William. Mercy leaned her head back against the pillows and closed her eyes. Aunt Rachel sprang to her feet in alarm.

"I'm surprised at you for spreading rumors, William," she reproved him. "They say no news is good news. Now, 'tis way past Mercy's bedtime. She looks white as a ghost." She hesitated. "Kit, you and William can lay a fire in the company room if you like."

Kit did not look up from her spinning. " 'Twould take a monstrous lot of wood to heat the room before midnight," she observed. William took the hint and pulled on his heavy beaver-fur coat and cap. Kit would not have risen from her place at all, but Rachel, with a meaningful nudge, handed her a candle, and she had perforce to see her suitor to the door.

In the hallway William did not seem disposed to hurry. He lingered so long that Kit was forced to shut the door behind them to keep the chilling draft from the kitchen.

"I've missed you, Kit," said William finally. "I had to come back."

Kit said nothing.

"You don't seem very pleased to see me."

How could a girl say that there had been a time when she had longed with all her heart to see him?

204

Besides, there was something more on William's mind.

"I don't want you to think that I hold anything against you, Kit," he said awkwardly. "Everyone knows that you meant well. They are all saying in the town what a help you have been to your aunt these past weeks. You'll find, when you come back, I promise you, Kit, that everyone is willing to let bygones be bygones, and that you can make a fresh start."

Kit looked down at the tip of William's great boot. "What do you mean by a fresh start?" she asked quietly.

"I mean that it is well over. The Widow Tupper is gone, and it won't be necessary to see much of the Cruff child. Don't you agree, Kit, that from now on it would be wise to use a little more judgment about people?

"Mind you, I'm not speaking against charity," he went on, seeing her mouth opening to protest. "We're supposed to care for the poor. But you overdo it, Kit."

"But it wasn't charity!" Kit burst out. "Hannah and Prudence—they are my friends!"

"That's just what I mean. We're judged by the company we keep. And in our position people look to us for an example of what is right and proper."

"And I'm to set an example by turning my back on my friends?" Kit's eyes glittered.

"Oh, Kit," pleaded William miserably. "I didn't want to quarrel with you tonight. But try to see it from my side. It would make a man uneasy never knowing what his wife would do next."

" 'Twould make a wife uneasy never knowing whether she could depend on her husband," Kit answered levelly. William had the grace to flush, but he held stubbornly to his position.

A month ago Kit's temper would have flared. But all at once she realized that William could not really anger her. She had had a long time to think, that night on the riverbank, and the longer night in the constable's shed. She had never consciously made any decision, but suddenly there it was waiting and unmistakable.

" 'Tis no use, William," she said now. "You and I would always be uneasy, all of our lives. We would always be hoping for the other one to be different, and always being disappointed when it didn't happen. No matter how hard I tried, I know I could never care about the things that seem so important to you."

"The house isn't important to you?" he asked slowly.

"Yes, in a way it is," she admitted. "I'd like to live in a fine house. But not if it means I have to be an example. Not if it means I can't choose my own friends."

William too had been doing some thinking. He did not seem surprised, only gravely regretful.

"Perhaps you're right, Kit," he conceded. "I've hoped all this year that you would forget your odd ways and learn to fit in here. If I thought you would just try—"

She shook her head.

"Then I won't be coming again?"

" 'Tis no use, William," she repeated.

At the door he turned and looked back, his face baffled and unhappy. There was in his eyes just the merest flicker of the look she had seen there on that first morning outside the Meeting House. In that instant Kit knew that she had only to speak one word or to stretch out her hand. But she did not speak, and presently William opened the door and was gone.

Now the long evenings about the hearth were seldom relieved by any visitor. For hours on end the whir of the spinning wheel and the twang of the loom were the only sounds. Except for a formal bow of greeting on Sabbath morning and on Lecture Day, Kit did not see William again till the day of Thankful Peabody's wedding.

Thankful's wedding was the first festivity Wethersfield had enjoyed since the sickness. Through drifts of snow waist-high, by sleigh and sled and snowshoe, young people and old folks and children gathered in the spacious Peabody house, relieved to shake off the labor and anxiety of the past weeks and to rejoice with the happy couple. The feast spread out on the board would be talked of for weeks to come. There were apple and mince and dried-berry pies, little spicecakes with maple sugar frosting, candied fruits and nuts, pitchers of sweet apple cider, and great mugs of steaming flip for the men.

"Seven different kinds of cake," Judith counted surreptitiously. "I'll never be able to have anything half so grand at my wedding."

Kit scarcely heard her. She was remembering the last wedding she had attended, could it be only a year ago? in Barbados. She could shut her eyes and see the long damask-covered table, set with gold and silver plate. The banquet had lasted for four hours. Light from crystal chandeliers had twinkled back from gold braid and jewels. Deep windows had opened out on curving formal gardens, and the sea breezes had filled the room with the scent of flowers.

An almost intolerable loneliness wrapped Kit away from the joyous crowd. She was filled with a restlessness she could not understand. What was it that plagued her with this longing to turn back? Was it that far-off memory of elegance and beauty, or was it just the look in Thankful's eyes as she stood, radiant in her rose-colored lutestring wedding dress, and listened to the toasts to her future?

Kit and Judith, each lost in her own thoughts, stood together near the wall, unable to join in the merrymaking. From across the room William watched them gravely, making no move.

When the bride and groom had driven off in their sleigh toward the snug new house that awaited them, the guests turned back to the laden tables. Two fiddlers in the corner scraped a lively tune, and some of the more daring young people began to dance. No one paid attention to the two tardy guests who appeared at the door, letting in a gust of wind, till suddenly a woman screamed and threw her arms about a snow-covered figure. Then abruptly the music stopped and the laughter was checked, and everyone crowded about the newcomers.

They were two Wethersfield men returned from Massachusetts with the detachment of militia. The story they had to tell put a somber end to the happy evening. Of the detachment of twenty, only eight had come back to Hartford. Just south of Hadley, before they could reach Deerfield, they had been ambushed by Indians who attacked savagely with both arrows and French rifles. Four men had been killed outright and two others had died of wounds on the trail home. The rest had been surrounded and taken captive. For a few days the survivors had attempted to follow the Indians, till a heavy snow had made it impossible to go on. They had found the scalped body of one of the captives lying by the trail, and they had little hope that in that weather any of the prisoners would have been spared. They had turned back and made their way on snowshoes, barely reaching Hadley before another blizzard set in.

The sobered guests crowded close, waiting for one answer. No, none of the Wethersfield men had been killed, but one of the captives was that young fellow who had been studying with the doctor, John Holbrook.

In the mingled relief and horror, few of them noticed the faint wail that came from Judith, or saw her waver and fall. Kit and Rachel sprang forward, but it was William who reached her first, and carried her gently to the settle by the fire, and it was William who later tucked her carefully into his sleigh and drove her home.

In the weeks that followed, watching Judith, Kit began to understand how the gray shadow that was her Aunt Rachel could once have been the toast of an army. Hopelessness had erased the color and animation from Judith's face, and set her lovely features into a still mask. Kit ached for her. But even more she was torn with pity for Mercy, whose grief could not find an outlet in a tear or word. Would Mercy's scant strength be equal to this burden? Rachel worried that her daughter did not gain, and fussed over the fire concocting nourishing stews which Mercy obediently tried to swallow. In some contradictory way grief seemed to have etched on Mercy's thin face a beauty it had never possessed. Behind the clear gray eyes the light still burned steadily.

Should I tell her? Kit wondered. Surely now Mercy has a right to know that John loved her. But watching Mercy's stillness she found a new patience to resist her own impulse. Someday the time would come when Mercy could know.

The Christmas season passed, unmarked by any rejoicing. There was no holiday in this Puritan town, no feasting, no gifts. The day went by like any other, filled with work, and Kit said nothing, ashamed that in this somber household she should even remember a happy English yuletide.

January dragged by, and February. It was the hardest winter most of the townspeople could remember. Old people shook their heads, recalling blizzards of their childhood, but it was impossible for Kit to visualize anything more bleak than this first winter of her experience. She no longer saw any beauty in a world muffled in white. She hated the long days of imprisonment, when there was nothing to see through the window but shifting curtains of pale gray, when drifts stood waist high on the doorstep, and it took hours of backbreaking labor to carve a passage to the well. She hated the drafty floors and frigid corners, and the perpetual animal reek of heavy clothes hung about the fireplace to dry. Every night she shrank from the moment when she and Judith must make the dread ascent to the upstairs chamber with only the meager comfort of a warming pan. But impatient as she was with the long days indoors, the outdoors promised only aching misery. She resented the arduous preparation for the journey to Meeting, the heavy leather boots, the knit socks drawn over them, the clumsy little footstove they had to lug all the way, that cooled off long before the sermon was finished and left one to sit with stinging fingers and toes, while the breath of the whole congregation rose like the smoke from so many pipes.

How could Hannah ever have endured it? Kit often shivered, alone in that cabin with the wind howling outside and no one to speak to for weeks on end but the cat and the goats. She hoped there was a cozy hearth at Nat's grandmother's house, and her own heart warmed at the thought of the two old ladies sharing it together.

Then her restless thoughts would drift after the *Dolphin*. Nat had offered to take her with him. Suppose she had accepted his offer? If she had never come back, would anyone here in this house really have cared very much? By now she would be in Barbados. At this very moment she might be— The broom in her hand, or the treadle under her foot would idle to a stop as she walked in imagaination up the wide drive to her grandfather's house, and stepped up to the long shady veranda. Then she would shake herself free. Such daydreaming was a weakness. The house was sold, and she was here in New England, and perhaps Nat had never really meant his offer at all.

One night she woke from a vivid dream. She and Nat had stood side by side at the bow of the *Dolphin,* watching that familiar curving prow carving gently through calm turquoise water. They came soundlessly into a palm-studded harbor, fragrant with the scent of blossoms, and happiness was like sunshine, wrapping her round and pouring into her heart till it overflowed.

She woke in the freezing darkness. I want to go back, she admitted at last, weeping. I want to go home, where green things are growing, and I will never see snow again as long as I live! Her tears, scalding her eyelids, froze instantly against the pillow. Lying tense beside Judith, she made a resolve.

After that, all through the cheerless days, she hugged the dream close. Sometimes, driven by her restlessness, she would talk about Barbados to Mercy. "Once when I was quite small," she would say over the hum of the flaxwheel, "my grandfather took me to see a great cave. You had to go to it when the tide was very low, and when a wave dashed across the rocks it made a sort of curtain across the opening of the cave. But inside it was very calm and still, and the water on the floor was as clear as glass. Underneath the water there was a sort of garden, made of colored rocks, and all over the roof of the cave there were queer hanging shapes, like those icicles outside the window, only pale green and orange and rose colored. It was so beautiful, Mercy—"

Mercy would look across at Kit's wistful face, and smile in understanding. She knows, Kit thought. When I tell them that my mind is made up, she will not try to keep me. She will be sorry, I think, but truly, won't they, all of them, be a little relieved?

In all honesty, she often argued, wouldn't she help the family most by leaving? Did the help she managed to give her aunt and uncle ever begin to make up for their trouble, and for the inescapable fact that she was another person to feed and clothe? Though no one ever so much as hinted at it, the grim truth was that where a short time ago two girls had been well provided for, there was now every likelihood of three spinsters in the Wood household.

No, she amended, Judith would never be a spinster. Kit had watched William's face in Meeting, and she knew that he was only biding his time. And Judith, in spite of her downcast eyes, was well aware of this. By every right of beauty and accomplishment, Judith belonged in the new house on Broad Street. In their secret hearts all three of them, she and William and Judith, had really known that all along. It needed only time now to bring about the match which Kit and John Holbrook had interrupted.

In March a fresh blizzard buried the town in drifts. The long days wore on, one as like another as the endless threads of the loom. Though the bitter cold did not abate, the daylight hours grew perceptibly longer. They lighted the candles a bit later every afternoon.

Judith had just set the brass candlestick on the table one late afternoon, and the girls were moving the table nearer to the hearth in preparation for supper, when a knock sounded at the door.

"See who it is, Kit," said Rachel absently. "I don't want to take my hands out of this flour."

Kit went into the hallway, leaving the kitchen door open behind her, drew back the bolt, and opened the door. A gaunt, ragged figure stood on the step, and as she shrank back a man pushed his way through the door and halted on the kitchen threshold. Judith suddenly let fall a wooden bowl with a clatter.

Rachel, wiping her hands on her apron, came forward, peering in the dim light. "Can it be—John?" she breathed tremulously.

The man did not even hear her. His eyes had gone straight to Mercy where she sat by the hearth, and her own eyes stared back, enormous in her white face. Then with a hoarse, wordless sigh, John Holbrook stumbled across the room, and went down on his knees with his head in Mercy's lap.

CHAPTER TWENTY-ONE

On a Lecture Day in April two marriage intentions were announced together in the Meeting House. John Holbrook and Mercy Wood. William Ashby and Judith Wood.

The Wood household was busy from dawn till close to midnight. There was so much to do if all were to be ready for the double wedding that was set for early May. There was the vital matter of two dowries. Judith had been carefully hoarding a small store of linens since childhood, adding one cherished bit from time to time, and her loom and needle had worked busily. But Mercy had never given a thought to a dowry. She had not a single pillowcase or linen napkin that she could call her own. Now, though Rachel fussed and stitched, Mercy still regarded the whole problem with indifference. Why did she need a dowry, she argued practically, when she was really not leaving home at all? She and John had already decided that for the first year at least they had best share the Woods' ample house. The company room was being readied with fresh whitewash and new linen curtains.

John had resumed his studies with Dr. Bulkeley. All his uncertainty had disappeared, and his steady eye and voice plainly revealed the core of strength that Kit had always sensed beneath his gentleness. In the days of his captivity, of which he never spoke, in the waiting for a chance to escape, and in the weary hunted trail down the Connecticut River, John had found his answers.

"Dr. Bulkeley is everything I ever thought him to be, a great scholar and a great gentleman," he explained. "In politics he is obeying his own conscience, but I think he is mistaken. We have come to an understanding. He will teach me theology and medicine, but I will think as I please." By June he would be ready to accept a call to one of the small parishes springing up to the south and west of Wethersfield.

William's house on Broad Street was nearly finished. Piece by piece he was assembling the costly treasures for its furnishing—fine hand-turned bedsteads and chests and chairs from the skilled Wethersfield joiner, Peter Blinn, glossy pewter plates and a set of silver spoons from Boston, real china bowls of blue and white Delft from Holland. Judith knew where every piece would go in the new house, and how to care for each lovely thing to keep it shining. She and William spent their evenings in happy planning, and their contentment was good to see. Kit had never found William so likeable before.

In the midst of all this preparation Kit silently made her own plans. She would not share them with anyone till every detail was carefully provided for. Her leaving would be a shock to them, she knew. Rachel, and Matthew in his own way, looked upon her as a daughter, but even a daughter, though welcomed and loved, could come to be a problem. There was no real place for her here. With John to help with the planting and Mercy still sharing the work of the household, there was no obligation now to hold Kit to the tasks she hated. They would protest, they might even sorrow a little, but in their hearts wouldn't they be relieved to see her go?

The ice on the river broke into great floating blocks, and gradually thinned and disappeared. The ferryboat began its daily journeys from Smith's landing back and forth to the opposite shore. Small boats slipped out of their winter moorings, and one day a bustling cheering crowd thronged along High Street to greet the first sailing ship up from New London.

That afternoon Kit climbed to the attic and surveyed the seven small trunks. She had not looked inside them all winter. Now, one after the other she threw back the lids and lifted the filmy dresses, holding them up to the dim light. How long ago it seemed that she had worn these things! Could it be not quite a year? The silks and muslins and gauzes still gleamed unworn and beautiful, and doubtless they were still fashionable. She touched them wistfully. It would be good to shed these shabby woolen garments and feel once more the softness of silk against her skin, and to hear the rustle of petticoats wherever she moved.

But the dresses must serve another purpose now. Would they bring enough to pay her passage on a ship? Fine cloth like this was rare in Connecticut. In many families, she had learned, one dress such as these would be handed down through three generations as a cherished possession. Surely in Hartford, or perhaps even here in Wethersfield, she would find willing buyers, even though she had not yet worked out a plan for approaching them.

As she lifted the peacock-green dress she hesitated. How radiant Judith had looked in this

216

dress. "If only William could see me in it," she had said. She laid aside the dress, and very thoughtfully she chose another, a fine blue-flowered muslin. These two she would take directly to Uncle Matthew, and this time she felt sure he would let his daughters accept them, because he would know now that she offered the gifts with love instead of pride.

All Kit's plans now turned toward Barbados. She had no illusions about the prospect before her. She would not be going back as Sir Francis Tyler's granddaughter. She would go as a single woman who must work for her living. Her best chance, she had decided, lay in seeking employment as a governess in one of the wealthy families. She liked teaching children, and hopefully there might be a library where she could extend her own learning as well as that of her charges. Whatever befell, there would be a blue sky overhead, and the warmth and color and fragrance and beauty that her heart craved.

One day in mid-April she walked alone down South Road. She could not go far, for the river was still very high from the melting snows. It had overflowed so that the fringe of poplar trees on its banks stood deep in water, and the cornfields were transformed into endless lakes. Blackbird Pond had been swallowed up, and Hannah's house, had it still been standing there, would have been flooded up to its thatched roof. Poor Hannah, how had she endured this ordeal year after year, watching while the water crept nearer and nearer, stowing her valuables higher in the rafters, moving away goodness only knew where to wait out the season in some deserted barn or warehouse, and creeping back when the water receded to scrub out her house and replant her soggy garden? Kit was thankful, as she had been so many times when the wind howled and the snow piled higher, that her friend was snug in a proper house. But she knew a pang of homesickness, nonetheless. The little cottage had been very dear to her.

She perched on a sun-dried rock and sniffed the air. There was an earthy indefinable scent that stirred her senses. The new shoots of the willows were a sharp yellow-green. The bare twigs of the maples were tipped by swelling red buds. A low bush nearby had blossomed in tiny gray balls. She reached to touch one curiously. It was furry and soft as the kitten that Prudence had held in her arms that summer afternoon. All at once Kit was aware that this New England, which had shown her the miracle of autumn and the white wonder of snow, had a new secret in store. This time it was a subtle promise, a tantalizing hint of beauty still withheld, a beckoning to her spirit to follow she knew not where.

She had forgotten that summer would come again, that the green would spread over the frozen fields, that the earth would be turned up to the sun and the seed sown, and that the meadows would renew themselves. Was this what strengthened these New Englanders to endure the winter, the knowledge that summer's return would be all the richer for the waiting?

Yet the spring air held a sadness too, sharper than all the loneliness of winter. The promise was not for her. I am going away, she thought, and for the first time the reminder brought no delight, only a deeper longing. She did not want to leave this place, after all. Suppose she should never walk in the meadows again? Suppose she should never sit in the twilight with Mercy, or see Judith in the new house, or the girl Prudence would grow to be? Suppose she should never see Nat Eaton again?

Suddenly she was trembling. She snatched at the dream that had comforted her for so long. It was faded and thin, like a letter too often read. She tried to remember how it had felt to stand on the deck of the *Dolphin* and see before her the harbor of Barbados. The haunting joy eluded her; the dream shores were dim and unreal. Why had she closed her heart to the true meaning of the dream? How long had she really known that the piercing happiness of that moment had come not from the sight of the harbor at all, but from the certainty that the one she loved stood beside her?

If only I could go with Nat, she realized suddenly, it wouldn't matter where we went, to Barbados or just up and down this river. The *Dolphin* would be home enough.

"There is no escape if love is not there," Hannah had said. Had Hannah known when she herself had not even suspected? It was not escape that she had dreamed about, it was love. And love was Nat.

It must have been Nat from the beginning, she admitted now, and with that knowledge came a sureness that she had never known in all the last bewildering year. Memories of Nat came crowding back to her— agile and sure-footed, as she had first known him, leaning far out on a yardarm to grasp a billowing sail—throwing back his head in laughter, or shooting hot sparks of temper—sitting on a thatched roof in the sunshine—coming miraculously out of the fog that morning, bending tenderly to lift a frightened old woman into the rowboat—and as she had seen him last, standing erect by the door of the magistrate's office, sending across the anger and confusion a steady reassurance and strength.

Nat is New England, too, she thought, like John Holbrook and Uncle Matthew. Why have I never seen that he is one of them? Under that offhand way of his, there is the same rock. Hannah has leaned on it for years. And I refused to see.

Was it too late? He asked me to go, she reminded herself. But what did he mean? Only that he could never bear to see anyone in trouble? And he came back. He risked the whipping post to come back and help me. But he took the same risk to rescue a yellow cat!

After a long time Kit started slowly home. The sun slanted low in the sky, and behind her there began a sweet, disturbing melody. Peepers, Judith had said, the little frogs that lived in the swamp, and why should the sound of them tear at her heart? "Too late? Too late?" they queried, over and over, and she fled along the road to the house where she could shut herself away from them.

From that moment in the meadow Kit ceased to plan at all. She only waited. Somehow she found a way to meet every trading ship that came up the river. How beautiful these proud little sailing ships were! She never glimpsed their spreading sails without an answering surge of her spirits. Yet every new mast that rounded the bend of the river brought at the same time a fresh plunge of disappointment. Always she waited, her eyes straining to make out the figure on the prow, and always, at the sight of those strange, glistening white figureheads, her heart sank. Why did the *Dolphin* not come?

On the second day of May, as she came out on Wethersfield landing, a trim little ketch was already tied up, fresh-painted, with clean white canvas and not a barnacle on its hull. It must have been newly launched.

The wharf was a confusion of unloading and bartering. A seaman in a blue coat bent to check a row of barrels, and as he straightened up, even before he turned or before she consciously recognized him, Kit began to run.

"Nat!" The greeting burst from her. He turned and saw her, and then he was running, too. As he caught her hands she came to a stop, the wharf, the ship, and Nat himself swinging in a dizzy arc before her eyes.

"Kit? It is Kit, isn't it? Not Mistress Ashby?"

"Oh no, Nat! No!"

"I thought the old *Dolphin* would never make it!"

The blue gaze was too intense. She had to look away, and abruptly she was conscious of the crowded dock. She pulled her hands away and stepped back, trying, too late, to retrieve her dignity.

"H-how is Hannah?" she stammered.

"Chipper as a sandpiper. She and Gran have been fine company for each other."

"And the *Dolphin*? Did something happen to her?"

"Just a heavy blow. She's hove down for repairs at the yard. What do you think of the new ketch?"

"She's lovely." Then something in his tone made her look at him more sharply. The blue coat with brass buttons was brand new, and pride sparkled over Nat like the shiny paint on the new vessel. "Nat—you mean—you can't mean she's yours?"

"All but a few payments. By the end of a good summer's trade she'll be every inch mine from stem to stern."

221

"I can't believe it! She's beautiful, Nat—even more beautiful than the *Dolphin!*"

"Have you noticed her name?"

Kit leaned sideways to see the letters painted jauntily on the transom. "The *WITCH!* How did you dare? Does Hannah know?"

"Oh, she's not named after Hannah. I hadn't gone ten miles down the river that day before I knew I'd left the real witch behind."

She did not dare to look up at him. "Can I see her, Nat?" she asked instead. "Will you take me on board?"

"No, not yet." His voice was full of decision. "I want to see your uncle first. Kit—" His words came in an unpremeditated rush. "Will he think it is enough—the new ketch? There'll be a house someday, in Saybrook, or here in Wethersfield if you like. I've thought of nothing else all winter. In November we'll sail south, to the Indies. In the summer—"

"In the summer Hannah and I will have a garden!"

"Kit—" He glanced ruefully about the busy wharf. "Of all the places to choose! I didn't plan it like this. Aren't you going to invite me home with you?"

Happiness brimmed over into shaky laughter. "Captain Eaton, we'd be proud to have you dine with us."

"Then must we stay here any longer?"

She took the arm he offered, but still she lingered, looking back. "I want to see the ketch. Please, Nat, before we go! I can't wait any longer to see my namesake!"

"No," he said again, leading her firmly toward the road. "That ketch has a mind of her own. She's contrary as a very witch herself. All the way up the river she's been holding back somehow, waiting. Now you'll both have to wait. I'm not going to disappoint her, Kit. When I take you on board the *Witch*, it's going to be for keeps."

GOTHIC MYSTERIES
*of Romance
and Suspense ...*

by Rae Foley

A CALCULATED RISK
DARK INTENT
FATAL LADY
GIRL ON A HIGH WIRE
THE HUNDREDTH DOOR
MALICE DOMESTIC
THE MAN IN THE SHADOW
OMINOUS STAR
SCARED TO DEATH
THIS WOMAN WANTED
WILD NIGHT

and Velda Johnston

ALONG A DARK PATH
THE FACE IN THE SHADOWS
THE HOUSE ABOVE HOLLYWOOD
I CAME TO A CASTLE
THE LIGHT IN THE SWAMP
THE PEOPLE ON THE HILL
THE PHANTOM COTTAGE

Dell Books 75¢

If you cannot obtain copies of this title from your local bookseller, just
send the price (plus 15c per copy for handling and postage) to Dell Books,
Post Office Box 1000, Pinebrook, N. J. 07058.